Dear Dr.

Our two fo

MW01289775

that GOD has taken care of us so well. We have nothing to regret in life. Friends like you are very valuable in my life. God bless you & your family.

TOMORROW WILL BE A BETTER DAY

By

Ramesh Babulal Shah

Ramesh B Shah

March 24, 2021

As told to

Richard Graves

A portion of the proceeds received from the sale of this book will be donated to charities of my choice.

Ramesh Shah

All rights reserved. No part of this book may be reproduced or transmitted in any form or by any means without written permission from the author.

Cover design by Sheila Bernal Ray at sheilaraycreative.com

Dedication

Dedicated to my caring parents,
Babulal and Savitaben Shah, my siblings, my wonderful
wife and partner of 43 years, Mina,
our daughters Sonal and Rita,
and our wonderful hassle-free grandchildren.

Contents

Introduction

Like most grandparents, I love the hours spent with my grandchildren. Watching them play reminds me of my own childhood in Bombay, India (now Mumbai). At ages nine and five, Sejal and Joshua already take an interest in the stories I tell of my journey from poverty to prosperity. As they grow up, I want them, and future generations, to understand the miracle of that journey and to appreciate how fortunate and blessed they are to raise their families in a country where ample opportunities exist for honest, law-abiding citizens and where hard work can lead to any level of success. I also want them to know and appreciate the people who helped me and inspired me along the way. Without that help and support, I would not have escaped the poverty trap into which I was born.

The importance of spiritual faith and of going out of one's way to help others in need—treating them just as one would hope to be treated—is another emphasis. I would love for that to be a family legacy. In the direst circumstances, my father would often say, "Tomorrow will be a better day." When we meet someone in need and help them with our time or our money, we make that statement true for that person in that situation.

For others who read my story, I hope they will gain an understanding of the culture and values of the Indian subcontinent and grasp that many similarities as well as differences exist between the cultures of East and West. If my story of a life spanning both cultures can help that understanding, I will be a happy and rewarded man.

Now, in my seventies and with several health issues, I still find life so sweet. I am breathing, laughing, and still able to do what I like most—play with Sejal and Joshua and travel the world. The most important lesson is that life is beautiful and that we can choose how we live it. Never let the dream die. God bless you all.

Acknowledgements

I would not have finished school, survived as an immigrant, adjusted to life in America, or succeeded in my career without the help of many people. My helpmates were humble people who did more than they needed with no personal gain. They are the heroes of my life story, and I want to honor them.

My father and mother head the list. They taught me honesty, resilience, tenacity, and unbelievable faith in Bhagwan Mahavir, the sage who laid out the central tenets of Jainism. I was born fifth of nine children. In the midst of poverty, our father, Babulal Kacharabhai Shah, taught us all to believe in and to strive for a better future. His teaching and belief that, "Tomorrow will be a better day," kept me going in the dark days of my own life.

My father was born in 1912 in Jamnagar, a town five hundred miles northwest of Bombay in Gujarat province. I do not know his precise date of birth. Even in poverty, his life displayed a generous spirit. I often saw him give what little change he had in his pocket to someone less fortunate. He would turn to me or one of my siblings and say, "We will find a way to buy milk tomorrow, this man needs milk today." At age seventeen, I watched my father die of a heart attack, a day of great sorrow for me. Yet he still plays an amazing role in my life; his voice of faith, generosity, and responsibility is always there to guide me.

My mother, Savitaben Zaveri, was the eldest daughter of Tribhovandas Zaveri, a cloth merchant from Jamnagar. Of eighteen siblings, only five girls survived. Savitaben stood five feet two inches tall, with medium build, brown complexion, black hair, and black eyes. She married my father as a young teenager in an arranged marriage. Like most Jain or Hindu brides of that era, she remained uneducated and devoted her life to keeping house and providing loving care to her husband and children. She did this with great humility. My parents were happily married until their final days together.

My older siblings Hasubhai, Bhupat, Nimuben, and Damuben, and my sister-in-law, Ramanbhabhi, all made sacrifices to help me stay in school and complete college. In difficult circumstances, they worked many extra hours and went without basic comforts to give me the opportunity to study in America. In time, that opportunity lifted our whole family out of poverty. We did this together.

I first met my wife, Mina, at age eighteen and was immediately captivated by her beauty. My family ranked beneath hers in wealth and social standing, and only when I had my degree from the University of South Florida (eight years later) could my oldest brother approach Mina's father and propose a meeting, the first step toward an arranged marriage. Today, she is the one who assures we do the right things for each member of our family. I would personally like to thank my lovely bride for supporting me for the last forty-three years, with many more years to come.

Another important person in my life is Mrs. Chandler, a cafeteria worker at St. Joseph's Infirmary in Atlanta, Georgia, who assumed the role of surrogate mother to me. I thank her from the bottom of my heart for her kind and caring attention during my lonely, depression-filled days when I first arrived in America. She was there whenever I needed to talk, and made a huge contribution by correcting my Indian English so that others could understand me. I lost contact with her when I moved from Atlanta in 1968, and my attempts to locate her have proved fruitless. If any reader knows of her, I ask that they contact me.

Robert (Bob) Boe worked as a dental intern at Crawford Long Hospital in Atlanta, Georgia. In 1967, he befriended a naïve foreign student with little money, a big language barrier, and a major dislike of Western food. He became a caring friend, helping me through periods of homesickness and depression. It was God's blessing that I met such a generous and unselfish young American man. Today, after forty-five years, Bob and I still maintain a great friendship and enjoy discussing the memories we have shared.

I am also thankful to Larry and John Glendenning who, as owners of Microlife Technics, sponsored my application for a work visa and subsequently for U.S. Permanent Residency.

There are many other wonderful American people who have helped me along the way. I will not attempt to name them individually for fear of missing someone, but I thank every one of them for their practical help, encouragement, and genuine interest in my personal well-being.

Finally, I want to thank the people who helped me put my story on paper. Without constant encouragement from my daughters, Sonal and Rita, and their husbands, Jonathon and Samit, this story would not have been written. Jonathan, in particular, urged, inspired, and bugged me to write my life story so his children could understand my roots and the people who shaped and influenced my life. Richard Graves, my longtime friend, helped research, write, and edit this memoir with great patience and creativity. My friends at the St. Charles Writers Group provided valuable feedback and encouragement. I would like to thank each one of them.

Author's Notes

Names

Indian culture places a high value on respect. One way we show respect is the way we address people, particularly our seniors. I have four sisters: Nimu, Damu, Pratibha and Sadhana. The first two are older. As a sign of respect, I add the extension "ben" to their names every time I address them (ben means sister). I call them Nimuben and Damuben. I do not add this extension when I address my younger sisters. Similarly, I add the extension "bhai" when I address my older brothers (bhai means brother). The same extension is used when addressing a work colleague or friend who is clearly senior.

This can lead to long names, so for those close to us, we often familiarize and shorten those names. For my oldest brother, Hasmukh, we shortened Hasmukhbhai to a more familiar Hasubhai. My daughters called him Hasukaka (kaka means paternal uncle). For my second oldest brother, Bhupendra, we arrived at the familiar form Bhupatbhai or simply Bhupat. For my sister-in-law, Raman, we shortened Ramanbhabhi to just Bhabhi (bhabhi means sister-in-law).

In this book, I use both given name and familiar name depending on who is addressing whom and the circumstance. That's how it is in real life.

Another point regarding names is that small differences in spelling are important. The words for grandpa and grandma are nana and nani. Uncle and aunt on the paternal side are kaka and kaki. On the maternal side, they are mama and mami (yes, mama is male).

The Indian Subcontinent

At the time I lived there, the nation of India comprised seventeen states and eleven territories. Each maintained fierce independence and unique identities. With 525 million people (1.3 billion people today), eighteen official languages, and close to eight hundred active dialects, India was (and is) a very diverse nation. This memoir covers my experiences in one small section of the subcontinent and does not intend to be representative of the nation as a whole.

The Jain Religion

Core teachings of the Jain religion are non-violence, truthfulness, enlightenment, and reincarnation. These are similar to the teachings of Hinduism, and Jain followers often go to Hindu priests for marriages and other special occasions as most Jain temples do not have priests. Both religions also have an abstract Supreme Being,

Although there is common ground, there are differences. The Jain religion has Bhagwan Mahavir as its central idol, whereas Hinduism has many gods and goddesses such as

Brahma, Vishnu and Shiva. Perhaps the biggest differences is the Hindu caste system compared to Jain teaching on fairness, equality, and the absence of personal desire.

In the area of Bombay where I grew up, the vast majority of the population was Hindu. Jain was a minority religion. Muslim mosques, Christian churches, and Buddhist temples also existed to serve other religious minorities.

In my generation, the inhabitants of this diverse religious landscape lived peacefully together. The government pledged religious freedom along with justice, liberty, and equality to all its citizens. Adherence to this pledge was not perfect, but we were truly a secular nation.

Discrimination

While religious freedom existed, other forms of discrimination were prevalent in our culture, including the caste system and discrimination against women. When property and possessions passed from one generation to the next, culture dictated that men benefited and women received nothing. Most parents did not consider the education of girls past high school. The cultural expectation was for girls to marry, have children, and look after the household and aging relatives. An underlying risk of sexual harassment and assault of young girls alone in public spaces promoted these parental decisions. Only rich families could afford private tuition for their daughters.

The caste system defined social hierarchy from birth. Brahmins (priests) were the highest level, followed by Kshatriyas (warriors, rulers) and Vaisyas (skilled workers, merchants). Shudra (laborers) came next and at the lowest level were the untouchables, who did jobs defined as unclean, such as cleaning toilets and sweeping the streets.

Memoir Accuracy

The events recorded in this book are as I remember them, but memory isn't perfect and details may differ and order of events may vary. Much of the dialogue took place in a different language. I have endeavored to stay true to character in what is written here. For a long period of time, my English was faltering at best. To make for easy reading, I have written a more fluent version of my speech. In some instances, to paint a scene and make the narrative flow, I have grouped memories from many typical days into the events of one day. I have also changed the names and the identifying characteristics of some people to protect their privacy.

1

Summer 1955 (Age 10)
Kalbadevi, Bombay

I woke to a rat scratching the floor inches from my head. I glanced up and made a hissing noise that sent it hurrying past Hasubhai, my oldest brother, who lay on the bed-mat next to me. Rats and house lizards were regular visitors to our one-room apartment, entering through cracks and openings in the rundown tenement building. As followers of the Jain religion, we believed in non-violence to all creatures, and did no harm to the rodents and other life forms that came into contact with us.

Beyond Hasubhai lay four other siblings: Bhupat, my second-oldest brother; Nimuben and Damuben, my two older sisters; and two-year old Pratibha, my younger sister. Our parents and baby Rashmi slept in a small kitchen area beyond a partition my dad had constructed for privacy.

I occupied a space between a storage closet and a window. When we moved to this apartment, the space fit me perfectly. Since then, I had grown and could no longer lay flat. I lifted my legs high in the air to ease the cramps that had developed while I slept. I could sense that dawn would soon arrive. Then traffic noise would start. Then Ma would come and rouse us.

We kept the window open at night to cool our third-floor apartment, and from my bed-mat, I could see a small section of night sky. Sometimes, I'd gaze at the stars and wonder if they would align kindly at important moments of my life. Astrology played an important role in our beliefs.

There were no stars that night; monsoon season had come early. I listened to the periodic "plink" as drops of water landed in several pans distributed around the room to catch drips from the leaking ceiling. Our apartment occupied the space at the end of the tenement building where the roof angled down and caught the worst of the storms. In monsoon season, mildew discolored the walls and the room always felt cold and miserable. Washed clothes hung to dry never dried completely.

A sewer smell drifted through the window from the toilet located next to our apartment and used by all residents on our floor. I turned to face the other way. At least my ear did not hurt this morning and my allergies were not bothering me. I frequently had infections in my left ear, and would wake with severe pain. I was not a healthy child.

Bhupat had bigger problems. He had contracted polio at age two or three and needed constant medical help. He had weak legs and a hunchback, and could not run or throw a ball, although his hands worked well and he had nimble fingers. We teased him about being the favorite because he had special shoes to help him walk, while the rest of us had only simple flip-flop sandals. When he was young, Ma and the older siblings fed him, bathed him, and carried him wherever he needed to go. Now, at age 16, he weighed around ninety pounds and managed to get most places on his own.

We slept on cotton bed-mats that were around two-inches thick. The girls wore cotton nightgowns and the boys wore undershirts and loose cotton trousers called lengha. Each morning when Ma woke us, we would clear away the bed-mats and stack them in one corner of the room. In the evening, we would return the living space to sleeping quarters, laying out the bed-mats beneath washed clothes hung out to dry. The total space was thirty-three feet by twelve feet, including the kitchen. Two light bulbs lit the apartment, one in the kitchen and one in the main area.

My stomach tightened and I pulled my knees tight to my chest to control the hunger pains. Soon Ma would make tea with three-part water and one-part milk and we would eat a spicy snack before going to school.

We were pure vegetarians, which meant no eggs. We could have milk and cheese and butter, but these were expensive. When we had them, the portions were very small. Mostly we ate wheat chapatti (an Indian form of tortilla), vegetables, rice, and watery buttermilk. I loved the taste of milk, and sometimes daydreamed of having a full glass all to myself.

In some ways, life had been easier in Jamnagar, the town five hundred miles away where I was born and where I started pre-school. Our wealthy maternal grandfather would visit us and bring us treats.

My father could not find regular work in Jamnagar, so he joined the multitude that came to Bombay for employment. He worked long hours and shared a room with eight others so that he could send money home to support us. He would return to Jamnagar two or three times a year and stay with us for a week or two. I remember the joy when he was with us, and the despair when he left.

He had a slim, five-feet-six inch frame with good looks, fair skin, and a big white smile. Each time he left, he would hug us and say, "When I have some place for us to live, you will come and join me. You'll get a better education in Bombay." I would cling to him and run my hands through his thick, black hair. None of us wanted him to leave. Then he was gone. I was overjoyed when we finally moved to Bombay and lived as a family again, even though life in Bombay seemed harder.

Every day, dad would arrive home from his job at a store that sold cotton fabrics, having used the money he'd earned to pay off a debt. What he had left would not cover our daily expenses, and the next day he would borrow again just to keep us afloat. Most evenings my parents discussed which debt should be paid next to maintain a reputation of honesty and integrity. The whole family joined the conversation. Many times I searched the pockets of every piece of clothing in the apartment looking for a coin or two that might help the situation. Often, my brothers and I took a detour on our walk to school to avoid shouts about unpaid bills from the vegetable vendor, milkman, and grain shop owner.

When we became discouraged, Dad would say to us, "Tomorrow will be a better day." He would grip the arm of my oldest brother, "We have Hasubhai studying commerce at the University of Bombay. When he has his degree, things will improve. You must all get an education. That's how we'll escape from poverty."

To me, it seemed like the college fees were making things worse. Even with Hasubhai working part time as a junior accountant while he studied, we never seemed to have enough money to survive. I wanted to believe Dad and tried to think positively, but so often tomorrow was no different from today or the day before: just more pain and misery.

***

A dull light crept through the window and I heard the first sounds of street life. Soon, the *Bombay Samachar* and *Times of India* newspapers would be delivered for Mr. Vakil who lived on the fourth floor. He was an attorney and the wealthiest tenant in our apartment block—a building that spanned the narrow road below like a giant archway. More than one hundred people lived there.

In our sector of Bombay, businesses, warehouses, and tenement buildings mingled together, and it was not unusual for rich and poor to live alongside each other. The very rich lived further south. Two miles away, the River Mithi flowed through the city center and formed an arc. It was known as the "Necklace of the Queen of England," because it looked so beautiful at night—with lights that lined the Arabian Sea illuminating the magnificent buildings that housed the super-rich. Four or five miles in the other direction were the slums of the untouchables, the people who performed tasks that Hindus considered unclean such as sweeping the streets, leatherwork, cutting hair, and cleaning toilets.

Some mornings I would sneak upstairs to Mr. Vakil's apartment and read the cricket news before he gathered the newspapers into his room. He was a kind man and would let me have the newspapers when he had finished with them, but I needed the information before I went to school so I could join in conversations with my schoolmates who had listened to the cricket commentary at home on the radio. That was a luxury we couldn't afford and I didn't want them to know that.

We all worked hard to hide our poverty within the four walls of our apartment. When mango season came, my school friends would talk about the wonderful mango they had eaten the previous evening. I would nod my head and say how nice mango tasted, even though we did not eat mango until the end of the season when quality dipped and prices dropped.

Family reputation impacted every aspect of life. It defined social status, how people treated us, who we would marry, and what job opportunities would come our way. With few exceptions, rich people married rich people and their children got all the best jobs.

When it came to marriage, my mother was an exception. She came from a wealthy family and grew up in a big house in a beautiful residential area near the Rangit Sagar Reservoir that supplied Jamnagar with water. Her father, Tribhovandas Zaveri, and her uncle had a family business that dealt in retail and wholesale cotton materials. But my mother received no suitors from other wealthy families.

The reason was that all the male children in her family—eight uncles I never knew—had bled to death at very young age for no apparent reason, and people decided that the family must have been cursed. Getting away from that superstition may have been one of Dad's motives for leaving Jamnagar, but no one ever said that openly.

***

"Time to get up. Quickly now," Ma's voice rang out. "The water tap will be shut off in forty minutes."

The tenement building had only one water supply—a municipal water line that terminated at a single faucet outside the building entrance. Fetching water each morning was one of our childhood chores.

At Ma's call, we all got up, stacked our bedding, and closed the windows to stifle the growing sewer smell from the constant stream of visitors to the toilet next door. Dad had already washed, shaved, and dressed for work. He moved to a framed picture of Bhagwan Mahavir that hung on the wall and, with his head bowed and his hands folded, murmured some mantras requesting peace at the start of the day. I would do the same before I left for school.

Sister Damuben fetched buckets from the kitchen and, together, we headed out the door.

"I'll catch up," I said as we approached the stairs. She nodded and descended to join the water line while I climbed to Mr. Vakil's apartment, slowing for the last few steps to make sure I missed the boards that squeaked.

Lifting one of the newspapers from his doorstep, I turned to the sports page and read the cricket news. My favorite players, Poly Umbriger and Vinoo Mankad, had scored runs. Umbriger worked for the Associated Cement Company and played for the company-sponsored team. Hasubhai worked for the same company and occasionally got tickets for home games at Bombay Brabourne Stadium.

The biggest matches were international matches played over five days known as "Test Matches." That year, New Zealand would visit India after the monsoon season and my brothers and I would follow every moment. Once I went with Hasubhai to Bombay Brabourne Stadium and saw a foreign team play. We were amazed by the physical size of the foreign players, almost twice the size of the Indian players.

A headline announced that England had rescued a match they were losing against South Africa. I grimaced. India had gained independence from Britain less than a decade earlier and I wanted South Africa to win.

Dad often talked about politics and I had begun to take an interest myself. I scanned the front page for news. Prime Minister Jawaharlal Nehru, the man who led the independence movement, had just returned from a trip to Moscow to meet Nikita Khrushchev, the Russian Premier. Although I didn't understand the details, I enjoyed having knowledge to discuss with Dad and others. I refolded the newspaper and returned it to the doorstep.

***

Downstairs at the water line, I found Damuben filling our buckets. I announced the cricket news to others waiting and helped her carry the buckets back to our apartment. There we filled a large tin container that stood in the corner of the kitchen. It held 60–70 liters (18 gallons), and each person got about ten liters of water per day for bathing. We bathed, cleaned clothes, and washed dishes at a three-foot by three-foot cement pad in the kitchen.

Next to the cement pad stood a small clay stove, about twelve inches by ten inches, with small openings in the side to collect ashes. Ma would place charcoal in the base, pour on kerosene, and light the charcoal with a match. The kitchen, with no ventilation, had a constant smoky, damp atmosphere.

For drinking water, we poured city water through a double-layered cheesecloth and collected it in a clay pot that had a small copper faucet on the side. The cheesecloth collected small insects, dirt and other debris. Some days we would find small worms—up to half an inch in length—and Ma would sacrifice some precious charcoal to boil the water before we drank it.

The girls bathed first, then the boys. While I waited, I filled a small tin container with water and joined the line of people outside our door waiting for the toilet. The smell of fresh fecal waste mixed with the ever-present smell of stale urine hit my nostrils.

When my turn came, I entered the closet-sized space, put my can of water on the floor and removed my loose cotton trousers. The toilet comprised a hole in the floor with a pipe that disappeared through the outside wall of the building. Placing one foot either side of the hole, I squatted down and did my business.

The pipe carrying waste ran along the outside wall of the building to a downspout that fed a collection pit at ground level. Untouchables came daily to remove solid waste from the pit. In monsoon season, a big storm sometimes overloaded the city's drainage system, and storm water washed through the collection pits and turned the streets into rivers of contaminated, mud-brown water.

Back in the apartment, my sisters had finished bathing. I fetched the clothes I would wear that day, filled a small bucket with water, removed my nightclothes, and stepped onto the cement pad. Beside me Ma tended the stove. I splashed water on my face and torso, rubbed my skin with a lump of hard soap, and rinsed off, shivering when the cold water hit my spine. Then I dried off with a thin towel already used by one of my siblings.

A random thought entered my head as I squeezed out the towel: Maybe one day we would own a radio, have a towel each, and I would drink a full glass of milk every morning. I smiled at the impossibility, but I had to believe that tomorrow would be a better day.

2

Values & Priorities

Laughter filled the apartment. Nimuben, my elder sister, had returned home to give birth to her firstborn. She had married a man from a Jain family in Jamnagar about ten months earlier and had conceived almost immediately. Both families were thrilled with this sign of fertility.

According to tradition, a girl returns to her family home where her mother guides her through her first birth. Her husband is not present at the birth and does not see her for a month or two while she recovers from the ordeal.

Nimuben's first pregnancy coincided with Ma's ninth, and mother and daughter were sharing a special moment comparing the size of their abdomens and debating who would give birth first. The rest of the family looked on, sharing the joy. Nimuben moved her hands across her belly. "I think I'm ahead of you."

Ma shook her head and they laughed.

"Please, not both at the same time," Dad said with his broadest smile.

This would be an important family milestone; soon Dad would hold his first grandchild. I had not seen him happier since the day Hasubhai got his university acceptance letter, another milestone in his dream for our family.

On that occasion, Dad arrived home from work to find Hasubhai waving the letter in his hand and the rest of us looking on. Dad gripped my brother's shoulders with both hands. For a moment, the lines on his forehead disappeared. "Son, this is wonderful news. You are the first in our family ..." His eyes scanned the rest of us, "but not the last."

Then the familiar lines returned to his forehead. "I have a distant uncle. I will ask him to lend us money. You must not let me down. Every penny must be repaid."

Hasubhai nodded. He understood. We all understood.

Dad turned to Bhupat. "Son, you are next. You have a bright mind and good hands. We will get you into technical school. There's a certificate for radio repair you could do."

Bhupat grinned. "Give me the chance. I'll not let you down."

My mind snapped back to the present when my sisters roared with laughter. They had seen Nimuben's baby kick from inside the womb.

After our evening meal, we set about rearranging the apartment to provide privacy for two expectant mothers.

Three weeks later, my new brother, Kirit, entered the world, followed a few days later by my first nephew, Mukesh. Dad could not have been happier than when he held his baby son and grandson, one in each arm. Two cribs that looked like cloth hammocks took center stage in the apartment, making the rest of the space even more crowded.

***

The bell rang to end the day at Esplanade Middle School. I slipped my writing book and pencil into a small cloth bag I carried each day and joined the other students putting books away on classroom shelves. The textbook I had used had pages missing and a broken spine; typical of government run schools that served the older sectors of the city. I took care to make sure no more pages went missing.

Outside the classroom, students chatted before dispersing for home. Conversation hushed when Jayant walked by. He towered over most other students, and rumors ran wild about his life outside school. At any given time, he could be friend or bully for no apparent reason. Even teachers and school staff avoided him. Some days, he came to school with alcohol on his breath, a big taboo in Hindu culture.

Why Jayant treated me better than most, I don't know. My undernourished frame and poor health meant I was no threat, and maybe my father's teaching that every human being has dignity impacted the way I treated Jayant. I never shunned him or avoided sitting near him in class.

For whatever reason, we got on okay and would sometimes walk home together along Kalbadevi Road for about half a mile, until I turned onto Hanuman Lane and he headed for Zaveri Bazaar, a busy local marketplace that was about a ten-minute walk from our apartment. The market was known for its trade in diamonds and gold jewelry, and

Jayant had told me his dad owned a small retail shop that sold hair oil near the Vithal Wadi area.

Jayant was also the smartest kid in our class. Whenever our teacher, Mrs. Desai, pinned the results of a test to the noticeboard, Jayant headed the list. Occasionally, I came second. Those were the times I had discussed the material with Jayant. He did this without appearing to study.

That afternoon, I slipped away from the other students and caught up with Jayant. The traffic was not heavy and I was able to walk beside him, yet he ignored me.

"Is everything okay?" I said.

No response.

"How is your father?"

He grunted.

I could tell something was bothering him and persisted with my questions. Finally, he confided, "I have a problem with the shop."

It seemed an odd thing to say. Why would he have the problem, not his father? "What does your dad say?"

He shook his head and continued to brood.

I moved a step ahead so I could see his face. "Jayant, why are you so worried?"

He stopped walking and stepped out of the flow of traffic beside a bamboo scaffold supporting a storefront. "I don't have a dad."

"What do you mean?"

"He died."

My jaw dropped. "When?"

"Years ago."

"But you said…"

"I know…I don't want people to know I'm an orphan."

Other pedestrians brushed past us and we squeezed closer to the building between the scaffold posts.

"What about your mother?"

He hesitated and looked away. His shoulders slumped. "I don't know who my mother is."

I didn't understand. "How can you not know your mother?"

"I don't want to talk about it. I really don't care anymore."

I leaned closer. His eyes looked dull and misty. "Tell me."

Eventually he spoke, "My mother's a Muslim. Dad met her at a Kothas." Once more, he avoided eye contact. "She was a Mujra dancer."

I didn't know how to respond. Mujra was a cross between art form and exotic dance, and Kothas often doubled as high-class brothels. Performing Mujra was a tradition passed down from mother to daughter amongst Muslim practitioners.

"Do you have relatives?" I asked.

He shook his head. "I have a stepbrother, but he's always drunk."

"Where do you sleep?"

"At the shop. Laxman sleeps there too. He worked for my dad for years and runs the shop when I'm not there. We sell hair oil."

I couldn't imagine what it was like to not have a family, and words escaped my lips before I had chance to think. "Come home and meet my family."

He shook his head. "They won't want me. No one wants me."

I wondered if that was true. What would my parents say if I brought home a homeless half-Muslim bully who drank alcohol?

Jayant stood straight and pushed past me, "Don't you dare tell anyone."

***

At the apartment, life was back to normal. Nimuben and baby had returned to Jamnagar and Ma was up and about, managing the household. That evening after our meal, I told my dad about Jayant and asked his advice.

"Be his friend, my son. You can't change his life, but you can be part of it."

"Can he come and visit us?"

Dad smiled. "Of course. You can invite him for tea or for a meal. We'll share whatever we have with your friend."

In bed that night, I listened to the rhythmic sound of my siblings' breathing and reflected on how much my family meant to me. Behind the screen, my new baby brother suckled at Ma's breast. Each sound brought a feeling of peace and contentment. I thought of Jayant sleeping alone and how hard that must be. I fell asleep wondering about my father's words—what did it mean to be a part of someone's life?

***

I woke with a start. Beside me, Hasubhai sat bolt upright on his bed-mat. From the kitchen, we heard Dad shouting abusive language that we had never heard from his lips. It sounded like he was arguing with a stranger. Between shouts, I heard baby Kirit crying and Ma trying to settle him. In the dull dawn light, I could see that all my other siblings had stirred.

The shouts came again. We looked to Hasubhai, our oldest brother. He seemed as scared as the rest of us. The shouting had happened once before, to a lesser degree, and we had attributed it to a bad dream. This time it went on for longer and sounded far worse.

"If he's dreaming we should wake him," I said.

Hasubhai shook his head. "It's not a dream. A spell maybe."

The shouting and yelling continued. I felt sick. "This is not good…"

"Quiet Ramesh." Hasubhai lowered his voice to a whisper. "There's nothing we can do. Something happens in his mind."

Fear gripped my heart. Dad was the backbone of our family. He provided stability. I didn't want to be like Jayant, with no one to guide me. Dad's leadership held us together and moved us forward. Maybe the stress of daily life had affected his mind. "If he needs a doctor…"

"Ramesh…" Hasubhai stared at me. I could see fear in his eyes. "We cannot afford a specialist."

The shouting stopped as suddenly as it had started. Seconds later, baby Kirit quieted. Siblings stared at each other in the dim light. I turned to the picture of Bhagwan Mahavir on the wall and prayed that the horrible sound would never return.

Moments later, Ma emerged from the kitchen. "Go back to sleep all of you. You must say nothing of this. Your dad is fine."

***

The next day at school I sat next to Jayant and whispered, "You can come to my house for tea on Saturday. My family wants to meet you."

Before he could respond, Mrs. Desai entered the classroom. Conversation stopped and we all stood to show respect. She left the door open, allowing air to circulate, and walked to the front of the class with her sharp eyes darting back and forth, missing nothing.

When she reached her desk, we sat down and I opened my notebook, ready for our English lesson. We had started to learn English that semester. If I made it to college, many of the lectures would be in English so I was keen to learn. I knew a boy who went to a private school and he had started to learn English in third grade. I wished all schools did that.

I turned the pages to the last thing I had written and looked up to see Mrs. Desai staring at me. Her gaze did not waver. I swallowed hard; it had to be my monthly school fee. The school was semi-private and parents had to pay a small fee each month for their children to attend. My fee was two weeks overdue. Dad had paid other debts instead. This had happened before, and on each occasion, the stare from Mrs. Desai had frozen me in my seat. Other students said the same thing about her stare. I wanted to turn and look the other way but that would show lack of respect.

Normally, after a few seconds, Mrs. Desai would stand and write something on the chalkboard to begin the lesson.

This time she remained motionless. "Do you have anything for me Shah?"

I squirmed. There were many in the class named Shah but everyone knew whom she meant. I lowered my head. "No, Ma'am."

"Then you cannot stay in class."

My stomach tightened into a knot. *If I miss class, I'll never get to college. My school days are over.* I felt paralyzed, unable to respond. She had never said anything like that before. I closed my book, picked up my bag, and walked to the door, a walk that seemed to take forever. My cheeks burned and I felt every eye in the room staring at me. Tears formed. One or two students smirked but most held back, knowing that next month it could be them. I gripped my bag tight, hoping my tears would not flow until I passed through the open door.

In the corridor, I leaned against the wall and wiped my eyes on my sleeve. *Dad says I must study hard, but how can I study if I'm not in class? Hasubhai has graduated from university and has a job, so why can't they find a few rupees for me? Bhupat will soon have his diploma in radio repair. Has Dad borrowed so much for his first two sons that there's nothing left for me? Will my education end here in middle school?*

From the classroom came the tap-tap-tap of chalk on the chalkboard. I remembered that Mrs. Desai had the habit of saying out loud everything she wrote. Maybe I didn't have to miss class. Glancing up and down the corridor I reached for my notebook. If I listened carefully, I could hear most of what she said. I crouched down with my back against the wall and began to write.

***

That evening Hasubhai worked late, so nine of us gathered in the apartment waiting for our evening meal. I sat by the window while Damuben helped Ma prepare food. Five-year-old Prathiba held baby Kirit, and Bhupat played a game with Rashmi and Sadhana (aged four and two).

I felt Dad's hand on my shoulder. "Son, you are quiet. What is it?"

I glanced at his handsome face. Beneath a gently furrowed brow, dark pupils framed with white enquired about my well-being. How could I be angry with a man who cared so much for me? Words tumbled from my lips, "I had to leave class today and everyone stared at me. I hated it."

He squeezed my shoulder. "Stares cannot hurt you."

"They all know it's the school fee. What about our family reputation?"

He crouched beside me, close enough for me to feel his breath on my cheek, and smiled the soft smile that made problems go away. "Son, your job is to study hard, not to worry." He reached in his pocket for some coins. He had maybe 10 rupees, the price of small bag of rice.

"I need milk, rice, lentils, and spices," Ma said, stepping from the kitchen with a plate for the table. "And I'll use the last of the cooking oil and charcoal tomorrow."

Dad grimaced. Normally, the discussion about finances came after dinner, but he had pulled coins from his pocket. Ma counted on her fingers the merchants she needed to visit and our outstanding debts to each one. "We owe Mr. Madan 50 rupees for last week's grain, 30 rupees to the vegetable vendor, and 40 rupees to the milkman. And Dr.

Malkan will want money when I collect Bhupat's polio medicine. We owe him more than 100 rupees."

Dad let the coins slide back in his pocket like water disappearing down a drain. They were but a drop in the ocean of what we owed. "Hasubhai will have money today," he said.

Ma returned to the kitchen and Dad turned his attention back to me. "Let's go for a walk after dinner. You and I."

The thought pleased me and I smiled.

***

After dinner, Dad reached for his tattered white Nehru jacket and we left the apartment. The style of his jacket, with its high mandarin collar, had been made popular by Jawaharlal Nehru, when he led India's independence movement. The tailor who did our clothing repairs had told Dad not to bring his jacket back, since there was no space for more patches.

On the stairs, we met Hasubhai. Dad whispered to him and Hasubhai indicated he had 90 rupees to contribute to the family budget. Dad grinned and slapped him on the back. "Tell Ma she can shop tomorrow."

In the street, Dad lit up a bidi, a cheap cigarette made of raw tobacco rolled in a tobacco leaf. The evening air hung dusty and damp, and noisy truck horns reverberated through the narrow single-lane road—a road that had no markings, no sidewalks, and no drains. Cars, trucks, bicycles, animals, and pedestrians battled for space, all making slow progress. My nostrils filled with the smell of urine, spices, and exhaust fumes. Dark clouds threatened rain.

Across the street, I saw Shankar the Estriwala (apparel-ironing vendor) at the door to his shop. "Hey, Shankarbhai," I shouted, and he waved back. He was barely five years older than me and I often stopped to talk with him, even though he was of a lower caste.

A few paces along the street, part of a residential building had collapsed and spilled onto the roadway. Old Hanuman Lane formed part of a rent-controlled district and landlords took no interested in building repairs. Most residential buildings were poorly maintained, yet the local municipality rarely took action. Our building, 64-D, was in worse shape than most.

We weaved our way past potholes, animal droppings, and scaffold poles that provided structural support to crumbling buildings. These temporary fixes had long ago become permanent structures. As we walked, Dad rested his arm on my shoulder and I leaned into him.

"You should buy a new jacket," I said.

"What with, fresh air?"

"Nehru gave us our freedom. Your jacket should not be made of rags."

"One day, Ramesh, when you are wealthy, you can buy me a Nehru jacket. For now, I must put food on the table." His voice softened, "Sometimes that's not easy."

"Maybe I could get a job," I said, and immediately felt him stiffen.

"No, you must study. It's the only way things can get better."

We reached the intersection with Kalbadevi Road, a two-lane street that had six-inch deep open-sewer gutters on either side of the road. Traffic at the junction had come to a standstill, and a disharmony of horns filled the air. Pedestrians shuffled along in the space between the gutter and shop entrances.

From the street corner, we could see the doorways of the vegetable vendor, grain shop owner, and milkman. I remembered Ma's comments and, in my head, I added how much we owed them.

Dad must have seen my lips move while I did my mental arithmetic. "How much?" he asked.

"One hundred and twenty rupees."

He grimaced. "If we pay half, and pay your school fees, how much is left for Dr. Malkan?"

I remembered what Hasubhai had said and what Dad had in his pocket, and made the calculation. "Thirty-five rupees. A third of what we owe him."

Dad looked thoughtful. "Dr. Babubhai Malkan is a good man. He will understand. A third is better than nothing."

I looked at my father and wondered how he could handle this juggling act every day of his life. It had to be stress that was driving him crazy and causing his night terrors. Perhaps the person he argued with in his sleep was Mr. Madan, the grain merchant. None of us liked him.

Dad gestured to turn right and we moved away from the stores where we owed money. In the doorway of an empty shop, a mother with three young children and a baby crying at her breast begged for small change. Dad reached in his pocket and handed her a rupee coin. When he saw my questioning look, he gripped my arm. "Son, we have a roof over our heads. Compared to her, we are rich, and rich people should be generous."

"It's a leaky roof," I said.

He smiled.

On the other side of the street, two half-naked laborers pulled large, cotton-bagged bundles behind them with straps of material wrapped around their heads. As they advanced, they shouted warnings to other streetwalkers to move to the side.

"What about them?" I said. "They have nowhere to sleep."

He thought for a moment. "They are on the other side of the street. Bhagwan Mahavir has not caused our paths to cross."

Further along the road, we came to an opening between the shops that led to the elementary school I had attended. The school stood at the far end of a square with residential buildings on either side. The school comprised two buildings, each three-stories high: one for boys and one for girls. There was no playground. I remembered playing chase in the streets with hundreds of other students during recess.

In class, there had been no chairs and forty boys sat in groups on the floor to learn, mostly by memorization. Our teacher had been a lady and, when I first arrived from Jamnagar, I had to learn Hindi. In my Jamnagar school, we had spoken Gujarati and there had been more than forty children in the class.

The darkness of night settled in, and the street scene changed. We turned for home, our path lit by dim streetlights and light spilling from shop doorways.

Homeless people and itinerant laborers crowded the streets searching for somewhere to lay their torn, dirty blanket for the night. Spaces that provided shelter from the monsoon rains were the most desirable, and shop owners were losing the battle to keep their entrances clear of prostrate bodies. A drunken laborer staggered toward us without equilibrium.

Dad turned to me. "Son, look at these people. See how blessed we are to have a roof over our heads, even one that leaks. Bhagwan Mahavir is on our side."

Questions raced through my mind. *Why did these people have such miserable lives? Had they hurt or exploited others in a past life? Perhaps things would be different for them in their next life if they bore this current misery with strength and fortitude.*

"How will you pay off our debts?" I asked. "They keep getting bigger. If you can't pay the grocer how can you send Hasubhai and Bhupat to college?"

He smiled. "Payments for college are not debts, they are investments." His arm rested on my shoulder. "And you are next."

How I wanted that to be true. My eyes moistened. "If you can't pay my school fees, how can I go to college? I will have to get a job."

He paused in a doorway and pulled me close beside him. Other people jostled past us. I could feel his breath as he spoke, "Ramesh, a poor man's job will not improve our life. Two poor-man jobs will not be enough. Only education can move us forward. You must think big and study all you can, like your brothers. We will find a way to make it happen."

I wondered if he knew about his mental lapses and how much his children worried about him. He would do anything for us and was constantly taking on more. He never took the easy way out. Could his mind handle it?

I decided he should be a Brahmin in a future life. No one ever questioned his kindness or his motives, and his trust in God was unshakable. He kept us moving forward, one step at a time, even when those steps seemed to leave us further behind than where we started.

His arm wrapped around my shoulder, "Son, tomorrow will be a better day."

3

A Visit to the Doctor

I sat in class, struggling with a fever. It had started during the night and increased in intensity during the school day. This was not unusual. I'd had ear problems since early childhood, maybe two or three times a month. I glanced at the rag I'd used and slipped it in my pocket; it had yellowed with pus.

Most times, the aching pain and yellowish discharge were accompanied by fatigue, cough, and fever. Sometimes the fever remained mild, but today the pain and fever were elevated. My concentration had suffered and by early afternoon, the teacher's words were avoiding my brain like people avoiding an untouchable on the street.

Ma had told me to stop at Dr. Malkan's office on my way home if I needed medication. Dad had glanced at me with a look that said "only if you have to." I hated to increase our financial burden, but this time I had to see the doctor.

I climbed the wooden steps to the doctor's office and stepped inside. Everything took place in a single room. Dr. Malkan sat at a small wooden desk in the corner of the room with a patient seated in front of him. Two other patients sat waiting on a row of wooden benches that lined the wall. With just three patients, my outlook brightened. This could be a quick visit.

The doctor glanced in my direction. His white lab coat accentuated his well-groomed black hair and wire-rimmed spectacles. Neat piles of documents, old papers, and a couple of reference books filled his desk. The books had scuffmarks and tattered spines. A large ceiling fan made a muffled click with each rotation.

I had spent many hours waiting in this room, either on my Ma's knee or by myself. During those hours, I had observed how the doctor's reaction changed depending on the appearance of the person walking through the door. Most patients received a nod of recognition. Well-dressed patients were welcomed verbally. A small number were greeted with a silent glance like the one I had just received. I guessed that he reserved that for people with unpaid bills.

Normally, a dozen or more people filled the waiting area between the entrance and the doctor. Some would be seated and others would stand. Each time the doctor finished with a patient, the line of people would shuffle forward one space. The doctor worked on a first-come, first-served basis and did not take appointments, at least not for the patients I observed.

Behind a screen at the far end of the room, a compounder (chemist) weighed, mixed, and dispensed the medications the doctor prescribed, usually enough for two or three days. It looked like many patients received the same prescription: a combination of liquid medicine dispensed in small, barely labeled containers and colored pills wrapped in old newspaper cutouts folded into small triangles.

The compounder also collected money from each patient before handing over the medication. In my case, he would add an entry to the ledger for unpaid bills.

I sat down to wait my turn, confident that Dr. Malkan would see me even though I had no money in my pockets. He knew my father well. Even so, his attitude bothered me. Why should his attitude change based on the number of rupees he thought a patient had in his or her pocket? Whether I had a rupee or not did not make me a different person, so why should I be treated differently? I didn't like it.

I felt the same about the caste system and all the discrimination that it created. *Was a child born to a Brahmin (priest) really superior? Who said Kshatriyas (warriors, rulers) should come below Brahmins and above Vaisyas (skilled workers, merchants). My family belonged to this third tier—Dad worked as a bookkeeper in a store that sold cotton fabrics and clothing. Did our work habits make us better than the fourth tier of laborers—Shudra—who performed functions of serving the other three? And what of the untouchables who did all the unclean jobs? Their blood ran red like mine...was there really a difference?*

I thought of my childhood in Jamnagar and the time a boy I sat with every day at school came to play at my house. My grandmother looked down on him because he was a barber's son. The day was hot and I asked for a drink. She offered me tea in a stainless steel cup and a snack on a stainless steel plate, but to my friend she gave an old glass cup and glass plate.

"Why can't my friend have a stainless steel cup?" I asked.

Grandma looked shocked. "Ramesh, we are higher-caste Jain. We cannot share our dinner dishes with a barber's son."

Her answer made no sense to me. I played with my friend every day: why should we eat from different plates? "Then I want a glass cup and plate. Like my friend."

Grandma stared at me. With a shake of her head, she walked away and returned with another glass cup and plate.

***

Back at the doctor's office, the patient ahead of me moved to the treatment chair. I took the seat he had occupied, happy that the doctor would soon be prescribing my medication. Three new patients arrived and sat beside me.

Minutes later, the patient ahead of me got up from the treatment chair. I waited for the doctor's nod to move forward. Instead, Dr. Malkan made notes in one of his files and then looked past me and pointed to the man sitting beside me. The man jumped up and occupied the treatment chair. I stared at the doctor and wanted to shout, "*You've made a mistake!*" Yet I knew it was not a mistake. The doctor was making a point. Unpaid bills had consequences. Because I had no rupee in my pocket, I could sit in pain a little longer.

All I could do was daydream about how I would act differently if I was a doctor and could make the choice of who to treat next. I felt confident my dad would choose differently. He often quoted Nehru and Gandhi about how we should all work for the well-being of others. I had seen Dad live by those standards, and I wanted to be like him.

Sometimes I sat in Dr. Malkan's surgery and daydreamed of becoming a doctor, until reality reared its head and asked, "Ramesh, where will you get money for medical school?" I had no reply. Today, I decided to think big, like my dad had told me. Maybe I *could* become a doctor.

Two hours later, after a dozen or more patients had passed in front of me, Dr. Malkan invited me forward and looked at my ear. He muttered the name of a specialist before prescribing medication and nodding to his compounder to let me pass without payment. He knew there were no resources for me to visit a specialist and that I would be back at his office in a week or two. The compounder opened his book and added another visit to our list of unpaid debts.

***

I exited the doctor's office with my medication and joined a throng of people rushing home to be with their families for dinner. If my fever followed the usual pattern, the pain would subside over the next day or two. Hasubhai would help me with my homework and I'd work hard to catch up with the rest of the class.

At our apartment building, I climbed the three flights of stairs and arrived at our doorstep short of breath and exhausted. An embrace from Ma comforted me.

"What did the doctor say? Did he give you medicine?" she asked.

Several seconds passed before I had enough breath to reply. "The doctor gave me medicine for three days. He says I should see a specialist."

A pained look flashed across Ma's face. I held onto her for several seconds, soaking in her warmth.

Dad joined the conversation. "Son, take your medicine and get some rest. If you need a specialist, I'll see what we can do." He pulled a bed-mat from the pile by the wall and laid it out for me in my usual spot. I followed his instructions and soon dozed off.

***

The noise of a radio with bad reception woke me. It took me several seconds to realize it came from inside the apartment. I rubbed my eyes and saw Bhupat sitting at the table with a large, ornate, box-shaped radio. He had removed the back with a screwdriver and was looking inside.

I moved to the table. "You have a radio?"

He nodded, "I'm repairing it. Mind the aerial. I've wedged the end in the window frame so it doesn't fall out."

I looked at the long wire that hung between the radio and the window. Nimuben and the young ones sat in the corner. Dad and Hasubhai were not there.

"Whose is it?" I asked.

"It's the grocer's. He said he'll take 10 rupees off our bill if I fix it."

"Ten rupees? That's a lot of vegetables."

Bhupat grinned. Like Dad, he had excellent teeth. We all did. I moved closer and watched him manipulate the screwdriver inside the box. "How do you know what to do?"

He gave me a look. "It's what I'm studying."

It looked like an expensive radio. The box was made of polished hardwood. I peered inside. Various components were joined together with wires. "How does it work?"

Bhupat put down his screwdriver. "Do you know about electrons and radio waves?"

I shook my head.

He thought for a moment. "The broadcasting company has transmitters which send out radio waves. They're like an invisible stream of signals floating in the air." He pointed to the long wire. "This aerial collects the signals and the components inside the box amplify them so you can hear them."

His knowledge impressed me, even though I didn't understand what he was talking about.

He pointed to a glass tube inside and glanced at me, "...forget it. You're not even listening."

Ma entered from the kitchen, "You can't do that now. It's bedtime for the little ones." She carried a plate of food for me. I had slept through dinner.

While I ate, Bhupat cleared the table. He laughed when I told him about my wait at the doctor's office. "He's done the same to me."

"Does it bother you?"

He shrugged. "Ramesh, that's nothing. People laugh at me all the time because of my hunchback. They think I'm dumb. One day I'll show them they're wrong."

"How?"

"I'll start my own business. Most people have no idea how a radio works, but everyone wants one. When they come to me for repairs, I'll charge them as much as I want."

"You'll make them pay for their faults!"

He grinned. "What about you? Have you decided what you want to study in college?"

I hesitated. "I don't think we can afford it."

"Ramesh, college for you is four years away. By then we'll have three incomes in the family. What is it?"

"Promise not to laugh if I tell you?"

He nodded.

"I want to be a doctor."

He paused for a moment. "That's good."

Saying it out loud made me feel good. "Do you really think it could happen?"

"You will need perfect grades for that."

I nodded. "That's why I need your help with algebra."

He groaned.

I fetched my notebook and we struggled for an hour with the questions that Mr. Soni, my math teacher, had assigned the class.

That night, I lay in bed thinking about how some of my classmates had additional, one-on-one tutoring lessons with Mr. Soni. To get perfect grades, I needed something like that. It made two things I needed that were beyond our financial reach: an ear specialist and private tutoring. I thought about which I would choose if I could have only one. I wanted to say tuition, but my ear said otherwise. Sleep came before my decision.

4
A Summer Trip to Jamnagar

A couple of years after we moved from Jamnagar to Bombay, Grandpa Tribhovandas began a tradition of sending money at the end of each school year so Ma could bring her children to Jamnagar and spend the summer there while Dad, and later Hasubhai, stayed in Bombay to work.

Ma's face broke into a big smile when a courier delivered a letter from her father in the summer of 1961. The courier service was more secure and took only two days from Jamnagar, compared to four or five days for regular postal service. Ma opened the envelope, counted the money, and handed it to Hasubhai. "Son, please go to the booking office. Get eight third-class round-trip tickets to Jamnagar and make arrangements for a carriage to take us to the station."

I groaned at the thought of a 500-mile trip in a third-class compartment. "Ma, why can't we go second-class? Then we're sure to get a seat."

Hasubhai pocketed the money. "Ramesh, be quiet. Grandpa has sent money for the third-class compartment."

Although I enjoyed Grandpa's luxury bungalow, I really wanted to spend the summer with Dad and Hasubhai in Bombay. "It gets crowded and takes so long," I said. "I don't want to go."

Ma looked at me. "Ramesh, your grandpa wants you to come. You'll be on your own all day if you stay here. Come with us."

I couldn't show disrespect to my mother, so I had no choice but to go.

***

On a map of the Indian subcontinent, the journey looks like a short distance but, in reality, it's like traveling to a different country. The State of Gujarat had a different language, different customs, and different cuisine. The government refused to adopt Hindi as their official language and refused to teach English in its schools. Even the railway tracks were a different gauge, requiring a change of trains in Viramgam, where the two track systems (broad gauge and meter gauge) met.

The day before our trip, Ma packed a large suitcase with clothes and a second suitcase with bedding and small blankets in case we found space to sleep on the train. She also prepared a set of stackable, round, stainless steel containers with a carrying handle, known as a tiffin. On the day of the trip, she filled the containers with cooked spiced vegetables, whole-wheat chapattis and some hot mango pickles so we didn't have to purchase food on the train that was scheduled to depart at 8 p.m.

As the day progressed, a pain developed in my ear and the prospect loomed of a long and painful journey. I put some balls of cotton wool in my pocket, ready to soak up the discharge. Early in the evening, a horse-driven carriage arrived outside our apartment. Dad and Hasubhai loaded our luggage while the rest of us squeezed into the seats for the one-hour ride to the station. Bhupat brought along a water jug.

The driver took the most direct route to Victoria station, which passed through the red-light district of Golpitha, where the government allowed licensed brothel houses. Women sat in open doorways lining both sides of the narrow street. Some wore colored saris, others just their undergarments. They all wore liberal amounts of makeup and pouted bright red lips. As we passed, I noticed them making hand gestures and trying to make eye contact. I had never seen anything like it.

"Ma, why are these women staring at us?"

"Son don't look. Don't think about these girls."

Many times, our horse halted to sidestep a man talking with a prostitute. Some of the men chewed tobacco and spat on the sidewalk while they negotiated. Street vendors shouted their wares. Garbage from their stalls spewed onto the street. Bhupat sat beside me, holding the water jug. I watched him look at the prostitutes and then avert his eyes.

"Bhupat, who are these women?"

"I'll tell you later. You'll understand when you're older."

Traffic crawled along. The air had a musty smell, mixed with occasional wafts of incense from the brothels or spices from street-vendors' stalls. I tried to listen to some of the conversations, but all the street noise prevented me from hearing them clearly.

***

At last we arrived at Victoria Station. Damuben held onto our four younger siblings while Ma paid the driver his fare, and Bhupat and I unloaded our luggage. We entered the large stone archways holding hands as best we could while each carrying a piece of luggage. Bhupat also had the precious water jug, and Ma had the tiffin. It was important to stay together. Around us, the high ceilings echoed with a thousand conversations. The noise and jostling movement increased the pain in my ear.

Ma headed toward a man wearing a railway-conductor uniform, "Which track for Jamnagar?"

"Track five," he replied, glancing up at a giant clock positioned high in the arched ceiling. He pointed to a bridge that straddled the tracks. "You'd better hurry."

Damuben urged the younger ones along and Ma helped Bhupat climb the steps. As we crossed the bridge, the putrid smell of human excrement wafted up. I looked down at the tracks littered with garbage. Homeless people occupied the tracks at night when the trains did not run.

Ma urged us on. "Look, I can see track five."

We arrived at the track with Bhupat limping badly. Hundreds of people crowded the platform, standing four to five deep beside the track where the train would arrive. It looked like every one of them had a piece of luggage. We stood no chance of getting a seat if we remained at the back.

Ma pulled a blanket and a gray scarf from one of the bags. She handed them to Pratibha and Rashmi, aged eight and seven. "When the train comes, you must squeeze through the crowd and get on the train first. Lay this blanket across seats for all of us. Sit down, one at each end, and don't move no matter what people say. Wave the scarf out the window so we know where you are." She took the water jug from Bhupat. "You and Ramesh wait with the luggage. When you see the signal, get our luggage on board. Damu and I will look after the little ones."

An engine whistle sounded in the distance and we watched an empty train roll toward us on track five. The rhythmic beat of the engine grew louder and everyone on the platform prepared for the melee to come. Some had paid one of the unionized station porters, known as coolies, to board the train in advance and hold seats for them. Everyone else had a plan similar to our own. We needed good execution to get a seat.

Before the train stopped, I nudged Pratibha and Rashmi forward. They squeezed their slim bodies past the people in front of us and rushed for the door. The engine let out a long whoosh of excess steam and the platform became a scene of total chaos. A thousand ants can enter a pinhole in good order, but not my countrymen boarding a train.

I watched for Pratibha's signal.

"There she is. Third window," Damuben shouted.

Ma confirmed it was her. "Go," she said.

Bhupat and I moved the luggage toward the nearest door and pushed our way onto the train in a scrum with a dozen other luggage-movers. Once inside, we pushed our way to where Pratibha and Rashmi had seats in two separate sections of the compartment. The seats were wooden benches positioned beneath overhead wire racks for storing luggage. Benches designed to seat four people already had five or six occupants.

Window seats were the best, and Rashmi sat in one of them. I helped Bhupat maneuver our luggage under our seats and onto the wire racks above, and then sat down beside Rashmi. I felt exhausted. I glanced at Ma; she also looked tired.

Gradually, the pandemonium quieted. Passengers settled and got comfortable with the people with whom they would share the overnight journey to Viramgam. One light bulb lit the compartment and two ceiling fans circulated air. Each one was housed in a cage to prevent theft. The fans did little to disperse the body odor of the strangers squeezed next to me.

Daylight dwindled and I changed seats with Rashmi so I could rest my head on the window frame in an attempt to make my throbbing ear feel more comfortable. My lips moved in silent prayer that I would be able to sleep.

Through the window I could see the station clock. When the hands reached eight o'clock, the stationmaster waved his green flag and the engine driver sounded his whistle. Moments later, the train shuddered into motion. I stood up and leaned out the open window. Some passengers who had not managed to board the train clung to the outside of the compartments. They would hang there until the train reached the next station, maybe twenty or thirty minutes away, and then try once more to board.

The whistle blew again and I saw black and gray smoke billow from the engine stack and head in my direction. I pulled back inside the compartment, but it was too late. A whoosh of warm soot blackened my face.

The train stopped after thirty minutes at a small station on the outskirts of Bombay. More passengers tried to board. Fortunately, everyone who looked in our compartment turned away in search of a less crowded one.

When we left the station, Ma opened the tiffin and distributed food. We drank water from the jug Bhupat had carried. Other passengers had also brought food. Ma cleaned our plates in the latrine sink, put them away, and then spread blankets on the bench and dusty compartment floor so we could all stretch out for the night. "Get some sleep," she said in a gentle tone. "We change trains at 6 a.m. tomorrow morning. In the afternoon, you'll see Grandpa, Grandma, and your four aunts."

I stayed seated at the window listening to a whispered conversation between two elderly men sitting across the aisle. They were discussing politics. Other passengers dozed or read newspapers in the dim light from the single light bulb. The train moved through the darkness at about seventy kilometers per hour. Eventually, I settled beside Kirit and fell asleep to the rhythmic beat of wheels on the track.

***

"Six o'clock," the conductor shouted. "Viramgam in thirty minutes."

Ma tapped us on the shoulder, "Get ready to change trains."

I roused and looked out the window. The first rays of light were creeping over the horizon. I leaned out and the rush of dawn air felt cool on my skin. The elderly men across the aisle smiled at me. Ma folded our blankets and checked that we had all of our luggage. "After the change, it's only six more hours."

Several trains waited at Viramgam Station. Passengers rushed to make their transfers, but with far less chaos than in Bombay. We moved to the Jamnagar train and found comfortable seating. Bhupat organized our luggage, ordered tea, and handed out snacks from the tiffin.

The narrow-gauge train ambled along at a much slower speed through barren countryside with hard, stony plateaus mingled with green patches of farmland. Farmers tilled the soil with plows pulled by oxen, followed by family members and hired hands with small axes to break the harsh clumps of soil. Many of them worked with bare hands.

Temperatures rose rapidly under a clear blue sky and I asked Bhupat to turn on the fan. He reached to flip the switch but nothing happened. He tried again. "It's not working."

I stood up. "I'll go find the conductor."

"Don't waste your time."

Ma agreed, and I returned to gazing out the window. "How much rain falls in this region?" I asked.

"Between three and five inches a year," Ma replied. "There's always a water shortage."

I thought of the hand-operated well pump in Grandpa's compound and how grateful the neighbors were that he let them use it for a couple of hours each day. They all treated it like a prized possession.

The hours passed slowly.

Finally, the train slowed. Ma nudged us. "We're nearly there. Look out for Grandpa. He'll be waiting."

Bhupat leaned out the window. "I see the sign."

A minute later, the train crawled past the large wooden JAMNAGAR sign at the approach to the station.

"I see him!" Bhupat shouted. "He's on the platform."

The train eased to a stop and we jumped out and hugged Grandpa. He looked very smart in a starched white Nehru jacket with white cotton dhoti (loose, silk-blend bottom wrap), a black velvet cap, and shiny black shoes. I wished Dad's Nehru jacket looked that good. Ma followed us with a big smile on her face. After embracing her dad, she started to cry. I didn't understand why.

"Get the luggage," Bhupat shouted.

Grandpa ordered his favorite porter, dressed in a red shirt, red lengha, and red turban to help. Together we loaded the luggage onto the coolie's two-wheeled cart and walked through the station gate together. Grandpa paused to chat with the stationmaster. It seemed like they knew each other well. The coolie called over two horse-drawn carriages, loaded our luggage, and helped us into our seats. We all laughed as each one of us pretended to be an important person.

The journey to Grandpa's house took about twenty-five minutes. The road leaving the train station had one lane of paved surface with an additional lane of fine, reddish clay on either side. Dozens of scooters and bicycles threw up dust clouds from the unpaved surfaces.

Roaming cows, water buffalo, and donkeys crossed our path. Camel-drawn wagons that carried whole families, hay bales, and other produce headed for the marketplace. At one point, our carriage driver maneuvered carefully through a flock of goats that had strayed onto the road. The summer sun felt hot.

"You must be careful," Grandpa said. "Afternoon temperatures can reach fifty degrees Celsius."

In town, the streets were less crowded than in Bombay. "There's far less beeping of horns," Bhupat said.

Grandpa pointed at a group of dogs fighting over a piece of garbage. "You children must be very careful after dusk. There are many wild dogs in Jamnagar."

We continued down the main street toward the Rangit Sagar water reservoir. Grandpa pointed out his bungalow with pastel-colored stucco walls and a carving of the Goddess Laxmi in the center arch. It looked stunning. The surroundings were clean without any smelly garbage piles like we had near our apartment in Bombay.

We passed through a gate into a large private courtyard with high stone benches. Grandma stood at the door to the bungalow. When we had dismounted, she hugged each one of us and led us inside.

The bungalow was a palace by Indian standards: It had twelve rooms, plus a separate kitchen and washroom, more than five thousand square feet of living space in total. The floors were Italian mosaic tile and the main living room had Victorian sofas and chairs. A beautiful English wall clock hung above the sofa. The walls were decorated with framed family portraits. Everything looked spotless—except for the eight people with fine charcoal soot covering their exposed skin.

We bathed with as much hot water as we wanted while Grandma collected our clothes for washing. After bathing, we put on clean clothes and sat down to the lunch Grandma had prepared.

I gazed at the family portraits, all in identical polished mahogany frames. Ma and Hasubhai were among them. Hasubhai was grandpa's closest male blood-relative, an important relationship in Indian culture. According to Hindu and Jain tradition, if a man hopes to reach Nirvana when he dies, his eldest son should light the flame at his cremation. Grandpa's sons had all died in childhood, so Hasubhai was next in line. Grandpa had once offered to adopt him, but Hasubhai had said no.

"For dessert, we have mithai," Grandpa said.

My mouth watered at the thought of the sweet delicacies; they were my favorite treat. Made from milk, sugar, and clarified ghee with different mixes of saffron, cardamom, nutmeg, and other spices, each individual flavor had a special name: peda, mesub, halwa, and gulab jambu.

After lunch, I spent time in my favorite room where Grandpa kept his RCA gramophone and a collection of records. He also had a radio. At night I shared a room with Bhupat.

Outside, the landscaped backyard had a rose garden and flowerbeds full of mums. The hired help kept the yard looking beautiful. Each morning Grandpa and Grandma took roses to the temple and placed them in the open hands of the Jain idol as an offering.

***

Each morning I played marbles or pick-up cricket with neighborhood boys who congregated outside grandpa's bungalow. It was too far for me to visit my old school friends who lived in the center of town. During the hot, muggy afternoons, I stayed indoors and found things to do to kill time. Most days we played card games and sipped cold water with the fan blowing at full speed. Grandpa had a small ice chest and bought blocks of ice from a local vendor to keep it cold. This was something we never had in Bombay. Occasionally, Aunt Jasimasi bought us cups of shaved ice flavored with local delicacies such as saffron, cardamom, or artificial strawberry. They were delicious.

Even with all this activity, the days in Jamnagar moved slowly. I wished Dad and Hasubhai were with us. Some days I walked a mile to the local temple with Grandpa, and on the way we talked about local politics or the Jain religion. If Bhupat wanted to join us, we went by carriage. Jamnagar was famous for its historic marbled temples. They were more than three hundred years old and had survived the uprisings between Muslims and British rulers.

Once when Grandpa and I walked to the temple, we talked about life in Bombay and the hardships the family faced. I felt him put his hand on my shoulder. "Ramesh, would you like to move here for schooling?"

The question surprised me—Dad had always said we would get a better education in Bombay. Then it dawned on me that Grandpa meant private schooling. Hasubhai had turned down his offer of adoption, so Grandpa had decided to ask me. He wanted a male heir close by when he died. I wondered if he'd had the same conversation with Bhupat.

Thoughts swirled in my mind. *I would never go hungry in Jamnagar. There would always be water for bathing. Grandpa would find work for me in his shop and teach me his business. Life could be good.* But I didn't want to be separated from Dad. I had spent years without him and had hated it. I didn't want that situation to return.

Put on the spot, I made the same decision as Hasubhai, "I want to stay with my family."

"I understand that feeling," Grandpa said. He remained silent for a few paces. "What about your health? The dry climate might help you."

I shook my head. I could live with my ear infections and I was not the only one with allergies. My eyes moistened and I felt my fists clench. "The education is better in Bombay."

From the corner of my eye, I saw Grandpa slowly nod his head. He paused and turned to me. "Son, you have a strong spirit. That is good. Please know you can visit us whenever you want. You are always welcome."

I thanked him for his kindness and walked on, wondering if I had made the right decision. When we reached the temple, I said different prayers than normal.

***

That evening in our room, I sat beside Bhupat and told him about the conversation.

Bhupat shrugged, "He's not as rich as you think."

"What do you mean?"

"Grandpa's brother has three sons. While Grandpa is alive, he owns an equal share in the family business with his brother. That will change when he dies and things pass to the next generation. Everything will be split equally between the males on each side of the family. Grandpa's side will get one share and his brother's side will get four shares."

I was shocked. "How do you know all this?"

Bhupat tapped my shoulder. "That's the way it is. Girls get nothing from the family fortune."

***

A few days before our return trip, Grandpa presented us with new clothes to take with us—pants and shirts for the boys, frocks for the girls. After receiving the gifts, we sat drinking tea when a courier arrived with a letter from Hasubhai. "Go and pack your new clothes," Ma said, with the letter still unopened.

I rushed to change and be first back in the room. Something must have happened for Hasubhai to send a letter by courier. When I returned, Ma's face looked pale. Grandpa stood beside her with his hand on her shoulder. The envelope lay open on the table and I recognized Hasubhai's writing.

"What is it?" I said.

"Get your brothers and sisters." Her voice wavered as she spoke.

I ran to the bedrooms, "Come quickly."

When all of us were there, Ma explained that Dad had experienced a mild heart attack. "He is resting at home and recovering well. Hasubhai is with him. Dr. Malkan visited him and has advised four weeks of total rest. We've sent a reply via courier that we will leave for Bombay first thing in the morning."

I couldn't sleep that night. *If I had stayed in Bombay would this have happened? If Dad can't work, how will we pay our rent?* I felt certain I had made the right decision about Jamnagar. I wanted to be with Dad.

Bhupat stirred and I turned to him. "Can't you sleep?" I whispered.

"No."

"If Dad died, what would happen?"

"Ramesh, don't say that. Hasubhai says he's recovering well. You must believe him. Think positive."

"That's not what I meant. If Dad died, would Hasubhai be head of our family or would it be Grandpa who made the decisions?"

"Hasubhai would decide."

I felt relieved.

The following morning, I rose before dawn and made sure I had everything packed; then I helped everyone else get ready. Before we departed, I heard Ma talking with Grandpa. He gave her an envelope containing money and told her she could always return home to Jamnagar.

The return trip to Bombay took forever.

***

When we arrived home, we all rushed to see Dad. He lay near my window on a triple layer of bed-mats. Seeing his smile made me happy. Ma approached him first and we waited while they spoke quietly for a minute or two. The apartment was so small compared to Grandpa's bungalow, yet I was pleased to be home. Several medicine bottles stood on the floor beside Dad and I wondered how much we owed Dr. Malkan. It didn't matter; it was worth it.

Ma stood up and beckoned the younger ones forward. Dad gave each of them a hug, and Ma moved to the kitchen to make tea. Then Dad gestured for Bhupat and me to sit beside him. I struggled to contain my emotion. Dad reached for my hand and squeezed it. "Son, I'm going to be fine. This is not my time to go." His words came out slower than normal. Bhupat and I had tears in our eyes.

"Does it hurt?" I asked.

"No, son, there's no pain. But I have to be careful. Dr. Malkan said my heart is like a glass jar that has a fine crack in it. It still works but it has a flaw. If I handle it carefully, it can last a long time. We will do what Dr. Malkan says. I will be fine."

Ma brought tea, "Leave him now and let him rest. Have your tea in the kitchen."

I gazed at Dad, "I've something important to tell you."

Dad gave a slight nod and the others left us alone. "What is it son?"

"Grandpa talked to me. He said I could stay in Jamnagar and study there. I said 'No.' I told him the education is better in Bombay."

He reached for my forearm and I felt his squeeze.

"I want to be here with you. I want to study to be a doctor."

Dad's eyes moistened and a smile creased his lips. He spoke quietly and I leaned close to hear. "You make me happy, son. Now I know you understand." I felt another squeeze on my forearm. "Remember, tomorrow will be a better day."

5

Religion, Friends & Arranged Marriages

Five Jain temples stood within walking distance of our apartment. Four of them had their own plot of land and ornate carved marble architecture. Dad had chosen the fifth, the Mahavir Jain Temple, located in a typical two-story residential building near Zaveri Bazaar. I began visiting the temple with Dad as a child and gradually transitioned to going on my own, often in the evening.

At the center of the temple, a five-foot-tall, milky-white marble statue of Bhagwan Mahavir sat in the cross-legged yoga position. His hands rested on his legs in the open position. The idol's face had a wonderful expression, with a pleasant smile and beautiful eyes that gazed at the worshiper with a truly humble look.

When life seemed difficult, I found peace of mind at the temple and a sense of forgiveness every time I had a whispered conversation with the statue. My unselfish requests were fulfilled every time, sooner or later.

One evening, I walked to the bazaar, planning to visit the temple and then stop by Jayant's shop. Our friendship had continued to grow, even though I nagged him whenever I smelled alcohol on his breath or saw him bully someone at school. He often visited my home after school, but I had never visited his.

At the door to the temple, I removed my shoes, rang a bell mounted from the ceiling, and entered barefoot. The bell was thought to dispel evil forces and help focus the mind on prayer. Some people rang the bell two or three times but I always rang just once.

Inside, there were two rooms joined by an archway opening. The inner room housed the statue of Bhagwan Mahavir. Only people who had gone through a full cleansing ritual entered the inner room. There, they would perform a special form of worship that included touching the idol with the tip of their right-hand ring finger. This kind of worship is known as pooja.

I was wearing my street clothes, so I remained in the outer room and found a place where I could see the idol through the opening without blocking others' views. Once I settled, I focused on the idol, bowed my head, and whispered a mantra several times. I knew two mantras by heart. My mom could recite many more that she had learned as a child. She also had a book of mantras that we referenced on special occasions.

When I finished the mantra, I said my prayer in the form of a simple conversation with Bhagwan Mahavir. I started with gratitude that Dad had made a good recovery and then shared my worries and requests. After that, I made a final bow to the idol and held that pose until I experienced a sense of peace and forgiveness. Then I walked backwards to the door making sure I did not turn my back to the idol.

Outside, I put on my shoes, descended the steps to the narrow streets, and pushed my way through the crowds to the dimly lit side street where Jayant's hair oil shop stood. The side street was little more than a narrow alley that provided access to stairs leading to a second level of shops and residential apartments above.

As I approached, I heard Jayant's voice ring out with a curse. I searched the crowd and saw him shaking his fist at a man crossing the alley. Jayant stood several inches taller than those around him. I pushed through the crowd to where he stood and smelled liquor on his breath. "Jayant, why are you shouting like that?"

He lowered his fist. "That moron owes me money."

"My friend, he will not pay if you talk to him like that."

For a moment I wondered if he would take a swing at me, but his body relaxed. "What are you doing here?" he said.

"I've come to see your shop. Where is it?"

He hesitated for a moment before turning to the stairway behind him. In the shadows beneath the stairs, a weathered dark-wood cabinet with glass-fronted doors stood against the building. One-gallon pots labeled *Hair Oil* lined the oil-stained shelves. An elderly man sat on a wooden bench in front of the cabinet, ready to dispense the oil. The whole arrangement occupied a space of about three feet by four feet.

"This is Laxman," Jayant said.

I gave the man a slight bow. "Laxmanbhai, my name is Ramesh."

Jayant smiled at my formality of adding "bhai" to the end of his name, something I did for every man older than myself, regardless of who they were or their social standing. He pointed to the store above. "My dad owned the hair oil shop."

The reality of his situation hit me. His shop was this space beneath the stairs.

"Where do you sleep?" I asked.

He chuckled and pointed to the bench. "I sleep here. Laxman sleeps on the stairway landing."

I felt sorry for them both. No wonder Jayant liked coming to my apartment after school.

***

When I arrived home from the bazaar, Dad was resting and my homework waited. Dad had taken Dr. Malkan's advice and avoided exertion whenever possible. At work, his boss had given him a desk job. At home, he refused to go out in the evening because of the thirty-nine steps he would have to climb. I missed my walks with him more than I can explain. Although we had conversations in the apartment, they seemed colorless compared to our times walking the streets together.

I pulled out my homework and Hasubhai spent some time conversing with me in English. He had become semi-fluent at college, where most of his classes were in English. He often said that choosing finance helped, because numbers are the same in any language. For me, things would be more challenging; studying medicine and becoming a doctor might depend as much on my English skills as on my understanding of biology.

We moved on to algebra and he pointed out an error in one of my calculations. While I made the correction, he pulled a photograph from his pocket and peeked at it.

I looked up from my notebook. "Show me."

He grinned and turned the photograph so I could see it—a young girl with long, dark hair, dark eyes, and a friendly smile. Her name was Raman. Ma and Dad were at an advanced stage of negotiation with her parents about an arranged marriage. The parents had agreed to let the young couple see a photograph of each other, but they had not yet met or spoken.

Both families originated from the Jain community in Jamnagar, and a mutual friend had suggested the match. The parents had presented the couple's astrological data to a Hindu jotish (astrologer), and a meeting would be arranged if the jotish gave a positive response regarding compatibility. If that meeting went smoothly, the engagement would be announced and elaborate wedding plans would follow. The photograph and first meeting were concessions—our parents had seen each other for the first time on their wedding day.

The jotish would also study the stars and planets associated with the couple's birth dates and predict when those stars would align for a happy and prosperous marriage. The parents would choose a wedding date based on his recommendations.

Hasubhai motioned for me to continue with my homework and slipped the photo back in his pocket.

***

A few weeks later, the family waited eagerly for Dad to return from the final meeting with Raman's father. Anticipation hung in the air like a grape on a vine waiting to be picked. Hasubhai paced the floor, fingering the photograph of the woman he had fallen in love with. I sat by the window with Bhupat, searching the street below for Dad.

The trip to Jamnagar was more than Dad should be doing, but tradition dictated that he must arrange the marriage of his eldest son. Once Hasubhai was married, he could perform that role for his siblings.

"What are your feelings?" Bhupat asked his brother.

Hasubhai smiled his broadest smile. "I can't describe…It's a good feeling."

Everyone laughed.

We all had a stake in these negotiations. Hasubhai's marriage would set the stage for when we arrived at that point in our lives. Raman came from a wealthy and respected family. If her father accepted Hasubhai, then other families of high standing would consider us as suitable candidates for their sons and daughters.

Reputation impacted every part of life. Dad's reputation as an honest and trustworthy man, faithful to his beliefs, created an advantageous backdrop for the negotiations. Raman's parents would be confident their daughter would be treated with respect and dignity, a fact that often outweighed financial consideration. Our efforts to keep our poverty inside the four walls of our apartment also helped. Raman's parents did not know how poor we were.

"I see him," Bhupat shouted.

Hasubhai leaped to the window. "Where?"

Awnings and scaffolding restricted our view of the street, and Dad had stepped out of view. "Bhupat, does he look happy or dejected?"

Bhupat shrugged. "I couldn't see his face."

"Was his head held high or were his shoulders slumped?"

"Dad has so many worries his shoulders are always slumped," I said.

My younger siblings all laughed. Hasubhai shot me a glance that said comments like that were best left unsaid.

"I still can't see him," Bhupat said.

On the opposite side of the narrow street, a boy my age sat in a third-floor window. I waved to him. "Hey Pravin, can you see my Dad?"

He leaned out his window and scanned the street below. "Yes, I see him."

Communicating between buildings like this was common practice. Very few people owned telephones and this inner-city version of the bush telegraph allowed us to communicate within the neighborhood.

Ma moved to the kitchen to stoke the coals, ready to make tea. A minute or two later, the apartment door opened. Dad looked worn out by the long journey and the steps he had just climbed, but he had a smile on his face so we knew the news must be good. He raised his hand to stop the questions and addressed Hasubhai.

"Son, Raman's father has agreed to your engagement."

The girls squealed with excitement. They would gain a new sister and get to take part in the wedding ceremony. Each member of the family congratulated Hasubhai with a hug.

"Did the jotish set a date for the wedding?" Ma asked.

"Three months," Dad said. "We must make plans."

To celebrate, Ma served tea with some sweet delicacies, and then discussions about wedding preparations started.

***

One evening, a few days later, discussions were in full swing when someone knocked at the door. Hasubhai jumped up to see who it was, "Ramesh. It's Jayant."

I got up to welcome my friend. He carried a manila envelope close to his chest.

"Jayant, is there a problem?"

He shook his head and grinned. "I'm rich. I need you to look after this money for me." He opened the envelope and showed me several wads of money—more than I had seen in my life.

"Where did you get it?"

"The man who bought my father's shop has paid the final installment. I need somewhere to keep this safe. I can't keep it at my shop. You're the only people I trust."

Dad had heard our conversation. He stood up, "Jayant, it is safe with us. First we must count it." He led the way to the kitchen where we counted the money and wrote the total on the front of the envelope. Dad placed the envelope in the cupboard, and there it stayed.

Some evenings, when the family discussed finances and I searched the apartment for a few pennies, I would pause by the cupboard and think about the hundreds of rupees inside. Yet we never took from it or borrowed from it. Whenever Jayant needed money, he would come home with me after school and we would remove the money and record the amount on the envelope.

Bhagwan Mahavir at the Jain Temple, Zaveri Bazaar, Bombay, India.

My father, Mr. Babulal K. Shah
From Jamnagar, India.
Born: 1912 Died: Jan.11, 1962

My Mother Savitaben B Shah
Daughter of Tribhovandas Zaveri from Jamnagar, India
Born: 1917 Died: July 1967

(L-R) Nimuben, Ramanbhabhi and Damuben Presenting wedding gifts to Mina in 1971.

Brothers: (L-R) Kirit, Bhupat, Ramesh, Hasubhai, Rashmi.

Brother: Bhupat

Sister: Pratibha

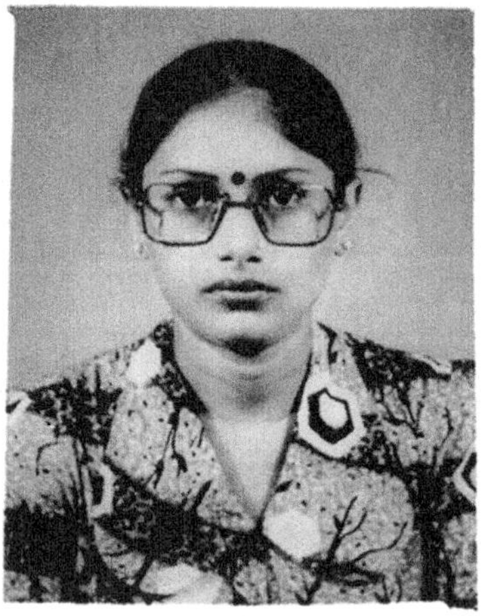

Sister: Sadhana

Maternal Grandma Maniben Tribhovandas in Jamnagar

Maternal Grandpa Tribhovandas Zaveri

Mina with my grandma and two aunts in Jamnagar

6

Departure of My Mentor

A month or two later, about five months after his first heart attack, Dad began to experience uncomfortable chest pains and made several visits to Dr. Malkan. The doctor advised him to see a cardiologist but Dad worried about the cost and ignored the advice. That worried us all, yet out of respect we had to accept his decision.

One evening, I was in the apartment when he had chest pains. Ma and I sat with him. "Dad, you should listen to Dr. Malkan and visit the cardiologist."

He gave a slight shake of his head. "Son, I know the doctor is right, but I feel fine now. The pain has gone. I'll take some rest and then I'll be okay."

"Ramesh, do your homework," Ma said. "Let Dad rest. He will be fine."

The next day he went to work as usual, but when he returned it was clear that things were far from normal. He had a fraction of his former strength and vitality.

In the following days, his cheerful, talkative nature disappeared and he stopped asking me about my daily school activities. Some days he would be like his old self, other days he hardly said a word.

On the evening of January 11, 1962, I sat by the window doing my homework when Dad arrived home. His face looked drawn and he felt exhausted from the exertion of climbing the stairs. I got up to give him a hand.

Ma rushed from the kitchen. "Are you okay?"

He had barely enough strength to nod his head.

We knew he was not okay. I helped him to a chair and he rested for a while. When his breathing stabilized he asked Ma to prepare some warm water so he could bathe. He also requested a clean white zabo (loose cotton shirt) and white dhoti to wear. He had never before made those requests during the evening hours. Ma stopped cooking the evening meal and placed a container of water on the charcoal stove.

While Dad bathed, Hasubhai and Bhupat arrived home from work. Ma got their attention before they entered the kitchen for a drink of water. "Your father is taking a bath. He is not feeling well."

They glanced at each other and then at me. I told them what had happened. There was nothing we could do. I tried returning to my homework but I couldn't concentrate. Our younger siblings huddled together and watched the unusual family dynamic in silence.

When Dad came through the kitchen door, he looked fine in his fresh white clothing.

Hasubhai stepped forward and reached for Dad's arm. "Are you okay?"

Dad smiled. "Son, I'm fine." His voice had no energy.

"Dad," Bhupat said, "we must call Dr. Malkan for a home visit."

Dad gestured to a chair and Hasubhai helped him sit down. The younger ones ran forward, wanting to sit with their dad. Ma stretched out her arm to stop them.

Dad looked at Bhupat. "Son, don't waste any more money. I am fine. Let me rest. I just need some rest." His voice trailed off and silence filled the room. He looked at Ma. "Serve dinner so we can sit and relax."

Ma moved to the kitchen and Hasubhai laid out a bed-mat for Dad to lie on after the meal. The room was subdued while we ate. So were our hearts.

Dinner ended around 8 p.m. Ma and Damuben got up to collect plates and clean the kitchen. Dad moved to the bed to rest. He had a pained look on his face. We all watched, wondering what to do.

When Ma finished in the kitchen, she rubbed some Vicks Vapor Rub slowly on Dad's chest. The smell of menthol reminded me of the times Ma had rubbed balm on my chest and how its warmth on my skin and tingling sensation in my nostrils brought comfort. Damuben joined Ma and massaged Dad's legs.

He did not complain of any pain, but his face looked pale and we could tell he was not comfortable. He whispered to Ma. "Get the Bhaktaman book."

Ma fetched her holy book of Jain mantras. Her hands trembled as she turned the pages to a mantra suitable for this situation. Her voice wavered as she read the first few words, and then she hit a tuneful pitch and proceeded to chant several different mantras. Dad gazed at the framed picture of Bhagwan Mahavir on the wall. Our apartment felt peaceful.

I felt drawn to the bed and sat next to him, reaching for his hand. He looked at me, gave me a smile, and squeezed my hand. I smiled back but couldn't contain the tears that welled in my eyes. I didn't want him to see sadness on my face, so I got up.

Hasubhai and Bhupat made eye contact with me. We had to do something. Hasubhai glanced at the wall clock; almost 10 p.m. "Dr. Malkan often works late. Maybe he's still at his office. Bhupat, go and check. If he's there, ask him to come quickly. Tell him Dad isn't well."

Dad heard the conversation and gestured to Hasubhai not to summon the doctor. "My time has come to see Bhagwan," he murmured.

"Don't say that!" Ma cried, the first time I had ever heard her disagree with Dad. She looked at Bhupat. "Go quickly. Get Dr. Malkan."

Bhupat left the apartment. Hasubhai moved to the window and hailed a friend across the street. "Narendra, I need your help. Please go to my father's uncle, Mr. Suderlal Shah. He lives on Marine Drive. Ask him to come and visit my father."

His action surprised me. Within minutes, the whole neighborhood would know something was happening in our apartment. Many knew of Dad's mild heart attack and would draw the obvious conclusion.

Hasubhai turned to me. "Ramesh, go to Mama's house. Bring Mama and Mami here." Mama was Dad's maternal uncle and the senior member of our family in Bombay. He owned a shop that sold churned butter (ghee) and was one of the people from whom Dad borrowed money. Both he and Mami (his wife) were in their late seventies and would need help getting to our house through unlit streets. They lived about half a mile away. I would have to escort them.

I rushed down the stairs and made my way to their apartment as quickly as I could through narrow alleys dotted with street sleepers. My mind kept wandering back to the scene at the apartment. Would Dr. Malkan have medicine that could help? Thoughts of Dad dying entered my mind, but I resisted them and convinced myself that wouldn't happen.

At Mama's apartment block, I climbed two flights of stairs. Out of breath and exhausted, I knocked on his door. His wife answered and invited me into the living room where the whole family relaxed on Victorian sofas. Two sons and their families shared Mama's luxury four-room apartment. On the far side of the room Mama raised his hand to welcome me, "How are you son?"

"Mama, please come quickly. My dad's not well. Dr. Malkan is on his way."

Mama nodded and motioned for Mami to get ready. Then he pulled his creaking joints out of his chair. "We'll be as quick as we can."

The wait seemed to take forever. I moved to their balcony and looked at the silent street below. In the stillness, I had a vision of my father's funeral pyre. Tears rolled down my cheeks and I prayed to Bhagwan Mahavir for his help.

Mama and Mami emerged and we moved slowly down the stairs. I willed them to move faster, but they were old and had poor eyesight. I wanted to run home, but I knew I must stay with them. Each step seemed to take forever.

When we reached our tenement building, the climb up three flights of stairs took even longer. I wanted to know what was happening in the apartment, but had to show respect and move at their pace. We reached the last few steps and I heard the wail of my mother's voice.

Inside the apartment, deep sadness filled the room. Ma cried hysterically and would not be consoled. My four younger siblings cried with her. Hasubhai hugged each one of them and told them that we would be fine. Bhupat and I did the same. In reality, we all knew the floor had been taken from under our feet.

Dad looked peaceful. He had known what was coming and had bathed and dressed for his passing. A white shawl covered his body leaving only his face exposed. His eyes were closed, his mouth open. Although contact with his dead body would make me unclean, I wanted one last physical contact with my dad and I touched the tip of his foot.

"Hasubhai, when did he die?" I asked.

338 | 9781503154094 | 1838

Location: B3

VOM.JQI

::	Tomorrow Will be a Better Day
d:	Good
r:	vo_list
tion:	DESKTOP-95EUL5F
e:	2021-11-30 21:35:31 (UTC)
count:	Veteran-Outsource
g Loc:	B3
SKU:	VOM.JQI
q#:	1838
it_id:	3564817
dth:	0.91 in
nk:	2,540,954

delist unit# 3564817

XXXXX

"It's difficult to say exactly when; he died so peacefully. When Dr. Malkan arrived with Bhupat, he examined Dad and pronounced him dead at 11 p.m."

I told Hasubhai of my vision on Mama's balcony. "It was the moment he died," I said.

Hasubhai nodded.

News soon spread that my father had passed away and neighbors began to arrive. He was a popular man and many people came. My brothers and I held up well, although inside we were in deep pain.

Dr. Malkan prepared a death certificate stating that Dad had died at age 50 due to heart failure. He apologized that he could not save Dad. When Hasubhai said we would pay his fees at a later date, the doctor said there would be no need for that.

We had to let family and friends know immediately so that people could join us and attend the cremation the next morning. The late hour made no difference. A dead body is considered a symbol of great impurity in Hinduism and Jainism, so cremation takes place as soon as possible after death. We also needed wood for the funeral pyre and to build a stretcher to carry the body.

Mama had experience with these situations. He gathered a group of younger men and sent them off to contact relatives and other members of our Jamnagar caste who were living in Bombay. One person rushed to the railway station to catch the last train across the city to inform an aunt who lived on the north side of Bombay. Another was dispatched to telegraph a message to Grandpa Tribhovandas in Jamnagar. He and Grandma would come to comfort their daughter, although they would not arrive in time for the cremation.

Hasubhai pulled me aside. "Ramesh, we do not have enough money for the funeral expenses. Go and ask your friend Jayant if we can borrow 200 rupees."

I took off in the direction of Zaveri Bazaar and found Jayant drunk and talking to no one in particular. When he saw me he looked puzzled, "Why are you here?"

"My dad has died. I need to borrow 200 rupees for the funeral."

For a moment Jayant sobered up and I thought I saw tears in his eyes. "You can take it from my envelope."

I rushed home, removed 200 rupees of Jayant's money, and noted the amount on the envelope. Hasubhai passed the money to some friends and sent them to buy wood and other supplies needed for the stretcher. While I was away, he had arranged for a Hindu priest to come the next morning and lead the procession to the cremation ground.

Caste members from all over Bombay began to arrive. Everyone came in clean white clothing. The women wore plain-white saris without any ornaments on their arms or face. The atmosphere in our apartment grew very somber as they tried to console my mother and other family members.

In a ritual that I found hard to watch, Mami and the other elder ladies removed my mom's gold bangles and gold necklaces from her wrists and neck to symbolize that she had become a widow. Mami also removed the red tika from Ma's forehead, the mark that symbolized her status as a married woman.

Ma would never remarry, and never again wear jewelry. From now on she would wear only a white sari and would be treated by society as if she were no longer a complete person because her husband had passed away.

It was painful to see her widowed in her mid-forties. Her welfare now rested with us, Hasubhai in particular. Her only assets were the gold jewelry, necklaces, and a few pieces of diamond jewelry given to her when she got married. They were her financial security for the rest of her life. From now on they would remain in her closet, unworn.

People continued to arrive through the early morning hours. Neighbors came and went. Family remained. Our small apartment overflowed with people.

In the center of the room, the elder males placed Dad's body on the floor with his feet pointing south, the direction of the dead. An oil lamp was lit and placed near the body. It would burn for three days. No one ate or drank anything. This complete fast would continue until after the cremation.

When Hasubhai's friends arrived with wood for the stretcher, Mama and some of the elder males started construction. They laid out the wood and tied pieces together with rope to form a frame that had four long handles for the pole bearers. Then they stretched cotton sheeting over the wooden frame to support the body. Amidst this activity, many of us were in a state of denial that our father was no longer with us.

***

The Hindu priest arrived at 8 a.m. to start the cremation ceremony. First, he chanted ritual mantras for a departed soul in the ancient Sanskrit language. Then we made a ritual offering to the priest of milk and rice for the Brahmins. We gave little more than a cup of each, although wealthy families would give more. This would be fed to a sacred cow or given to the poor.

Hasubhai, Bhupat, and I wrapped Dad's body in plain-white cotton cloth and then placed the body on the wooden stretcher. Only his face remained exposed.

Hasubhai, Bhupat, Mama's eldest son, and I were the first to carry the stretcher. We moved as carefully as we could down the three flights of stairs, and then raised the stretcher to our shoulders for the two-mile procession to the Hindu cremation ground near Marine Drive. People on the street moved from our path as best they could. In keeping with tradition, Ma and the other females stayed at the apartment and did not join us on the last journey of the deceased. A total of ten hours had passed since his death.

The procession moved slowly through the streets. Some of the funeral party members chanted Jain mantras in a gentle voice, while others walked in silence. Every few minutes, four new relatives or friends relieved the pole bearers at the front of the procession.

At the cremation ground, we presented the body to government officials who ran the operation and showed the death certificate signed by Dr. Malkan.

A wall surrounded the open area where burnings took place. Workers prepared a pyre and then laid the stretcher and corpse on top with the feet of the corpse facing south so the dead person could walk in the direction of the dead. The official in charge covered the body with wooden logs and then with ghee. While this took place, the priest spoke to Hasubhai about his role in the ceremony.

Hindu and Jain followers believe that the physical body dies and is consumed during the cremation, but that the individual soul has no beginning and no end. Depending on its karma—the consequences of actions over lifetimes—the soul may or may not pass to another life.

The priest took over from the government officials and chanted mantras over the body. Then he handed Hasubhai a vessel containing water and ghee and instructed him to walk around the pyre three times sprinkling the contents onto the pyre. Then the priest handed Hasubhai a clean white cloth and asked him to cover the face of the corpse. The preparations were now complete. Hasubhai took a flaming torch and set the pyre alight. This moment initiated the traditional mourning period that would continue until the morning of the thirteenth day after death.

It took about four hours for the fire to consume the body. At that time, most attendees left the cremation ground to go home, take a bath, and return to their daily activities. Close relatives returned to our apartment to mourn.

***

At home, Hasubhai, Bhupat, and I took a quick bath and dressed in white shirts and lengha. Nobody spoke while the ladies served tea and food to break the fast of those who had returned to the apartment.

The following days were filled with sorrow. Some of our aunts and uncles stayed with us for several days, making sleeping arrangements very crowded in our apartment.

Grandpa and Grandma arrived from Jamnagar, and a constant stream of visitors came to pay their respects.

Ma cried a lot and remained in a state of shock. The stream of visitors made her loss fresh every day, yet tradition dictated that everyone who knew my father should pay a visit. We could not change that.

A few days after the cremation, when things had quieted, an untouchable who worked in the apartment block as a janitor knocked at our door. He cried as he told us how Dad went out of his way to treat him with respect and how much it meant to him and his family that Dad often gave him a few rupees so he could send his son to school. It was an act of generosity we knew nothing about and it lifted our spirits.

7
Starting College

Our grandparents stayed for a month to help us through our first weeks of mourning. Grandma spent long hours consoling Ma. Grandpa contacted Raman's parents to postpone the wedding; it was customary to mourn for several months, even a year, before a big family celebration. Before they departed, Grandpa left some money with Hasubhai to ease our financial pain for a while.

During those weeks, my ear problem flared up and drained my strength both physically and mentally. I missed a few days of school and fell behind at an important time. In less than three months, I would take my final high school diploma exam. I needed a top grade to follow my dream of becoming a doctor.

Hasubhai, Bhupat and I sat down one evening to talk about our budget. They did most of the talking and I just listened. "The money from Grandpa will soon be gone,"

Hasubhai said. "When that happens, we have a big hole in our finances."

"But you earn a good wage," Bhupat said, "and word is getting around about my radio repair. I'm getting more work each week."

Hasubhai shook his head, "It's not enough. We lost Dad's income and he had no life insurance. The company he worked for provides nothing for death benefits."

Bhupat frowned, "No one from that company has even visited to see how we are doing."

For a moment, we sat thinking of our father and lamenting our fate. Then Hasubhai turned to Bhupat. "I will have to look for a second job, and you must take every repair job you can find."

Bhupat slowly nodded his head.

"I could look for a part-time job," I said.

Hasubhai gave me a hard look. "How are you doing at school?"

"I'm okay."

"Ramesh, okay is not good enough. You need good grades on your final exam, or who knows what will happen to us? Our father had a dream, and we are not going to let that dream die."

Bhupat wagged his finger. "Hasubhai is right. Don't worry about home. You must study. You need a top grade to go to college."

I swallowed hard. I doubted whether I could improve my grade.

"Besides," Hasubhai said. "If we work longer hours, you will often be the only one at home to look after Mom and encourage the young ones."

I felt the weight of added responsibility descend on my shoulders, and I wasn't sure I could handle it. But I had no choice, and nodded my head in agreement.

***

In the following days, Hasubhai found extra part-time work and Bhupat reached out to his friends for additional radio and other electronics repair jobs. He had some good friends who helped. Among the three of us, Bhupat was the most optimistic for the future.

For my part, I studied long hours. When I found it hard to concentrate, I remembered the walks I had with my dad and told myself I had to be strong for him, my mentor and spiritual teacher. Although life would never be the same without his smile to lift my spirits and make the worries of the day disappear, he remained with me in spirit. I could not let him down.

At the temple, I constantly reminded Bhagwan Mahavir that I needed help to get through this phase of my life. Frequently, I felt a response that things would be okay and left the temple with a smile on my face.

On my way home, I would visit Jayant and spend time with him. We were talking one day when a man walked by. Jayant raised his fist and shouted, "Where's my money, Manu. Pay up before next month or you'll have a bloody nose."

The man disappeared into the crowd.

"Jayant, don't forget I owe you money."

He looked at me. "Don't worry about it. I know you'll pay when you can."

***

My hard work paid off. I graduated high school with grades good enough to study science at Kishanchand Chellaram (K.C.) College at Churchgate, a well-respected school three or four miles from our apartment. It meant I could live at home. All we needed was money for tuition.

Hasubhai decided we should visit our father's distant uncle, Mr. Suderlal Shah, who we called Kaka (Uncle). We had attended the wedding of his eldest son, Chandu, earlier that year. Kaka had a business that traded in cloth and his office was not far from our home. Kaka's younger brother, Bachubhai, also had a trading company that dealt in the import and export of handicrafts, but the brothers did not work together and did not have a close relationship. We didn't know why.

Hasubhai arranged a meeting. When we arrived, Kaka was busy with customers, so Chandu greeted us. He offered us chairs to sit in, and ordered tea for us while we waited. After a few minutes, Kaka joined us and invited us to his private office. He wore starched, white clothing on his almost six-foot frame, and had a strong personality that matched his appearance.

His office felt cool. Hasubhai leaned close and whispered, "He has air conditioning." It was something very few people had at that time.

Kaka poured himself a cup of tea. "How is your mom moving along with her life?"

Hasubhai gave a non-committal response.

"And how are you boys coming along?"

"We are okay. These are tough times, but things are not so bad. As you know, I work at Associated Cement Company, and Bhupat has plenty of work as a radio repair technician."

"I'm glad to hear it." Kaka sipped his tea and looked in my direction. "Ramesh, what is your plan?"

Before I could speak, he turned away and continued his conversation with Hasubhai. "Now he's graduated high school, we can find him a good job in the cloth market. That will help your finances."

Hasubhai's jaw tightened. "Kaka, that's not our plan. We're here to ask if we can borrow money for Ramesh's college fees. He will join K.C. College in August."

Kaka frowned and I knew the conversation was going nowhere.

"It's been a tough year in textiles," he said. "Business is slow, and I've had additional expenses...like Chandu's wedding." There was an awkward silence. "Hasmukh, I can't promise you now, but come back and see me later. We will talk about it. How is your family in Jamnagar?"

We both knew it was time to leave. Hasubhai thanked Kaka for his time and we exited to the street. I felt dejected. Hasubhai placed his hand on my shoulder to encourage me just like Dad used to do. "Ramesh, we will be fine. We will find the money."

***

That evening we discussed the situation with Ma. Our younger siblings sat in the corner of the room listening to every word.

"Ramesh must go to college," Hasubhai said. "That is what our father wanted."

Bhupat nodded, "Taking Kaka's job would be like quitting."

Ma sipped her tea, "I have my gold and diamond jewelry that I don't wear anymore. Gold prices have gone up. They will pay for a year or two of college."

My eyes welled up with the thought that Ma would give everything she had for me. I spoke in a forceful voice, "No, we are not going to sell your gold. That's your security."

Hasubhai agreed. "Ramesh is right. We will not sell your gold. We will find additional loans. We'll ask Grandpa for help if needed."

"But I have no more use for gold. Better to pay for college. We don't want more loans."

Bhupat raised his hand. "Ma, I have two good friends I work with, Ishwarbhai and Dhirubhai. They will not say no to me."

Hasubhai consoled Ma. "We will be fine."

***

A few days later, Bhupat came through with the loan he had promised, and together we visited K.C. College to pay my first semester's fees and complete my registration. He turned to me on the walk home. "Ramesh, you cannot fail. However hard it is, you must keep going."

I nodded, conscious that my brother set a high standard for persistence and determination. Despite his curved spine and stunted right leg, we were walking along at a good pace. He had also made good progress in the world of radio repair and wanted to start his own business one day. I asked him about it.

"My friend, Ishwarbhai, is showing me how he runs his business. He says he will help me. A few more months, Ramesh, and I'll be ready."

***

On opening day of college, I got up early and dressed in a long sleeve shirt, long pants, and a pair of Indian leather Kolhapur sandals that Hasubhai had helped me purchase. Ma eyed me with a grin on her face. "You look sharp. Don't forget to take the bus. It's too far to walk."

I nodded my head and picked up my cotton handbag with my course books, obtained for free from the Jamnagar Visa Oswal Jain Charitable Trust.

At 7 a.m., I boarded a red double-decker bus operated by the Bombay Municipal public transportation system (BEST) at the corner of Old Hanuman Lane and Kalbadevi Road. The weather was warm and humid, and the bus had no air conditioning. I sat in an aisle seat at the front of the bus with a good view through the front window. I felt sorry for the driver as he weaved between cars, taxis, pedestrians, cyclists, hawkers, handcarts, and an occasional horse-drawn carriage.

The bus stopped frequently and soon filled with students heading to school and workers on their way to offices and factories. Soon, all the seats were taken, and new passengers had to stand in the aisle holding onto straps that hung from a safety bar fixed to the ceiling of the bus. Sweat stains on peoples clothing gave a measure of the day's heat.

An elderly lady boarded carrying a heavy bag and she struggled to hold on when the bus lurched from side to side. Remembering my dad's teaching, I got up to offer her my seat. She thanked me with a soft smile. More passengers pushed their way on board and I felt physically trapped. I dabbed my handkerchief to my forehead to wipe away the sweat.

At last, the bus reached my stop, a few yards from the college, and I disembarked into a posh residential and commercial area. The four mile journey had taken twenty-five minutes. I breathed in the fresh air and observed the clean streets. There were no piles of garbage or bamboo scaffolds. The roads were pothole-free.

I entered the college gates with a sense of pride. This was the next important step in my father's dream. The college building stood four stories tall. Well-dressed students stood joking in the courtyard and around the entrance door. Some smoked. Others sipped Coca Cola. Chauffeured sedans dropped off a stream of other students. I felt like an alien and looked around to see if there were others like me, but before I could locate anyone, the doors opened and I had to go in.

The brightly lit classroom had around eighty polished wood chairs arranged auditorium-style, facing a large chalkboard with a pedestal and podium in front. Each chair had a hinged writing surface for taking notes. I chose a seat near the front so I would be able to hear clearly.

The teacher entered and the room quieted. He spoke English with no pauses for explanation in Hindi or Gujarati, and used technical terms I had never heard. My upbeat mood turned to despair. I opened the textbook to the first chapter and realized I understood about one word in three. My high school English classes had focused on greeting people, asking street directions, and reciting verbs. I had never seen or heard this scientific vocabulary. My chest tightened and my breathing became erratic.

Students around me seemed to be having no problem. Most wore expensive clothes and I guessed they had attended private schools. The lesson was being taught at their level. I felt helpless, like a soldier sent into battle without a sword. What could I do? I couldn't let anyone know my predicament or I might be dismissed from the class. I had to try to fit in.

When those around me wrote in their notebooks, I wrote in mine—mostly gibberish. When the class recited something, I mouthed in silent mime. In our first lab class, I focused on a student standing on the opposite side of the lab bench. Whatever he did, I copied a second later.

I went home exhausted, pondering what to say to my family. They had high expectations and I didn't want to disappoint them. I had to say something positive. Ma would be the first to notice my anxiety, so I put a smile on my face at the apartment door. "Wow, what a day," I said.

Her eyes lit up. "Tell me about it."

"Learning in English is tough, but the laboratories are fantastic."

That evening, I opened my textbook and my English dictionary and started to translate the text, line by line. Each technical term I didn't know, I listed in the back of a notebook with its meaning.

"They gave you homework on the first day?" Ma said.

I couldn't say yes, and I didn't want to say no. "I'll have homework every day."

That night, I lay awake thinking about the task ahead of me. It seemed impossible. Yet my dad had faced impossible situations and he never gave up. I had to tackle my problem the same way, like Bhupat had battled polio, one day at a time. Today had been exhausting, but tomorrow would be a better day.

***

Later in the week, as students poured into the lecture room, I saw a face I recognized. "Hey, Pradip. Is that you?"

A boy about my size glanced in my direction and a smile creased his face. We knew each other from school, although we had never really become friends. Before we could talk, other students pushed between us, some of them much bigger than us. Finally, we maneuvered our way together.

"Ramesh, I didn't know you were here." He pointed at two empty seats and we sat down.

"Do you understand this teacher?" I asked.

He shook his head, "Not very well. He speaks fast."

"Me neither. We must help each other."

He nodded.

For the first time at K.C. College, I no longer felt alone. Pradip was Jain and from a poor family. He lived in an apartment building somewhere in my neighborhood. We were kindred spirits, trying to keep our heads above water like two pieces of driftwood in an ocean of affluence.

8

Addition to the Family

I had been at college about a month when Grandpa Tribhovandas informed us that Raman's father, Mr. Babulal Zaveri, had visited him regarding his daughter's marriage to Hasubhai. Ma agreed that after nine months of mourning, we should contact a jotish to establish a new date for the wedding.

We hoped the excitement would lift Ma out of her severe depression. Ma asked Mami, the elder lady of our Bombay family, and me to accompany her on a visit to Jotish Sharma, the family jotish.

We took a bus ride to the Bhuleshwar suburb of Bombay, and the jotish's wife welcomed us to their second-floor apartment. The small, windowless room was dimly lit by an oil lamp on a stand. A big astrological image with Sanskrit descriptions of the twelve individual Zodiac signs filled one wall. I did not understand a word of it.

We removed our sandals, bowed to show respect, and sat beside the jotish on a well-worn rug in front of the Zodiac signs. Ma held two small envelopes containing the horoscope charts, known as kundli or janampatri, drawn up after the birth of each child. The jotish's wife offered us tea, but we requested water instead; it had been a hot journey.

After quenching our thirst, Ma opened the envelopes. "Jotish, here are the kundli for Hasmukh and Raman. Please find the auspicious Shubh Muhurt (most beneficial time) for their wedding. We want events to proceed without any obstacle."

Jotish Sharma nodded. "Choosing the right time will nullify evil influences and make the result of the wedding most fruitful." He took the birth charts and laid them out in front of him. For several minutes, he studied the charts in detail and drew astrological signs on a clay slate while murmuring Sanskrit words that Ma, Mami, and I did not comprehend. His drawings looked like a child's version of a spider web. He stared back and forth between the large Zodiac signs and the marks on his clay slate before addressing Ma. "The planets and other astrological factors will focus their energy in an auspicious way during the third week of December."

Ma nodded her approval and paid the jotish 25 rupees for the information.

***

The families chose December 19, 1962, for the wedding in Jamnagar, and agreed to keep celebrations simple, because we were still in the mourning period for Father's death. A simple celebration pleased Hasubhai, who was worried about the expense. He arranged a loan and asked his very good friend, Pransukh, to be his best man. The loan meant we could proceed without financial concerns, although every new loan increased our debt and became another drain on our finances.

Ma decided to give some of the gold jewelry she had received at her own wedding as a gift for Raman. She set aside about 20 tola (around 235 grams) of gold for this gift, and presented it to Raman with new saris and other new clothing. This gift maintained our family prestige and camouflaged how close we were to the poverty line.

We stayed at Grandpa's bungalow for the wedding. All the gifts and jewelry were displayed on large, decorated, stainless steel plates for all to see. Grandpa hired cooks to prepare special food for the occasion.

On the day of the wedding, Hasubhai wore a tailored navy blue suit with a starched white shirt, a patterned red tie, and black shoes polished to a bright shine. Grandpa had also purchased new clothes for each sibling. We all felt very special dressed up for the family occasion, and it was sad to see Ma wearing just a plain white sari, no jewelry, and no red tika on her forehead.

***

The fragrance of carnations, roses, and mums filled the wedding hall. A group of musicians played traditional Indian instruments including the shehnai (a double-reed conical oboe), dhol (double-skinned, barrel-shaped hand drum), sarangi (stringed instrument like a steel guitar played with a bow), mangira (small cymbals), and harmonium.

A special structure used only for weddings, called a mandup, stood at the front of the hall. It had decorative pillars and a canopy decorated with colorful fresh flowers. Two bright-red bamboo chairs sat center stage for the bride and the groom. Side chairs for parents and a pedestal with a clay pot for the sacred fire filled the rest of the space. Chairs for the guests were set up in rows facing the mandup.

Pransukh and Hasubhai led our family group into the hall where two hundred guests stood in small groups, sipping sweetened milk flavored with saffron, pistachios, and almonds. The room had a wonderful party atmosphere. Many guests had not seen each other for months, and they were busy catching up on family news.

My ear throbbed as we passed the musicians on our way to the mandup. At the mandup, Ma broke away and joined the elder ladies of the family in the front row. Tradition held that a widow seated on the mandup might bring bad luck to the newlywed couple.

A few minutes later, the bride entered, escorted by her father. Her eleven younger siblings followed, with the rest of the wedding party behind them. The musicians played traditional wedding tunes. Raman wore a red sari edged with a detailed weave of gold thread and a matching blouse. Her jewelry sparkled. She wore a beautiful gold and diamond necklace, matching earrings, a diamond stud in her nose, and diamond bangles on both wrists. Her arms and hands were adorned with intricate mehndi, temporary tattoos applied using extracts from the henna plant. Her long, silky black hair intensified the beauty of her eyes, and her smile showed her joyful mood, although she remained serious for the occasion. Her father led her to the mandup and seated her in one of the red bamboo chairs at center stage. Her younger sister, Suman, sat close by as her bridesmaid.

Raman's parents then greeted the bridegroom and his family, an informal moment in the formal occasion. When the greetings were complete, Pransukh escorted Hasubhai to the second red bamboo chair to sit beside Raman. The pundit (priest), selected by the bride's family, gave a signal to the musicians to stop playing. Then, to begin the ceremony, he took a red powder (kum-kum) and placed a mark on the foreheads of the bride and groom.

The pundit lit the sacred fire and recited in Sanskrit the mantras for a traditional Hindu wedding. The whole ceremony lasted about three hours. During that time, the pundit spoke Sanskrit and the local Gujarati language, so guests could understand the proceedings. Hasubhai and Raman held hands and participated when prompted by the priest. Raman's parents also played a role.

My favorite moment came when the pundit requested Hasubhai and Raman to walk slowly around the sacred fire seven times and then take seven steps together reciting a vow at each step. The seven vows were commitments the two of them were making to each other. Step one: we will share responsibility in our marriage. Step two: we will strengthen each other in mind, body, and soul. Step three: we will strive for wealth and prosperity by righteous means. Step four: we will acquire happiness through mutual love, trust, and respect. Step five: we will raise strong, virtuous, and courageous children. Step six: we will maintain spiritual values and longevity. Step seven: we will remain best friends in lifelong wedlock.

Only close family paid attention throughout the ceremony; other guests returned to conversation in small groups. At the end of the ceremony, the priest and the elder family members, including my mom, gave a blessing on the young couple for a long and prosperous life. At that moment, Raman became a member of our family. Tears rolled down the cheeks of her parents. Ma and my grandparents consoled them, assuring them that Raman would be well cared for, and that they could visit her in Bombay any time they wished.

The party continued at Grandpa's house for close relatives and friends. Throughout the wedding, no alcohol was consumed and only pure Jain vegetarian food was served (no garlic, onion, potato or other root vegetables). For financial reasons, Hasubhai chose not to have a separate reception party after the wedding.

***

The next day, all family members making the return trip to Bombay gathered at Jamnagar Railway Station, including Hasubhai and his new bride. Bhupat had booked third-class tickets for all of us. The bride's relatives joined us at the station to give her a rousing and joyful send-off.

Raman, whom we now addressed with the familiar yet respectful name Ramanbhabhi, had several suitcases to bring along that her parents had packed with new saris, clothing, gift boxes, and a selection of homemade sweets. Ramanbhabhi also had gold jewelry her parents had given her and the gold bangles and necklaces that Ma had presented.

During the long train ride, we got to know Ramanbhabhi better. Her friendly personality soon shone through and my younger siblings loved having a new big sister. She also had a tender, loving nature. At one point, I sat near her and talked. "Ramanbhabhi, I heard you talking to Ma about how you have been looking after your sick grandma. What is wrong with her?"

"Rameshbhai, she is bedridden with very severe diabetes. She is a most wonderful person and I have learned so much from her." The smile disappeared from her face and I saw sadness in her eyes. "Now my younger sister, Suman, will take care of her. I am not worried. Suman will look after her well."

Later, I noticed Hasubhai standing by the window getting some fresh air. I joined him, gazing out at the arid landscape. "You've married a very nice girl."

He grinned, "I feel very lucky. Her whole family is nice." We passed a clump of bushes nestled in a rocky outcrop. "I wish Dad had been here. He worked very hard for this."

I nodded my agreement. "Have you seen how the young ones have taken to her? We're all lucky to have Ramanbhabhi join our family."

I shifted my position and noticed Ma listening quietly to our conversation. She smiled.

***

Back at the apartment Ma organized post-wedding activities, inviting neighbors and relatives who did not make it to Jamnagar to come and welcome Ramanbhabhi to her new neighborhood. At night, Ma joined us in the main room so the newlyweds could enjoy some privacy in the kitchen area.

Compared to the bungalow where Raman had grown up, our apartment was tiny and overcrowded. Yet she never complained about this or the loss of any other comforts and conveniences she had left behind. This endeared her to every member of our family. She quickly adopted my four younger siblings, aged four to nine, and never seemed to raise her voice to them. With Dad no longer around, she brought much needed sunshine to our home, and soon we were using a shortened, more intimate form of her name: Bhabhi (sister-in-law).

Our conversations about daily finances were hard for her to comprehend and she was shocked to learn the true financial status of our home. Her family had never struggled to pay bills, even for luxuries or vacations. Her decision to maintain the prestige of her adopted family and not disclose this information to her parents was a true blessing to us, and a sign of her deep respect for her new husband. Revealing our true financial situation would have impacted marriage prospects for others in the family, including myself.

Bhabhi and I bonded well. Five or six years my senior, she became a dear new sister. One afternoon, I came home from college to eat a late lunch and she sat with me on the floor. Ma was busy in the kitchen washing pots and pans.

"How are your studies going?"

I sighed, "Don't ask."

She raised an eyebrow, "It can't be that bad. You study so hard."

I looked up from my chapatti. Her eyes showed genuine interest and her friendly nature softened my reluctance to talk. "I guess I'm doing okay."

She smiled, "You don't sound convincing."

I took another bite of food and thought of a positive spin. "I'm doing better than I expected."

Her brow furrowed. "Did you expect to do badly?"

I lowered my voice so Ma couldn't hear. "My English is very poor. At first I didn't understand a word the teacher said."

Her jaw dropped. "Did you tell anyone about it?"

I shook my head, "No! I feared I'd be told to go home. All classes are in English."

"What did you do?"

"Each evening, I read the textbook and look up every word I don't know."

Her eyes widened. "Is it working?"

I shrugged. "Today, I understood some of what the teacher said."

She laughed. "I'm impressed. You're studying two subjects at once: science and English."

Her words cheered me, I'd not thought of it that way. My situation was like Hercules pushing two rocks up a hill instead of one—and I was making progress. I smiled and put my food plate to one side.

Bhabhi reached for the plate and served me another chapatti. "Rameshbhai, you need energy. You know how sick you get. You must eat more to stay healthy."

I opened my mouth.

She grinned and pushed the whole chapatti inside.

***

As the weeks passed, my understanding of both English and science continued to improve and I even began to enjoy laboratory classes. On my way home, I would sometimes stop at the David Sassoon Library, a private library at another nearby college. Hasubhai had membership through his work, and family members were welcome. It had quiet, comfortable places to study or take a nap. I also started sessions with a teaching assistant for extra help with physics and analytical chemistry.

At home, we had more family excitement with the marriage of my sister, Damuben, to a young man named Navin Kumar, who came from the Jamnagar caste family living in Bombay. He worked in his family's business of manufacturing jewelry boxes located near Zaveri Bazaar.

With so much financial drain after Dad's passing, Ma decided to have a low-key wedding with little spending. She gave Damuben a few pieces of gold jewelry and some new clothing. Although the groom's parents were financially better off than us, they understood our situation and cooperated with us. We were fortunate to find so humble a family for Damuben.

***

The end of the academic year approached, and I felt I had a good chance of surviving until the second year. My biggest concern was the end-of-year exam. It would be closed book, and my final grade would depend one hundred percent on the outcome.

A week or two before the exam, I suffered an ear infection and Dr. Malkan prescribed medicine to reduce the fever. I did my best to ignore the pain, but my studies suffered. One day, when I sat with Bhabhi to eat lunch, she leaned forward and touched the back of my hand when I reached for a chapatti.

"Rameshbhai, you still have a fever. Did you take your medicine?"

"Yes, I'm feeling better today. Thanks for asking."

Ma put her head through the kitchen doorway. "How's your ear discharge?"

I sensed a conspiracy. "It's much better."

They seemed satisfied and I bit into my chapatti. Bhabhi watched while I chewed. "Your elder brother told me last night about your big exam. Are you ready for it?" She didn't use her husband's name, an important sign of respect in Indian culture. She would speak his name only to him and only when they were alone.

"Bhabhi, I'll be fine. My sessions with the teaching assistant are really helping."

Her look of concern softened a little. "Your brother says the exam is important."

I nodded. "Very important, but I'm feeling much better. I'll go to the library this afternoon and study for several hours."

Ma's head appeared once more. "Be sure to take a bus. It's very hot today."

I said nothing. I had no money for the fare and didn't want a fuss.

Bhabhi's tone lightened, signaling that my interrogation was over. "Will you be home on time?"

I gave her a puzzled look.

"My cousin Mina is coming to see me. She has just returned from Jamnagar and has family news."

***

I arrived home early, before a storm hit, and sat by an open window in the apartment taking a break from my studies. The afternoon had been very hot and humid. Outside, lightning flashed against dark, rumbling clouds and I felt a gust of wind. The rains would soon arrive. I looked out the window and watched street vendors folding up their stalls and covering their merchandise.

Ma and Bhabhi were in the kitchen, and I could hear their conversation.

"You have several cousins in Bombay. Which one is visiting you?" Ma said.

"You remember Jasiben who lives nearby? It's her daughter, Mina."

I felt splashes from the first drops of rain and got up to shutter the window and turn on the fluorescent light Bhupat had installed to replace the single light bulb. It gave much more light.

"Ramesh, there's no reason to turn the light on so early," Ma shouted from the kitchen.

"I have to study."

Bhabhi joined in. "Ma, its dark. And Mina will be here soon."

Ma did not reply.

I returned to my seat thinking Bhabhi's cousin would be very wet when she arrived.

Before I could open my notebook, there was a knock at the door and I went to open it.

My jaw fell when I saw the girl standing in the doorway. She had light skin and big, beautiful black eyes. Her long braided hair, silky and black, gave perfect contrast with her bright white smile. She looked healthy, not at all malnourished, and wore a printed frock that radiated sunshine in the dark hallway. I swallowed hard. "Can I help you?"

"I'm looking for my cousin, Raman. Is she here?"

"P-please come in. She's expecting you."

I stepped to one side and called to the kitchen, "Bhabhi, your cousin is here."

Bhabhi ran to the doorway and embraced her visitor. When they parted, Bhabhi turned and formally introduced us. "Rameshbhai, this is my cousin Mina. Mina, this is my brother-in-law, Rameshbhai. He's in college."

Mina smiled and brushed some small droplets of water from her sleeve. "I just missed the heavy rain."

"Nice to meet you," I mumbled, too shy to say more.

Mina removed her sandals and Bhabhi led her to the kitchen. I remained motionless, gazing at the expensive, black high-heel sandals set neatly by the door.

***

From where I sat I could see Bhabhi and Mina through the kitchen doorway. They were laughing and talking about her family in Jamnagar. I tried to concentrate on my studies, but my mind was in the kitchen. If I leaned slightly, I could catch a glimpse of Mina's face. I tried reading the newspaper but still couldn't concentrate, not even on the cricket news. My eyes kept drifting to the kitchen.

Bhabhi came to the doorway. "Rameshbhai, Ma has prepared tea for us. Would you like to join us?"

For some inexplicable reason, I said, "No." Maybe I knew that Mina was out of my league. I couldn't compete for a girl who wore polished black sandals like the ones decorating our entrance. Or maybe it was the fear shy people experience when they meet strangers and fall in love.

After a while, their voices went quiet. I looked up and noticed that Bhabhi was crying. Mina was holding her hand.

I got up to see what was wrong. "Bhabhi, why are you crying?"

"I'm okay. I just miss my mom and dad."

I wanted to say more but my tongue wouldn't move, so I retreated to my books. Outside, the storm had subsided. I opened the shutters and a cool breeze entered the room. Moments later, I heard Jayant shout my name from the street. I leaned out the window and waved, "I'll come down."

***

When I returned from walking the streets with Jayant, the polished black sandals were no longer by the door. Bhabhi and Ma were in the kitchen. When Bhabhi saw me, she ran and grabbed my hand. "Isn't Mina pretty? I saw you peeking at her."

I grinned. "She is very pretty."

"Guess which school she attends?"

I shook my head. I didn't want to play guessing games.

Bhabhi smiled. "She attends the Shakuntala Jain Girls High School on Marine Drive."

It was a very prestigious girls' school. For a moment, I dreamed of marrying Mina. "How old is she?"

Bhabhi grinned, "You're too young to be asking."

She was right. I was too young…and too poor. My momentary dream wilted like the petals of an orchid struck by monsoon rain. What was I thinking? Mina's father would never give his beautiful daughter to a boy like me.

Perhaps Bhabhi saw my disappointment and wanted to cheer me. "We must keep her in mind when you are ready for a wife," she said.

I looked away and mumbled a reply. "We're too poor…"

Bhabhi reached for my arm. "Perhaps…when you're a doctor…" She looked serious. "Her father believes in strong family values. You pass that test easily."

I thought about her words several times over the next few days and began to study with renewed vigor.

9

Second Year of College

My friendship with Pradip grew stronger during our second year of college. He lived a five-minute walk from my home. Each morning I walked to his apartment block and shouted to an open window on the third floor. He or his brother would respond and, a minute later, Pradip would join me. In the afternoon when classes ended, we retraced our steps and parted company at the corner of his street.

One day, toward the end of the school year, we had just parted company when my foot hit a raised cobblestone and the strap on my flip-flop came loose. I bent down to fix it and noticed a folded piece of paper covered by dust and rubble in a nearby pothole. I picked it up to investigate and discovered it was a 5-rupee note! My spirit lifted. Five rupees would buy a new pair of flip-flops. I quickly put the money in my pocket.

As I walked along, my Jain conscience spoke to me. "It's not your money."

I pushed the thought away. I needed new flip-flops and this 5-rupees would pay for them.

"It's not your money," my conscience insisted. "That money belongs to the person who lost it…the person who earned it."

I tried to ignore the voice in my head, but it would not go away. What would my dad say, I wondered?

"It's not your money."

I walked on with the note weighing heavy in my pocket until I reached the corner where I could turn for home or continue on to a nearby shoe shop. I paused there for some time before heading home. The 5-rupee note remained unspent in my pocket for many days.

***

During that time, the University of Bombay posted the schedule for the crucial end-of-curriculum exams that would determine future options for study and, ultimately, future careers.

Based on the results of these exams, many hundreds of science students from all colleges affiliated with Bombay University would decide whether to apply for specialist fields like medicine, dentistry, and biotechnology, or to enroll for a Bachelor of Science degree in a less demanding discipline.

I was very conscious that I would need a first-class grade to advance to medical college and that my next few weeks of study and how I performed in these exams would determine my future.

The exam schedule was very demanding, and generated bad feelings among the student body. That afternoon, Pradip and I walked home in somber moods.

Pradip kicked a small piece of wood that littered the street. "Eight exams in four days. Can you believe it?" he said.

I shifted sideways to return the kick. "And each one is three hours long."

"With only an hour break for lunch."

The piece of wood, a broken end of a walking cane, hit a pothole, popped in the air, and landed a few feet into the road. When Pradip moved to retrieve our newfound toy, a loud horn sounded. I grabbed his arm and pulled him from the path of a passing truck. "Take the exam first, before you kill yourself," I shouted.

I regretted the words before they were out of my mouth. A boy from our apartment block no longer appeared in the water line because of suicide. It wasn't something I should joke about. "Sorry, that wasn't funny."

We walked on until Pradip broke the silence. "Have you ever considered suicide?"

I hesitated, not sure what to say. When pain from my infected ear pierced deep inside my brain, I'd often thought I'd rather be dead. And I hated when shopkeepers shouted about unpaid debts, but I'd never done anything to hurt myself. "I've thought about it few times, but not seriously…have you?"

For a while he didn't answer. "No, not seriously…but if I fail these exams, my life won't be worth living."

I nodded my agreement. "Did you know Hari, Vinod's brother, from my building?"

Pradip shook his head.

"He couldn't swim. Last summer he walked to Chawpatti Beach and continued out into the Arabian Sea without stopping."

"Why?"

"No one knows. But it was around the time exam results were announced."

Pradip frowned. "It's crazy that exams count for everything. One bad day can ruin your life."

I nodded. "I wish I could take my notebook into the exam room."

"And an English dictionary."

I thought of my conversation with Bhabhi about my studies being doubled. Pradip was right. In these exams, our understanding of English would be as critical as our understanding of science.

We approached the intersection where we parted company, and I wanted to end our conversation on a positive note. "Pradip, tomorrow will be a better day."

He grunted and turned onto his street.

I shouted after him, "Things will be fine in the end. Have faith, I promise you."

I continued on, praying silently that I would not get an ear infection during the exams like I had the previous year.

***

That evening Hasubhai sat beside me at the dinner table. He put his hand on my shoulder. "Ramesh, you are quiet. What's bothering you?"

"We got our exam schedule today. They start in three weeks. We have eight exams in four days!"

"That's tough," Bhupat said. "Any help you need, just ask."

I nodded.

"Which exam is first?" Ma asked.

"English, the hardest one for me. I'll do well to get a passing grade. I'll need top grades in most other subjects for a chance at medical college."

"What are the other subjects?" she asked.

Ma had a sharp mind, but had never received an education, so I knew she would struggle with my answer, "Biology, physics, organic chemistry, inorganic chemistry, calculus, algebra, and geometry."

She looked at me with a blank stare, "I'm sure you'll do well."

Hasubhai cleared his throat. "Bhupat is right. We must all do what we can to help Ramesh." He glanced round the table. "Pratibha, Rashmi, you will take on his chores until these exams are over. He must do nothing but study."

My eleven- and ten-year-old siblings both scowled, but didn't complain.

***

For the next few days, I went through my notebooks and put together a plan for the exams. For each subject, I picked out topics I felt confident would be included in the exam and focused on those.

For each topic, I summarized the history, listed important facts, wrote out equations, and drew the diagrams that professors had drawn on the chalkboard during the school year. I planned to memorize the notes and use them as the core of my essay answers.

Sir Hans Adolf Krebs, British biochemist, credited with discovering the cycle — 1937.

Acetyl-CoA + 3 NAD+ + Q + GDP + Pi + 2 H2O --> CoA-SH + 3 NADH + 3 H+ + QH2 + GTP + 2 CO2, where Q is ubiquinone and Pi is inorganic phosphate.

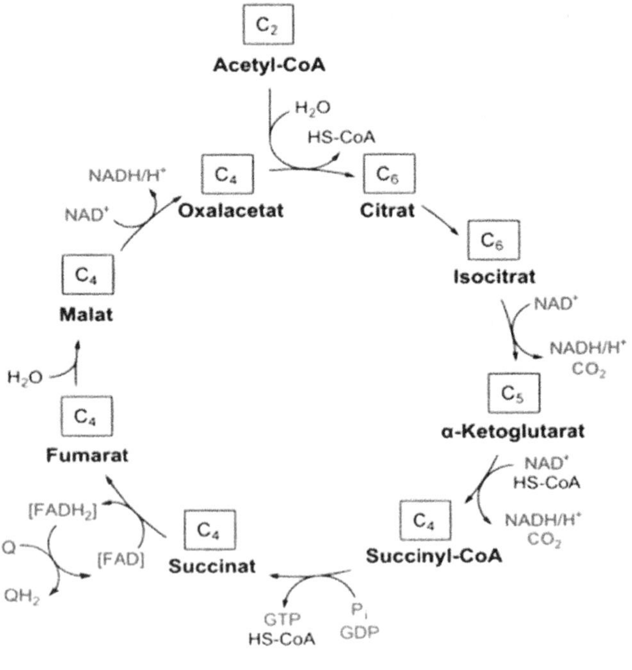

All this time, the 5-rupee note remained untouched in my pocket. I woke one night with thoughts bouncing back and forth in my mind.

Don't spend the money. It belongs to someone else. Spending money that is not yours is like stealing. You should return it. But who lost it? That will never be known. Discarding it would be a waste. Then give it to the poor. We are poor, so why not spend it?

The debate continued until I fell asleep again.

The next day, I paid a visit to the temple to ask for good health and spiritual calm during the buildup to my exams. With trembling hands, I removed the note from my pocket and held it up in front of the idol. In my heart, I felt Bhagwan Mahavir supporting my father and my conscience. *Do not spend money you have not earned.* Before departing the temple, I placed the note in the receptacle for monetary gifts and prayed that Bhagwan Mahavir would bring good fortune to the person who had lost it.

***

One evening, when we sat down for our meal, Bhupat raised a finger and said he had some good news. He waited a few seconds for suspense to build. "I'm going to start my own business. I'm calling it Blue Star Radio Repair."

Hasubhai almost choked. "You need money to start a business."

Bhupat shook his head.

Hasubhai counted on his fingers. "You need money for rent, money for inventory, and money to buy tools."

Bhupat grinned. "I have tools and some spare parts, and my landlord friend says I can pay rent in installments as my business grows."

"Is that your friend, Ishwarbhai?" I said.

He nodded. "He's offered me a small space for rent. He has many customers who own radios and gramophones. Many of them already know me and like the service I provide."

Hasubhai absorbed the information, "That sounds great. He's a good friend."

"Why Blue Star?" Ma said.

Bhupat shrugged. "It sounds good. I think people will like it."

***

Days flashed by and exam time arrived. I had stayed healthy and felt a sense of inner well-being as I entered the room to take my English exam. The seats were placed two feet apart, and no students talked for fear of discipline by the moderator. When the bell rang, I turned over the exam paper and started to read. My grasp of English was very basic, and I knew I would struggle with questions about complex sentences, verb tense and even simple grammar.

For the multiple-choice questions, I was able to eliminate one or two of the answers and then rely on guesswork and good fortune. For the essay question, I made sure I used some sentences I had practiced beforehand and knew were correct. I exited the exam room, having answered all the questions and with hopes of a passing grade.

The next two exams went smoothly and I approached my biology exam feeling nervous, yet confident. A good result from this exam would be crucial for acceptance into medical college. I found a quiet corner and calmed myself.

When the exam room doors opened, I entered and took my usual seat. Three hours later, after forty or more multiple-choice questions and four essays, I headed for the door with a smile on my face—it couldn't have gone better. The essay questions were all topics I had included in my revision studies.

I exited the building and saw Hasubhai waiting to greet me. He smacked me on the shoulder. "You're smiling. You must have done well."

"I nailed it. Let's wait for Pradip. I want to compare notes."

When Pradip emerged, I beckoned him over. "He looks happy too," Hasubhai said.

Pradip and I reviewed the essay questions. "How did you do on the endocrinology question?" he asked.

I frowned. "What endocrinology question?"

"The second essay question."

My heart missed a beat.

I closed my eyes and pictured the exam paper, the second question, the wording…and realized I had misread the question. I had written an essay about enzymology, not endocrinology…enzymes, not hormones. My detailed, well-structured description of enzymes in the digestive system would score zero. They wanted to know about the pituitary gland. With one stupid mistake I had blown fifteen percent of the exam.

I buried my head in my hands. I knew about hormones. I could easily have scored twelve percent on that question, and the difference between first class and second class was ten percent. I had blown it and there was no way I could recover on the remaining exams.

Hasubhai tried to console me, but we both knew I was in trouble.

"You mustn't dwell on it. You still have four exams to take."

"How could I be so stupid?" I said. "Why didn't I read the question twice?"

I felt Hasubhai grip my shoulders and wobble me to get my attention. "What's your next exam?"

"Mathematics."

"Study for that. You have to move on." He guided me, almost supported me as we left the college grounds. Pradip walked with us. There was nothing they could do to cheer me.

***

At the end of the week, all exams were done and I felt drained of energy and emotion. Over dinner, we had a candid family discussion about the likely outcome.

"A first-class grade is out of reach," I said.

Bhupat tried to cheer me, "But you did well in some exams."

I had to agree. "I've a good chance at securing a high second class."

Ma handed me some food. "That's still a good grade."

"Not for medical college."

I thought of Mina's visit to our apartment and Bhabhi's comment regarding the chance of Mina's father accepting me as a match for his daughter: *"Perhaps…when you're a doctor."* I could discard that dream.

"Not all doctors have first-class degrees," Ma said.

Hasubhai nodded, "That's true. But those who don't probably knew some politician who could influence the admissions committee."

"Some families make a financial donation to a college," Bhupat said.

Ma glanced at him, "How much?"

Hasubhai wagged a finger, "More than we could afford."

Bhupat reached for some coriander and mint sauce. "That's true in Bombay. But outside the city, maybe a modest donation would work."

An ember of hope glowed, but another thought soon doused it. "I'd have accommodation costs. I couldn't live at home."

The discussion faltered.

"We mustn't jump to conclusions," Hasubhai said. "We must wait for the results. If Ramesh is close to a first-class degree, we will visit a medical college and see what they say." He turned to me, "When will the results be posted?"

"Eight weeks. First on the notice board at college, then in the newspaper."

"We will go to the college early on the day they are posted. We must be prepared to take quick action."

I agreed to collect an application form from Grant Medical College in Bombay.

Hasubhai lowered his voice to a whisper. "Through my job, I know Mr. Natvarlal, the Trust Secretary of the Mahavir Jain Vidhayalai Charitable Trust. When we have a plan, I can approach him for a loan and a letter of recommendation. I'm sure he will help."

"That is good," Bhupat said.

My oldest brother turned to me, "Ramesh, you must also think about your alternatives. What other courses could you study?"

"Hasubhai, I really don't know."

Bhupat tapped me on the shoulder with a big grin on his face. "Ramesh, you can join me. My radio repair business is growing and I need help. What do you say?"

"That's a wonderful idea," Ma said, "Bhupat can repair and you can deliver the radios."

Hasubhai laughed. "Ramesh, you just went from doctor to delivery boy in ten seconds."

I grimaced. "Let's wait until the results come in."

10

Decision Time

Eight anxious weeks followed. I became confused and depressed, and wished more than ever that Dad was there to give advice. I prayed to Bhagwan Mahavir regularly and made frequent visits to the temple to seek his direction, but no answers came. On some occasions, standing in front of the statue, I even questioned his truthfulness and concern for devoted followers like me. *Why do you pay no attention to my heartfelt cries about physical pain and mental anguish? Do you want me to be hurt by insults from shopkeepers?*

When news came of the precise day the science department would post results, Hasubhai and I made plans to get to the college early. We arrived to find a throng of students and parents waiting for the doors to be unlocked. The jostling for position reminded me of Bombay Central Railway Station. We maneuvered to a good position and were in the first hundred to enter the building.

The scene at the bulletin board was even more chaotic. To maintain confidentiality, the college had omitted student names from the list. Only student ID numbers and grades were shown. Students took several seconds to locate their number and read the result. Frequently, the crowd pushed them off balance before they completed that task, and they had to start again.

I pushed and shoved my way to the bulletin board, found my ID number, and saw that I had achieved an upper second-class grade, equivalent to a B+ in the letter grading system. I was four percentage points short of a first class degree. My shoulders slumped. It was what I expected, but I felt intensely disappointed.

Back home, there was no joy or celebration. Hasubhai and I had something to eat and then set out to visit Mr. Natvarlal. We planned to give Grant Medical College a try.

Our meeting with Mr. Natvarlal went very well. He smiled frequently as Hasubhai explained the situation. I could tell he welcomed the opportunity to help a needy Jain student. He gave us a recommendation letter for a loan, and scholarship money from the Mahavir Jain Vidhayalai Charitable Trust. We thanked him for his kindness.

It took a few days to get the loan money from the charitable trust. While we waited, I collected my college transcripts and completed the application form. When the money came through, Hasubhai and I headed for the admissions office at Grant Medical College.

We arrived early in the morning to a room jammed with students and parents peddling their grade sheet and recommendation letters to officers sitting at a row of small desks. We joined the throng. Whenever the Dean of Admission stepped from his office at the rear of the room, a clamor of noise erupted from parents shouting out the names of influential contacts.

We finally made it to one of the officers and handed him my transcript and the letter of recommendation from Mr. Natvarlal. He looked at the documents and shook his head. "It's very unlikely…"

***

I tossed and turned that night wondering what to do. I couldn't stop thinking about my exam blunder and the limited options it left me. Some students had talked about dentistry if they didn't make it to medical college. Should I go in that direction? I prayed for guidance. At one point, Bhupat got up and touched my shoulder. He spoke in a whisper. "Ramesh, go to sleep. We can talk tomorrow."

"Bhupat, we are in trouble. I have no chance of medical college. We can't afford to go out of town. What do you think of dentistry?"

He shrugged, "Would you like it?"

"I think it will be okay."

Ma heard us talking. "Son, it's three o'clock. Go to sleep. We can talk in the morning."

Bhupat and I continued to whisper.

"I have a good chance of getting into a dental college in Bombay. Financially, it will be better. I can live at home."

A clap of thunder sounded in the distance and I glanced out the window. Monsoon clouds hid the stars that I hoped were aligning at this important time in my life. Soon more thunder sounded, followed by a flash of lightning. I decided to get up early and take a trip to the Dental College at Nair Hospital.

Rain started to fall. Splashes from the open window fell on my bare chest, refreshing but unwanted, so I got up to close the shutters. When I lay back down, I began worrying about the streets flooding. That could prevent a dawn ride to Nair Hospital.

I continued to toss and turn.

Finally, I slept.

***

The next morning, the streets were passable and BEST busses were operational. Hasubhai accompanied me and we arrived around 9 a.m. The admissions office was far less crowded than the one at Grant Medical School the previous day. After submitting my application, we met with the dean for an informative and pleasant conversation. He assured me that my grades were good enough to be accepted. I made the decision to go ahead and we paid my first semester fees from the loan money. At last my future seemed secure.

We boarded the bus to go home. Both of us felt physically and mentally exhausted from all the activity. We had walked many miles and struggled with many decisions in a few short days.

"We should celebrate," Hasubhai said. "Where shall we have tea?"

I chose the Metro Tea Shop near the Metro Cinema, about a mile from our apartment.

While we sipped tea and munched on light snacks, I wondered what life as a dentist would be like. I had visited

Dr. Malkan's office many times and had a clear image of the functioning of a doctor's office, but in nineteen years of life I had never visited a dentist.

Everyone in our family had excellent teeth. Our vegetarian diet and poverty meant we rarely ate items that caused tooth decay. Sugary items were limited to special family celebrations and our summer stays at Grandpa's house.

The rainclouds rolled in and we started our walk home. Office workers in smart clothes and factory workers in laborer clothes rushed past us on their way to catch buses and commuter trains. When we turned onto Old Hanuman Lane toward our residence, we heard a familiar voice. "Hey, Hasmukh."

It was Dr. Malkan. He motioned us to join him. I expected questions about our unpaid bills, but instead he addressed me, "Ramesh, come in for a chat. I want to know about your college plans."

When we were inside his empty office, he made eye contact with me, "What did you decide?"

"I have good news."

He beamed through his wire-rimmed spectacles. "Excellent. Which medical college will you attend?"

Hasubhai cleared his throat. "Ramesh will attend the Nair Hospital Dental College starting this fall."

Dr. Malkan's jaw dropped. "Did you say dental college?"

"Yes," I said, sensing his displeasure.

He tapped his pen on the table, "Let me ask you a question. Hasmukh, when did you last visit a dentist?"

"Never," Hasubhai replied.

"Ramesh, what about you?"

I started to feel uneasy. "You are right, sir. I never visited a dentist."

"And did you ever see your father visit a dentist?"

There was silence. We all knew the answer.

Dr. Malkan pounded his fist on the desk. "Ramesh, do you want to be poor the rest of your life? You will have huge debt after dental college. How will you repay it? People in our world don't go to the dentist. Only rich people go to the dentist. Do you think rich people will come to this part of the city to visit a dentist from apartment 64-D?

Hasubhai and I looked at each other. Dr. Malkan made sense. I felt confused and scared. "Dr. Malkan, what would you recommend?"

He thought deeply for several seconds. "I think you should consider a degree in medical microbiology, maybe with a minor in chemistry. Take a look at St. Xavier College. It's close by in the Dhobi Talav area and has an excellent reputation for microbiology. After graduation, you can get a job in a pathology lab or as a pharmaceutical technician or salesman."

We thanked Dr. Malkan for his candid opinion and headed home through spotty rain. I didn't care about getting wet: I had a major issue to resolve.

When we entered, Ma and Bhabhi noticed our dejected faces. "Rameshbhai, did you get refused at dental college?" Bhabhi said.

"No, Bhabhi. I got accepted."

Her eyebrows narrowed. "Then why do you look sad?"

Ma approached and touched my face with her palm. "Son, what has happened?" She spoke softly.

"We'll change our wet clothes and tell you over a dinner," Hasubhai said.

A few minutes later, we sat down and described our day, ending with what Dr. Malkan had said about dentistry. I looked at Bhabhi. "I don't know what to think."

"Let's eat before we discuss the matter," Ma advised. "Bhupat will be late. He acquired some additional repair work this afternoon."

Bhabhi prepared our dinner plates, but I had no appetite. I felt confused and worried about my future. While we waited for Bhupat to arrive, I searched through the Nair Hospital Dental College papers. "Hasubhai, we have to pay a ten percent penalty for withdrawal."

Hasubhai groaned.

Bhupat arrived tired and wet after a long day. Ma gave him a towel to dry off. It was the one I used every day after my morning shower and was so threadbare it would not dry his skin, even after several rubs.

After he had eaten, we sat together for a family discussion. We agreed that it did not make sense to attend dental college for four years if future success was uncertain. Dr. Malkan was right. Two years at St. Xavier College for a degree in medical microbiology would be a better option. Hasubhai and I decided to return to Nair Hospital Dental College the next day and ask for a refund of our admission fee minus the penalty.

The Dean of Admission listened to us sympathetically. He suggested that I had made the wrong choice and should take some time to rethink my decision. I remained firm and he returned our admission fee minus the penalty.

We pocketed the money and boarded a bus to St. Xavier's College. At the front office, a secretary provided me with application forms for the microbiology program. I sat down and started the admission process all over again.

When I had completed the application, we waited in the reception area to be seen by the Dean of the College. A tall, slim, white-robed Christian Father of Indian decent appeared at the doorway and greeted us. "Ramesh, please come to my office. My name is Father Pereira."

In his office, Father Pereira directed us to a pair of highly polished wooden chairs that sat in front of a spotless wooden desk lit by a beautiful ornate lamp. Behind the desk, a well-stocked bookshelf filled the wall. He sat down on a matching, high-back chair, put on a pair of eyeglasses, and studied my application form and last two years of college transcripts.

"Ramesh, your grades are fine in math and science, but they look very weak in English."

I nodded agreement. "Yes, it's true. But I'll work hard to make sure that does not become an issue."

Father Pereira placed my papers neatly on his desk, removed his glasses and looked deep into my eyes. I felt transfixed by his gaze. Eventually, he spoke. "Ramesh, I'm sure you will do well. You are welcome to come here for further study."

A smile appeared on his face and my breathing returned to normal. I glanced at Hasubhai with a big grin and he grinned back.

"St. Xavier College has been awarded the highest ratings of A+ and Five-Star by the agencies that monitor education establishments. It was founded in January 1869, and named after Francis Xavier, a sixteenth-century Spanish Jesuit saint. The college is administered by the Society of Jesus, part of the Roman Catholic Church."

For a moment I had doubts. Was religion a barrier?

Father Pereira must have sensed my concern. He smiled, "We have many Hindu and Jain students here. Attendance at church services is not obligatory. We care for all good students."

His words comforted me.

"I'll arrange a tour of the campus before you make a final decision."

***

Minutes later, a graduate student named Mr. Lopez arrived and led us out the building to a manicured courtyard where he began a well-rehearsed speech. "St. Xavier's stands on a 2.9 acre campus in the Dhobi Talav locality. It is built of black-gray stone in the Indo-Gothic style." He pointed to a building to our left. "This is the hostel. It has room for sixty foreign students with two occupants to each room."

We followed him across the courtyard to a building with green stained-glass windows, arching vaults, and marble stonework. "This is the chapel and prayer hall," he said.

The structure impressed me.

Mr. Lopez relaxed a little. "Father Pereira says you will be part of the microbiology department. I'll take you there. The head of department is Dr. Freitus. She's a very nice person."

Dr. Freitus gave us a warm welcome. She explained the microbiology program and emphasized strong future job prospects for microbiology graduates. I began to get excited about St. Xavier as the next chapter of my life. "I like this place," I whispered to Hasubhai. "I can feel it. And it's only fifteen minutes from home."

"Then let's pay the fees."

Dr. Freitus beamed when I announced my decision.

That evening, I visited the temple. Standing in front of the idol, I spoke audibly. "Bhagwan Mahavir, thank you for the guidance you provided through Dr. Malkan and for the feeling of inner peace I experienced at St. Xavier College."

***

The academic year started in the first week of August 1964. Students were of many different faiths and from all walks of life, although affluent students outnumbered poor ones. There were even children of famous movie stars and producers, although I didn't recognize the names because I rarely went to the movies. It made for a lively atmosphere.

I noticed that the rich dressed in expensive foreign clothes, rode in chauffeured cars, and focused their conversation on movies, music, and the social events they would attend over the weekend. Poor students, with no social calendar to divert their attention, helped each other with homework and dreamed of one day riding in a chauffeur-driven car.

At home, our financial struggles continued. Fortunately, Bhupat's fledgling business grew steadily and he was able to increase his contribution to the family budget. One evening, Bhupat said nothing when Hasubhai expressed concern over a payment due for my college loan. He let his brother agonize for several minutes before removing some banknotes from his pocket. "Hasubhai, don't worry. I have 100 rupees more for you this week."

Hasubhai relaxed and we all laughed. "Where did you get this?" I said.

Bhupat grinned. "I raised my price for same-day service. Everyone wants it. People don't want to be without their radios for even a day."

Another evening, Hasubhai announced we must not purchase or commit to anything but essentials for at least a month. Later that week, Dr. Freitus announced a field trip to Pune, where the class would visit the Electron Microscopy Laboratory at a government research center. She said the cost of the trip would be 40 to 50 rupees. I desperately wanted to see and touch an electron microscope, but I dare not ask Hasubhai or Bhupat for more money, so I withdrew from the trip, citing an ear infection and high fever.

Word of Bhupat's business skills reached Jamnagar and, in early 1965, Grandpa Tribhovandas informed Ma of a matrimonial invitation for Bhupat from a Jain caste family there. Ma beamed as she shared the news. "Bhupat, it's from Mrs. Hemlataben Parekh for their daughter Pravina. We are invited to visit them."

Bhupat beamed, unable to hide his excitement. Many families passed over young men like him when they sought a partner for their daughter, fearing that his physical disfigurement might pass to his children and bring shame to their daughter. Things such as birth defects were often blamed on the mother of the child.

Hasubhai turned to Ma, "What does her father do?"

"He died a few years ago. Hemlataben has five daughters and a son. Pravina is the oldest daughter. They live near our old house in the Shatrukhana area. They are poor like us, but they are nice people."

Ma, Hasubhai, and Bhupat traveled to Jamnagar and returned very happy. Everything had gone well. The families had visited a jotish together, and a wedding date had been agreed upon.

The marriage took place on May 11, 1965, in Jamnagar. The ceremony and the celebrations were subdued affairs compared to Hasubhai's wedding. Both families were poor and had no incentive to take on more debt.

Pravina wore an attractive red sari embroidered with silver and gold colored thread. Her arms and hands were artfully decorated with henna, and she wore a beautiful gold necklace and matching earrings. Even the poor find gold for a daughter's wedding. Pravina had a very pleasant smile and Bhupat beamed throughout the ceremony. We were all thrilled for him.

To give the newlyweds some privacy, Hasubhai added a partition in front of the kitchen, which meant I lost my sleeping space. I considered it fair trade for a new sister-in-law. Pravina settled in and became like a sister to Bhabhi, and I became next in line in the family marriage stakes.

11
Job Hunting

My two years of study at St. Xavier College passed quickly, and I enjoyed the learning process that had less formality and more open discussion. Dr. Freitus and other members of the faculty were very helpful. On one occasion, when an ear infection left me behind the rest of the class, Dr. Freitus gave me personal help to catch up.

The college had a great track record for graduate employment. Employers considered St. Xavier a prestigious school for microbiology, and I expected to walk into a well-paying job when I graduated in June 1966, with a Bachelor of Science degree with Honors Distinction.

I prepared my resume and applied for entry-level positions at all the pharmaceutical companies in the Bombay area. Most of them were multinationals. With my honors degree and an excellent letter of recommendation from Dr. Freitus, I felt ready for any interview. To my surprise, I received few invitations for interviews and zero job offers.

Responses often emphasized the employers' desire for candidates with workplace experience, but when classmates with no experience and less academic qualification began landing jobs, I realized my lack of high-level connections was the real reason. It was no different than when I applied for medical school.

In one interview, a Bombay native with piercing eyes questioned me, "Do you speak Marathi?" Marathi is the native language of Bombay.

"No. I speak Gujarati and Hindi," I replied.

His expression changed and I knew immediately that he disliked "outsiders." His prejudice would eliminate me from consideration, even though everyone in Bombay spoke Hindi, and language would not be an issue in the workplace.

I became frustrated and discouraged that I couldn't contribute to my family's financial needs. As a 21-year-old college graduate, I still depended on my older brothers for pocket change.

Bhabhi encouraged me. "Be patient. Things will turn around."

"Have faith," Ma urged.

I tried to have faith, but depression ate away at my resolve. Instead of my life moving forward after graduation, it was in decline. Education seemed to mean nothing. My father's dream was just that: a dream. I began to feel isolated and marginalized to the point where thoughts of suicide played hide-and-seek with my psyche. This time, the thoughts were real and I became scared.

Late one evening, after another job rejection, I passed Dr. Malkan's office. He was winding down his clinic for the day, so I knocked on his door, "Hello Dr. Malkan."

He glanced up from his patient files, "Ramesh, come in." He gestured me to a chair near his desk, "Any news on the job front?"

I shook my head. "No, sir. I have applied to every pharmaceutical company I know. They all want candidates with experience."

He thought for a moment, "Have you considered pathology labs? They need technicians too."

I hadn't considered that.

He reached for a sheet of letterhead paper, "I'll write you a note for Dr. Dufftary, the pathologist at GT Government Hospital. He's a friend of mine. Please go and see him."

He scribbled the note and handed it to me. I took it from him as if it were a fragile orchid flower. "Dr. Malkan, thank you so much."

"Be sure to go. I'll call him and let him know to expect you."

I skipped down the steps to the street. At last I had a connection with someone influential. Surely this would get me a job.

At home, Ma was mopping the floor in preparation for beds to be laid out, and Bhabhi sat stitching a button on one of Hasubhai's shirts. A plated dinner waited for me in the kitchen, and for the first time in days I felt hungry.

"How did your interview go?" Bhabhi asked.

I took a bite of chapatti. "Nothing new. They all want experience."

She stopped sewing and looked at me. "Something happened. You're not depressed."

I smiled at her perceptiveness. "Dr. Malkan gave me a letter of recommendation. He knows the pathologist at GT Government Hospital."

"That's great news. Does he know the man well?"

I nodded. "They're personal friends. Dr. Malkan said he would call him and tell him to expect my visit."

"When will you go?" Ma said.

"Tomorrow. I have no other plans."

***

The next morning, I dressed in an ironed shirt and clean pants, placed my college transcripts and recommendation letters from Dr. Malkan and Dr. Freitus in a folder, prayed my usual prayer at the framed photographs of Dad and Bhagwan Mahavir, and set out for GT Government Hospital. I had passed the Gothic-style Victorian building many times on my way to St. Xavier, but had never gone inside. The hospital provided free and subsidized healthcare to poor and needy people in South Bombay.

I prepared myself mentally as I walked: I wanted to impress Dr. Dufftary. Near the building entrance, I paused to check my appearance in a glass window, and then walked confidently through the entrance door into a courtyard that did not care about its appearance. Straggling weeds and patches of brown grass covered parched soil that begged for water. Overgrown bushes protruded onto the walkway. The hospital's first impression needed urgent care.

I found the pathology lab and entered a waiting room lit by one small window. Patients in torn and threadbare clothes occupied all of the chairs and most of the floor space. Some were barefoot, all looked malnourished. I felt sorry for them. The receptionist took my name and I asked to see Dr. Dufftary before securing a spot by the window to wait. A clock on the wall ticked away the seconds.

The hospital was two blocks away from St. Xavier College, where fancy cars lined the streets. Though geographically close, the two landmark buildings in this sector of Bombay were worlds apart.

Outside, the sky darkened with black-gray clouds, and the room became eerily dark. Thunder, lightning, and heavy rain soon followed. Thirty minutes passed, and I wondered if the receptionist had forgotten me. Finally, she called my name. To reach her, I had to step over patients sitting on the floor.

"Do you have an appointment with Dr. Dufftary?"

I handed her my papers with Dr. Malkan's letter on top. "I recently graduated with a degree in microbiology and I'm hoping to find work in the pathology lab." I pointed to the letter. "Dr. Dufftary knows Dr. Malkan very well."

She studied my papers like someone who regularly screens job applicants. "I'll check with Dr. Dufftary for his availability. Please wait here."

I took a deep breath and prayed for a positive response. Dr. Malkan's letter had got me past the gatekeeper.

A minute or two later the receptionist returned. "Dr. Dufftary will see you at 2:30 p.m. today."

I gave her a big smile, "Thanks for your help."

To keep my pressed shirt looking good, I stayed in the hospital building, out of the rain, and made my way to the canteen to wait with the crowd there. For 2 rupees, I bought two potato wadas (spicy potato balls about two inches in diameter, dipped in chickpea batter and deep fried) and some mint chutney. I asked for a glass of tap water to drink. The wadas were tasty and filling.

At 2:15 p.m., I returned to the pathology lab and the receptionist escorted me to Dr. Dufftary office. A middle-aged man with well-groomed salt-and-pepper hair pointed to a chair by his desk. He wore a white lab coat over a white shirt and a tie. "Please sit down."

Papers filled his desk on both sides. I sat down and tried to ignore a housefly that buzzed about my face. "Sir, thank you for seeing me."

The room was hot and humid, even though the rain had stopped and an open window allowed a breeze. Above us, a three-bladed ceiling fan made a ticking noise with each rotation.

Dr. Dufftary studied my college transcripts. "How do you know Dr. Malkan?"

"He's my family doctor."

I waited for the next question but it never came. Dr. Dufftary thumbed my papers for a few more seconds then removed his spectacles. "Ramesh, your qualifications are excellent…but I don't have an opening at this time."

My jaw dropped. "Doctor, I will do any job in the lab. I have a Bachelor of Science degree with honors from St. Xavier. I need a job to help my family."

He looked straight in my eyes. "Ramesh, I understand that, and I'd like to help. But this facility is government-run, and I don't have funding to hire you…although I'm hopeful that something will open up in the next six months." He glanced at my transcripts again. "If you are willing to work as a volunteer, I'll sign you up and train you. You will learn a lot, and you'll become certified as a medical laboratory technician. But I cannot pay you at this time."

I didn't know what to say. The thought of volunteer work among needy people appealed to me, but I needed money to support my family. I felt dejected.

Dr. Dufftary rose from his chair and walked toward the open door, "Why don't you think about it for couple of days and let me know? Six months of training is all I can offer."

I thanked him and said I'd be in touch.

***

The monsoon had flooded the streets. Dirty brown water gushed through the roadside gutters and jumped in the air at every obstruction. I made a detour to avoid the worst areas and pondered my future as I stepped between puddles. Was working for no pay the best I could do? I felt helpless. More rain came and I got wet. There were no bright spots.

At home, Ma read my body language and gave me a sympathetic look. "Ramesh, change your wet clothes, then sit down and tell us about the interview."

I nodded silently and changed my clothes. When I sat down, Ma and Bhabhi joined me. I could feel their love envelop me.

"Dr. Dufftary has no job openings. It was no different than yesterday or the day before. There are no jobs."

Ma reached for my hand and squeezed it. "What did he say?"

"He liked my qualifications and said I could work as a volunteer. He may have funding in six months."

Ma put her hand on my shoulder. "Son, don't worry. Remember what your dad taught you. Tomorrow will be a better day. Keep your faith in Bhagwan Mahavir."

My frustration overflowed and I responded with anger. "Ma, there is no tomorrow. No one cares, not even Mahavir." Tears rolled down my cheeks.

Bhabhi and Ma cried with me.

***

When Bhupat arrived home, he had a radio under his arm. I watched him as he removed the back and let out a muffled laugh.

"What is it?" I said.

"A loose wire."

"What's funny about that?"

"The owner made a big fuss. He talked like he knew all about radios. Said it had to be the valve. In the time he spent talking, he could have fixed it himself."

"So will you charge him?"

"Of course. He wants a new valve, so I'll give him one."

"But it's not broken."

"I'll use this one on another job."

"Will you charge him for it?"

"Of course."

"How could you do that?"

He gave me a wry smile. "I'm doing no harm."

I raised an eyebrow to question his logic.

"Ramesh, this owner has a big ego. If I tell him his diagnosis is wrong, he will not like it. If I tell him I changed the valve just like he said, and now the radio works, he will be pleased. He gets exactly what he wants. There's no harm in that."

"You benefit from it."

"We both benefit. That's good business. And because he's pleased, he'll come back to me the next time something goes wrong. The customer is always right, Ramesh."

I smiled and shook my head.

"He also demanded double-quick service."

"So you'll charge extra?"

Bhupat nodded. "If he wants priority treatment, he must pay for it. I'll tell him I worked late into the evening just for him. That will boost his ego." The wry smile returned to his face. "He will feel good giving a crippled technician a few extra rupees."

***

After our evening meal, Hasubhai, Bhupat, and I talked about the benefits of volunteer work at GT Government Hospital and agreed that I should seek the advice of Dr. Freitus. I visited St. Xavier College the next day.

Faculty members greeted me and I relaxed in the familiar surroundings. I knocked on my mentor's door. "Dr. Freitus, may I come in?"

She smiled, "Of course, Ramesh. Have a seat. Did you find a job yet?"

I grimaced. "No. They all want experience."

Her eyes showed sympathy. "I know it's not easy, but don't give up. It will take time."

I explained to her the opportunity for volunteer work at GT Government Hospital and asked her opinion. She put down her pen and leaned back in her chair.

"I think you should take it. You will gain experience and get training. In the meantime, you can keep looking for a paying job. I'm sure Dr. Dufftary would understand if you found something."

Bhupat had said the same thing. It was the way to go.

Dr. Freitus retrieved a letter from a pile of papers on her desk. "Ramesh, do you remember Prakash Mehta, one year senior to you?"

"Yes, I worked in the lab with him once."

"Prakash is in America studying medical technology. His letter says there are many opportunities at American hospitals for one or two year courses, and that some hospitals pay a stipend."

"What's a stipend?"

She smiled. "The hospital will pay you enough to live on while you study. Why don't you explore that opportunity?"

A glimmer of hope stirred inside me. Every schoolboy knew America was the land of opportunity. "Where can I get that information?"

She reached for a pen and wrote down Prakash's address in America. "Start by sending Prakash a letter. You can also make enquiries at the U.S. Embassy here in Bombay."

For the first time in weeks, I felt energized. Could I possibly study in America?

12

Volunteer Work

Early the next day, I visited Dr. Dufftary and signed up for volunteer work as a laboratory technician. He said my training would start the following Monday and would cover microbiology, hematology, serology, histology, parasitology, and blood banking. I would start at the blood bank.

Next, I visited the U.S. Embassy and obtained addresses of two-dozen hospitals that had medical technology certification programs. I wrote to all of them requesting application forms for the coming year.

I knew little about America. My school curriculum had included nothing about its history or geography or climate. What I knew came from folklore and news media, which portrayed America as a land of opportunity where citizens were rich and lived in beautiful homes. There were no poor people, and even janitors drove big cars. I had heard people say that America was heaven on earth.

***

My training at the blood bank started, and I was soon drawing blood from professional blood donors. These were people from the poorest communities who sold their blood for 10 to 12 rupees a pint. For health reasons, they were instructed not to come more than once a month.

As we conversed, I discovered that many lived on the streets in makeshift dwellings of tin or cardboard. I wished I could help these unfortunate people in some positive way, but all I could do was draw their blood. They were humble men who talked with pride about their children.

One particular donor named Mohan came with a big smile on his face. His teeth were stained dark red-orange from chewing tambaku pan (betel leaves filled with ground tobacco and spices). He smelled like he had not bathed for days.

"Hello, Mohan, how are you?"

"Very good. My wife is expecting child number three. The others are well." He climbed onto the wooden bench. His body looked like a layer of skin draped over a skeleton and sucked tight by malnutrition. I offered him a clipboard with a simple donor form to sign.

"You know I can't read or write."

"Then mark it with a cross."

He pushed the clipboard away. "I'll let you forge my cross." An eruption of laughter followed.

I examined both his arms for a vein to puncture, but his veins were small and difficult to access.

"Mohan, when did you last give blood?"

"Last week."

I stopped. "Where?"

He gave me a big grin. "Different hospital."

"You know I can't take your blood today."

His eyes pleaded with me. "Sir, I need the money for my family."

I felt torn and asked my supervisor what I should do. He gave me permission to proceed so I cleaned a vein on Mohan's left arm with alcohol and inserted the needle. "Mohan, it's bad for your health to draw blood this often."

His eyes flashed. "My blood is all I have. I give it for my family."

I shook my head wishing our society had support systems for people trapped in such deep poverty. I finished the draw and applied a dressing. "Keep it clean. Dirt can infect even a small wound." He nodded, grabbed his receipt, and moved to the next room to see the cashier.

Twenty minutes later, I took my lunch break and passed through the lobby on my way to the cafeteria. I saw Mohan sitting in the corner gambling the money he had just earned with other donors. That pitiful image stayed with me for days. Who was to blame for the ignorance and misery of Mohan? I shared the episode with Bhabhi and Ma, and we agreed that only education could help people like Mohan understand right and wrong.

***

Large envelopes from America began arriving in the mail. Hospitals in Georgia, California, North Carolina, and Massachusetts informed me they had openings in their programs. I felt excited until I sat down and calculated the cost just to apply.

Each application had a processing fee of between $10 and $20 and required copies of my college transcripts, my high school certificate, recommendation letters from people with good academic standing, and two passport-sized photographs. Each page of my college transcript had to be certified by the college, which added a cost of up to 4 rupees per page for a stamping fee. Finally, there were airmail charges to return the large, heavy envelopes. Ma frowned when she saw me sifting through the information. She did not like the thought that I might leave home.

Around mid-morning, Bhupat returned home from work with a cold and feeling weak. Ma headed for the kitchen to get the Vicks balm while Pravina, Bhupat's wife, fetched a warm blanket and arranged bed-mats so he could rest in a reclining position. After a few minutes, the smell of menthol filled the room and Bhupat glanced in my direction. "Ramesh, you don't look happy. Why?"

"These applications to America are expensive," I said. "I think I'll have to choose just one or two hospitals."

Bhupat wagged his finger. "Apply to them all. You will have a better chance."

I got up and showed him my calculations, "It will cost 200 to 300 rupees per application. We don't even know if I have a chance of acceptance."

"Three hundred rupees?" Ma wailed. "We can't afford that." Her pent up emotions flowed in a way I'd never seen before. "Son, we don't know anyone in America. Where will you eat and sleep?" She wiped her eyes on her sari. "I don't want you to go."

"Ma, we've talked about this. The college will help me find somewhere to live."

Her tears streamed, "What if there's no temple?" She gestured to Bhupat reclined on his makeshift bed, "Who will care for you when you are sick?" Her voice faltered, "We lost your dad. I don't want to lose you."

I exchanged a glance with Bhupat, wondering how to respond. Bhabhi stepped forward and reached for Ma's hands to comfort her. She spoke with a strong voice.

"Ma, I met Dad only once, but I know he had a dream for his family. He dreamed that his sons would be educated and that his family would not live in poverty. Rameshbhai must apply to study in America. It is part of that dream. We must have faith that Bhagwan Mahavir will watch over him. He will come back after two or three years, and we will ask Mina's parents for marriage."

We all had tears in our eyes. Ma leaned forward and clung to Bhabhi.

When she had recovered, she wiped her eyes on her sari, took the jar of Vicks balm from Pravina, and returned to the kitchen.

Bhupat gestured from his bed, "Ramesh, my business is doing well. Don't worry about the mailing money. Send all the applications." His optimism inspired me and I agreed to do what he said.

When Ma returned to the room, Bhupat gave her a big smile. "Don't worry, Ma. Your second son is not going anywhere." He lay back and closed his eyes.

***

After several days collecting documents and preparing applications, I arrived at Kalbadevi Post Office with my mailers. The day was hot and humid, and my ear throbbed with infection. The crowded room had no ventilation.

The government-run post office paid lip service to customer service. I waited in line for over two hours to get the envelopes weighed, buy the stamps, and hand the envelopes to the clerk at the airmail window. While I waited, I prayed over the applications and decided to visit the temple on my way home to ask Bhagwan Mahavir for a positive response from one of the American hospitals.

On my way to the temple, I stopped to visit Jayant. His elderly servant Laxman stepped into the street to greet me. He looked frail.

"Hi Laxmanbhai, where is Jayant?"

"Shhh..." he said. "Rameshbhai, he is drunk and has been very abusive all day. Please don't disturb him. Let him go to sleep."

I felt sad. My friend's life was spiraling downhill and there was nothing I could do to help him. He could end up living on the streets like Mohan. "Laxmanbhai, please watch him. Make sure he sleeps."

Laxman nodded.

I continued on to the temple and prepared to worship. Normally, I didn't ask for anything specific from Bhagwan Mahavir other than peace in my heart. Today I wanted more. I paused at the top step to calm my cough, then rang the ceiling bell twice and entered the worship hall.

Inside the temple, I found a spot by a carved marble pillar. Facing the statue and repeating my mantras, I soon sensed an energy within me that made me feel very much at peace. The pain in my ear subsided and I felt like my soul was somewhere else.

With my hands folded, I stared at the statue's eyes and felt emboldened to speak my mind. *"Bhagwan, I need your help. You know how much financial trouble we are in, but I cannot find a job. I am an obedient servant of your teaching. Knowingly, I have never harmed anyone and you know it. Then what is wrong with you Bhagwan? You know I want to help my family. You gave my father a dream. Please get me admission to study in America. Please listen to me. I have no one who can help but you."*

I felt sure he heard me and left the temple feeling peaceful. Outside, the streetlights of the bazaar were lighting up and shopkeepers were closing their shops for the night. Workers rushed by to catch buses, trams, or local suburban trains. I decided to check on Jayant before I left.

Laxman saw me coming. "Rameshbhai, Jayant is better. He vomited. I have cleaned it up and now he is sleeping. Don't worry, I will stay close to him."

"You are a dedicated servant."

Tears came to his eyes. "He gets drunk so many times. I'm over sixty years old and want to go back to my village, but who will take care…"

I put my arm on Laxmanbhai's shoulder and consoled him. "I'll come and see Jayant tomorrow."

***

A new month started at the pathology lab, and I was excited to move on to the serology department. Here I would study antibodies in serum taken from patients with infections that impacted their immune system. Mrs. Patil, the department supervisor, greeted me.

"Welcome, Ramesh, to Serology Department. You will be collecting body fluid samples from the vital parts of men who have sexually transmitted diseases. Do you know about VD?"

I'd never heard a woman speak that way about such things before. "I know a little," I said.

"Syphilis and gonorrhea are contracted by sexual contact with an infected person. Many people in the red-light district have one of these diseases." She raised her voice for emphasis, "We have to be extremely careful during the collection process."

I swallowed hard.

"Good laboratory practices are essential. This includes washing hands, using rubber gloves, careful handling of serology slides, and proper disposals of all waste materials. Your own health is at risk. If you are careless, you can become infected."

As we toured the lab, I listened carefully to her every word. "Now let's visit some patients," she said.

We exited the lab and she paused at the door to a hospital ward. "These men are sent by Public Health Services. Spread of VD in the red-light districts is a huge problem. These men have visited prostitutes and then given the disease to their wives. Regular testing for antibodies is part of their treatment, along with prevention education."

We entered a ward filled with pathetic looking men.

"Oh Bhagwan," I whispered.

Every one of them looked broken. No hint of a smile existed on any face. I had never seen expressions so devoid of hope. I felt disheartened and silently thanked Bhagwan Mahavir that I had better fortune than these patients.

"Are you okay, Ramesh?"

I nodded. "How do people get this way?"

"Through ignorance. This can happen to anyone who visits with a prostitute. There are many ills in our society."

I thought of Jayant. Did he know the risk he was taking? I wished he could see this scene.

For the rest of the day, I learned about preparing slides for microscope analysis and waste disposal. The next day, I worked alongside a serologist taking and analyzing samples. After that I worked on my own.

Dressed in gown and gloves, I approached my first patient. He knew what to expect. I lifted his gown to expose his inflamed penis and asked him to squeeze it so I could collect a sample of the discharge for analysis. His face contorted when he squeezed. I collected the sample and looked away; the expression on his face scared me. I had no strength to talk to him about his lifestyle.

On another occasion, when I asked a patient to squeeze, the discharge splattered onto my gloves and gown. "Not that much," I shouted, "All I need is one drop." Years later, I could laugh about it, but at the time it scared me.

When my time in serology ended, I went to Mrs. Patil and thanked her for what she had taught me the first day.

She looked at me down her nose like a schoolteacher addressing a student. "Good practices are important in any laboratory, Ramesh. Follow them, even when your life is not on the line."

I nodded my understanding.

Mrs. Patil relaxed. "Apart from good practices, what have you learned in serology?"

I thought for a moment. "I've learned that many lives are wasted."

"And why?"

"Because of ignorance."

She nodded, "Our country is poor, Ramesh. Everyone is left for themselves."

I wondered if those in government anguished over these issues like we did.

***

By the end of September, I had heard nothing from America and began to worry. I had no plan B, other than hoping Dr. Dufftary would receive additional government funding, and my time at the hospital gave me little confidence that would happen.

I sent another letter to each hospital in America asking if it had made a decision. I also checked the English language newspaper want ads regularly for technician jobs at local pharmaceutical companies and continued to visit the temple to pray for a job. Finally the responses from America trickled in…we have no openings at present.

My heart sank further with each response. My internal struggle with faith intensified and I started to lose trust in Bhagwan Mahavir. I became angry and started complaining to him that he hadn't opened a path for me.

Soon I stopped going to the temple altogether, although I didn't tell Ma. It was a hard decision that went against the habits of a lifetime, but I couldn't pretend to have faith. If I didn't believe, I wouldn't go. Every night, I played an internal debate over and over in my mind.

You are Jain. You should visit the temple.

But I don't feel a connection any more.

How can you connect if you stay away?

I need help—a job or study in America.

Your father remained faithful in difficult circumstances. You should too.

I am not my father.

Then be yourself; tell your mother about your decision.

She wouldn't understand.

Then visit the temple. You are Jain.

No! I think I am done with you.

This tug of war continued for weeks. My mentor, my dad, was not there for dialogue and I had no one to lean on. Hasubhai and Bhupat recognized the tension. They said laughter and happiness had vanished from my face and that my leisurely singing had evaporated. Bhupat reassured me that if things didn't work out, I could join him at Blue Star.

Then, one afternoon in late October, Mom shouted to me from the open window as I approached our apartment building, "You have another letter from America."

I ran up the stairs and Ma handed me the envelope. It was from St. Joseph's Infirmary, Atlanta, Georgia. Everyone at home gathered round. "Open it, open it," Bhabhi urged.

I opened the envelope and pulled out a letter and a Student Visa Application Form.

Bhabhi's excitement overflowed, "What does it say?"

I read the first sentence and adrenalin surged through my body. "I've been accepted in Atlanta," I shouted.

Bhabhi cried with delight and hugged me.

I raised the envelope above my head, "Yes, Bhagwan Mahavir, you do listen. Thank you."

I glanced at Ma, wondering how she would take this news. Without hesitation, she threw her arms around me and we hugged. "Son, I'm happy for you. Hasubhai and Bhupat will be delighted...but I will miss you." Tears welled in her eyes.

I sat down and read every word of the acceptance letter, announcing the main points as I read. Bhabhi and my younger siblings cheered and applauded each statement.

"It's a one-year medical technology class..." *Hooray!*

"It starts on the first of January 1967..." *Woo hoo!*

"I have a sponsor named Dr. John T. Godwin..."

"I get a stipend of $90 a month..."

"And a free lunch every day..." *Wonderful!*

I thought of my nighttime struggles and regretted my despair and anger. I had to put that right. "Ma, I'll be back soon. I'm going to the temple."

My heart pumped in overdrive as I walked quickly through the crowded streets. I felt out of this world. This was the best news ever.

At the temple, I stared at the statue and prayed. "Mahavir, you are great. You sure listened to me. Thanks for making this happen." I sensed a connection and felt a smile radiating through the marble statue toward me.

By the time I returned home, Hasubhai and Bhupat were there. I showed them the letter and visa application form and we celebrated together.

"We have a lot of work to do in two months," Hasubhai said. "You will need a passport before you can apply for the visa."

"We should book the flight as soon as possible," Bhupat said. "Ishwarbhai has a friend who flies often. He says fares go up at short notice."

Hasubhai paced the floor. "We will have to borrow money. Ramesh, prepare a budget of everything you need."

I nodded. "I also need certificates from the Bombay Police Department and the Income Tax Authority."

"What for?"

"To prove I have no criminal record and no liens."

"Keep copies of everything," Bhupat said.

Ma joined in. "You will need new clothes."

"Western clothes," Bhabhi said.

Bhupat raised a finger, "Where is Atlanta? Some parts of America get very cold. You may need a thick winter coat."

I had checked an atlas at the library when I mailed the applications but couldn't remember "I'll check tomorrow."

"Don't forget I still have gold jewelry we can sell," Ma said.

Hasubhai shook his head, "Ma, don't worry about that. We will manage." He stood up and spoke to everyone. "Ramesh has a lot to do tomorrow. Let's get the beds ready early." He looked at Ma, "Can you prepare puran puri (sweet chapatti) and bhajia (vegetable fritters) for tomorrow evening? We must celebrate."

13

Preparing for America

I woke the next morning ready for action. When Hasubhai and Bhupat had left for work, I sat by the open window and read the detailed instructions included with the visa application form.

Within minutes, my stomach tightened when I noticed a section of the application form had a signature missing. The hospital in Atlanta had completed a section requesting information about the sponsoring institution, but had left the signature block blank. The instructions clearly stated that an authorized officer of the institution had to sign the form.

Surely this was an error, but what should I do? Fear and uncertainty surrounded me like a huge, dark cavern. I breathed deeply to calm myself and decided to send a telex message to my sponsor, Dr. John Godwin, Head of Pathology. I would explain the error and request that he send the correct paperwork as soon as possible. Minutes later I set out for the post office.

Ten days passed without a response and I became anxious. Had he received my telex? Did anyone in Atlanta care? I couldn't start my visa application without the correct paperwork, and my acceptance letter stated that if I wasn't in Atlanta for the first day of class, my admission would be cancelled. I tried to arrange a phone call, but couldn't find anyone with an overseas-linked phone who would let me use it. All I could do was send another telex highlighting the urgency of a response.

The wait seemed like Chinese water torture with negative thoughts landing like drips inside my head. The more I tried to ignore the thoughts, the stronger they became.

While I waited, I sent off my passport application and gathered budget information for Hasubhai. I learned that a one-way ticket to Atlanta on December 30 would cost around 3,500 rupees plus 250 rupees for airport taxes. If I included the 600 rupees of foreign exchange allowed, the total came to almost six months of Hasubhai's salary as a degreed accountant.

That evening, while Ma and the others cleaned the kitchen and laid out the bed-mats, Hasubhai, Bhupat, and I sat down to discuss finances. In addition to travel costs, we estimated 3,500 rupees for new clothes and luggage and added a contingency for things we hadn't thought of yet. Our total came to almost 12,000 rupees (U.S. $350–400), a huge amount for us to borrow—way more than Hasubhai's annual salary, and four times what Dad earned each year.

"Let's drop the contingency," Hasubhai said.

Bhupat shook his head, "That's risky."

I agreed. "If there's a balance left over, I'll give it to Ma for household use."

Bhupat nodded. "Good idea."

I had no idea where we would get that much money. We had no bank to go to and still owed money to local vendors. "Who can we ask for a loan this size?" I said.

"It has to be someone in the family," Bhupat replied.

Hasubhai tapped his pencil on the table while he thought. "Sunderkaka could do it. But he will find some excuse not to."

I nodded, "He didn't want to help with my college fees after Dad died."

"I agree he's not the right person," Bhupat said. "What about Mama and Mami? They are well off."

Hasubhai shook his head. "Don't count on them. They are old. Mama will not spare much."

"How about Grandpa Tribhovandas?" I said.

Hasubhai frowned. "A few rupees maybe, but not 12,000."

My mouth felt dry. There was no one else.

"Wait a minute," Hasubhai said. "How about Bachukaka, Sunderkaka's younger brother. He offered to help us once. We didn't go to him because it would have offended his older brother. They don't get along."

We glanced at each other and no one disagreed.

Hasubhai relaxed and sat back in his chair. "I'll call him this week and ask if he'll see us."

***

I continued gathering the documentation I needed for my visa application. My trip to the police station went smoothly, but the Income Tax Authority proved difficult. My supervisor at GT Government Hospital agreed that I could make a call from there. After two or three false starts, the switchboard operator transferred me to an agent who could help.

"Hello, I'm applying for a student visa and need a certificate that confirms I have no outstanding liens."

"What's your tax ID number?"

"I don't have one."

"You must have one."

"No. I've never paid taxes."

The agent paused for a moment and the tone of his voice changed, "What's your name?"

I gave him my name, and then my address.

"Are you working?"

"Yes, but only…"

"Employer's name?"

"GT Government Hospital. But it's volunteer work. I'm not being paid."

A longer pause.

"If you're not being paid, you don't owe taxes."

"I know that."

"So there are no liens."

"I know. But I need a certificate that confirms that…for my visa application."

"Let me put you on hold?" Click.

I listened to silence for two or three minutes before he came back on the line. "Sir, to issue a lien certificate I need a tax ID number."

And so the conversation continued. Without a tax ID number I didn't exist. Eventually I got what I needed, plus a tax ID number and a warning that I could be liable for tax on overseas earnings. I decided not to debate the difference between a stipend and a salary.

***

Finally, in the third week of November, a letter arrived from St. Joseph's Infirmary. It contained a blank visa application form with the signature block signed. This time the sponsor information was missing. I sat down and copied the information from the old form to the new form hoping that no one at the embassy would check my handwriting.

With the necessary documents in place, I finally visited the U.S. Embassy late in November and found a notice taped to the door stating that embassy staff were observing the U.S. Thanksgiving holiday and that the embassy would reopen the following Monday. I grimaced; four more days lost.

I returned the following Monday and submitted my application. The agent said I would receive a notice in the mail informing me of my interview date.

***

Later that week, Hasubhai and I visited Bachukaka at his import/export office in the commercial and financial hub of the city known as the Fort Area of Bombay. Kaka had told Hasubhai that he wanted to meet me.

His office stood close to an area of imposing Gothic buildings constructed in the early nineteenth century that housed government departments, the Bombay High Court, and the prestigious Elphinstone College.

Inside Kaka's office, boxes of goods from foreign countries overflowed into the aisles and even the lobby. All of the employees were busy attending wholesale customers when we arrived, so we waited. A few minutes later, the store manager escorted us to Kaka's personal office, a medium-sized room filled with knick-knacks from around the world. The room felt pleasantly cool. Hasubhai leaned close and whispered, "He has air conditioning, like his brother."

Kaka got up from his padded leather chair and greeted us. He stood five feet eight inches, well-built and well dressed.

"Kaka, this is my younger brother, Ramesh."

Kaka inspected me like a general on the parade ground. "Ramesh, we met at your father's funeral. You look well. How is your mother?"

His posture and tone informed me this would be a better visit than the one we'd had with his brother. "Ma is doing fine, thank you," I replied. "It's so nice to see you Kaka."

He smiled and ordered tea and light snacks for us to share. "Hasubhai tells me you're going to school in America. Tell me about it. I'm happy for you."

I told him all I knew about St. Joseph's Infirmary and the medical technology course I would study.

"In which state is Atlanta?"

"It's in Georgia, in the Southeast."

"I visited England once and had a wonderful time. It's good to travel. I learned so much and I'm sure you will too." His face turned thoughtful and he addressed Hasubhai, "How exactly can I help you?"

Hasubhai spoke in a soft voice. "Kaka, we need a loan of 12,000 rupees for Ramesh's trip to America. We will start repaying you as soon as Ramesh gets a job."

I watched Kaka's face. He nodded twice and seemed deep in thought. Then his expression eased into a smile. "Don't worry about it. Your father was a very honest man. He died too early. I'm sorry to see you boys having a tough time, and I'm happy to help your family." He stood up. "Why don't you come to my home next Saturday afternoon around 2 p.m.? Kaki will be delighted to see you. You know where we live?"

Hasubhai nodded. "Thank you Kaka."

We shook hands with very broad smiles and Kaka walked us to the street to say goodbye.

Out of earshot, Hasubhai nudged me. "Kaka is very different from his brother!"

I grinned. "Are you sure they are brothers?"

Hasubhai rested his arm on my shoulder. "Plan on buying your tickets and clothing after next Saturday."

***

Saturday came and we rode a bus to Churchgate, another prestigious area of Bombay adjacent to the Arabian Sea. At high tide, waves splashed against an embankment no more than a stone's throw from Kaka's high-rise apartment sending spray high in the air.

We registered at the security gate and waited while the guard called Kaka's apartment to confirm we were expected. The air smelled saline clean.

Inside the complex, we paused in the parking lot to look at luxury cars before taking the elevator to Kaka's apartment on the fourth floor. A servant answered and, a moment later, Kaka came to greet us. We removed our shoes and he led us to the main living room. It looked like a larger, neater version of his office, filled with knickknacks and artwork from around the world.

Kaka gestured us toward a white sofa in the center of the room and sat in a matching chair next to us. The rug felt wonderfully soft. Moments later, a very attractive woman dressed in western clothes entered the room and welcomed us. Kaka smiled. "This is Shanta Kaki."

After some small talk about family and how Kaki had met Hasubhai once before but not me, our hostess asked what snack we would like with our tea. With proper etiquette, we politely declined and she insisted, intent on observing the custom of serving guests a tasty treat with afternoon tea.

When she left the room to instruct her servant in the kitchen, Kaka rose and went to his office. He returned a few seconds later with a brown envelope that he handed to Hasubhai. "Don't open it here," he whispered.

He had settled back in his chair and we were in an animated conversation about the upcoming cricket match against England when his wife returned. It was clear that he did not want Kaki to know about the contents of the envelope.

Our very cordial visit lasted about an hour. As we shook hands at the door, I quietly thanked Kaka for his help. He smiled and wished me good luck.

Once the door closed we ran down the stairs like school kids too impatient to wait for the elevator. I wanted to open the envelope and check the contents there, but Hasubhai said we should wait until we were in a taxi. He felt that would be safer than riding on a crowded bus.

The gatekeeper hailed us a taxi, and a mid-sized, box-like black car with a yellow roof pulled up. Hundreds of them roamed the streets of Bombay. Hasubhai gave the driver our address and we were on our way.

"Open the envelope," I whispered so the taxi driver did not hear.

Hasubhai lifted the flap and we looked inside at a bundle of bank notes. A small handwritten note accompanied it and Hasubhai removed the note and held it so I could read.

> *Hasmukh & Ramesh,*
> *I am so pleased to hear that Ramesh is going to America for further studies. I hope Rs. 12, 000 will help you move forward. If you need more, please let me know. Your father was the nicest man I ever met. I am so proud of you guys.*
> *Good Luck.*
> *Bachu Kaka.*

Hasubhai punched the air in jubilation. "Can you believe it? Dad got us this loan."

My eyes clouded with tears. We savored the moment for several seconds and couldn't wait to share the note with Ma.

"We don't have much time," Hasubhai said. "Tomorrow we'll go to the Air India Travel Agency and book your flight. You also need to meet with Tailor Kanu in the Fort Area to get a suit and winter jacket made."

"We have sixteen days," I said. "I'll go with Bhupat. He knows the tailor well."

I leaned forward in my seat so my hands were out of sight of the driver and took the money from the envelope. Holding 12,000 rupees made me feel lightheaded with excitement.

"Have you heard from the U.S. Embassy?" Hasubhai said.

I shook my head. "Not yet."

"Your passport?"

"I picked it up last week."

"You should check with the embassy."

"Why? They know when I have to travel."

"Ramesh, only the agent you spoke with knows. Maybe he didn't write it down. Maybe there's a delay. You should go there tomorrow. Your visa is the last hurdle." He leaned forward, took the money from me, and returned it to the envelope.

"I'll go tomorrow," I said.

Hasubhai lowered his voice. "You know the fastest way to repay this loan is for you to get a job in America when your studies are complete."

"I don't think I can. My student visa doesn't allow that."

Hasubhai nodded his head. "It's possible. Someone at work that knows about these things said that, while you are there, you must find a company that will sponsor you—one that wants to employ you. Then you can apply for a work visa."

I sat back and pondered this new idea.

***

At home, we described every detail of our visit with Kaka and his wife and showed everyone the money. Ma handed me a letter that had arrived from the U.S. Embassy. My visa interview was scheduled for 10:30 a.m. on December 28, two days before my departure date.

That night, lying on my bed-mat, I listened to my family around me—the quiet breathing of my siblings, an occasional grunt or snore from Ma, a muffled giggle from the screened areas where the married couples slept. Reality struck home. Soon, this would be a memory. Soon, I would be in a far-away country and I would sleep alone.

Prior to our visit with Kaka, going to America had been a dream. With the money, it became reality. Tomorrow I would buy a plane ticket. In a few days, I would leave India for a world I did not know, where I had no friends or family. If Hasubhai's idea came to fruition, it would be years before I returned to live at home. That thought did not sit well.

I stared at the ceiling, my stomach tense with anxious thoughts. Would my English be good enough? Who would care for me if I fell sick? What if I got lost? I was not an experienced traveler.

I knew I had to stop these negative thoughts and gave myself a pep talk.

Ramesh, be bold like your father. He moved to Bombay with nothing more than a dream to give his family a better future. You are part of that dream. Hasubhai went to college. Bhupat started a business. Your role is to go to America. Have courage. Do this for your family. You must complete the journey your father started.

I lay there thinking of people I wanted to spend time with before I left. I would visit Dr. Dufftary and Dr. Freitus and tell them my news. I would spend time with Jayant and Pradip. I would stop by Dr. Malkan's clinic one evening and thank him for his help.

What could I say to Jayant? His life was heading in the wrong direction and I wanted to say something to help him change his ways. No one else cared for him. I decided to visit him in the middle of the day when he was sober.

14

Shopping Spree

The next morning, Bhupat accompanied me on a shopping spree. Hasubhai knew the owner of a fabric store and had already negotiated a discount with his friend. We started there and selected several cotton fabrics for shirts and underwear, plus padding for a winter coat.

We would take these to Kanu Tailor for him to make the garments. Everyone in India did this, even for simple garments such as nightwear. There were no stores that sold affordable ready-made clothing.

For suit fabrics, we had to go to a store that specialized in high-quality textiles. On the way, Bhupat coached me on how he wanted to negotiate. "Put the fabric you like best to one side and then show me two others," he said.

I nodded.

Inside the store, the owner greeted us.

"This is my brother," Bhupat replied. "He's going to study in America and needs a suit."

The owner showed us a selection of fabrics. I pushed the one I liked best to one side and wavered over two others.

Bhupat picked one of them. "What is the cost for this?"

The owner looked at the bolt of material. "It's 50 rupees a yard."

Bhupat laughed. "Give us your Indian price, not your American price."

The owner scowled like we had insulted him. "I can do 45."

Bhupat shook his head. "Give me your starving student price."

The owner eyed my ninety-five-pound frame. "You'll need three yards; 125 rupees total."

"We have 100 rupees, cash."

"I can't do that."

Bhupat shuffled his feet and snapped at me, "Ramesh, pick a cheaper material." Before I could barely move, he grabbed the bolt of fabric I had put to one side. "This looks good to me." He thrust the bolt of material into the owner's arms. "Three yards of this material for 100 rupees cash… or we leave."

The negotiators faced each other, Bhupat with his hunchback and withered arm, the owner with a bald head and pencil behind his ear.

"I can do 110."

"With a lining?"

"No."

"We also need fabric for a winter coat. Something waterproof."

The owner hesitated and Bhupat turned to leave.

"Okay. With a lining."

***

Thirty minutes later we entered the Air India Travel Agency and learned that the fare I had budgeted was a ticket that could not be rescheduled or refunded. I hadn't yet had my interview at the American Embassy, so I wondered if it was a wise choice. "Bhupat, what if they refuse my visa application?"

"Ramesh, it's a study visa and you have a sponsor. Why would they refuse you?"

"I don't know. But it's an interview. That means they can say no."

"It's very unlikely."

"But it's so much money."

"If we wait, the price will go up."

He was right, yet I still felt uneasy when he counted out the money and handed it to the travel agent.

A few doors down the street, we entered a shoe shop. I tried on a pair of lace-up leather shoes which squeezed my toes. "They don't feel right."

The sales assistant smiled. "You'll get used to them. They're the right size for you."

I glanced at Bhupat, "They're so expensive."

"Ramesh, you can't wear flip flops to school in America. Get what you need. They look smart and we have the money. Just go and study hard."

We made the purchase and headed to Tailor Kanu's shop in the Fort Area. Kanu had known our father and had made clothes for the family on several occasions. He greeted us at the door. Inside, three tailors sat working. The oldest, was cutting material for a suit. The other two were sewing shirts.

"Kanubhai, this is my brother, Ramesh. He is going to America and needs Western-style clothes: undergarments, shirts, a suit, and a winter coat with extra padding."

I handed Kanu the materials we had bought. He eyed the suit fabric and then looked at me. "Three buttons … double breasted?"

I glanced at Bhupat. I knew nothing about suit design.

Kanu smiled. "Don't worry, Ramesh. When I'm finished, you'll look like a Bollywood movie star. Like Dev Anand."

"How much for everything?" Bhupat asked.

Kanu laid out each piece of fabric, totaling the number of garments as he went.

"Maybe 900 rupees."

Bhupat shook his head. "I don't want your movie star price."

A smile creased the tailors' lips. "My stitching is the best. Have you seen how good the movie stars look?"

"Kanu, don't lie to me. No one from Bollywood comes here."

Kanu looked at the fabrics again, "My rock bottom price is 750."

I looked at Bhupat, "Are you sure Kanu is the right guy? That's close to two months of your wages."

"You're right, Ramesh. Anything will look good on you. The stitching hardly matters." We both smiled.

Kanu shook his head. "Alright, 700 rupees."

"Six hundred," Bhupat said. "No more."

The tailor paused. "Your departed father was a good man. He would have given me 700."

For a moment Bhupat seemed stumped by Kanu's response, but he recovered. "I have cash. My father rarely had cash."

Kanu sighed, "That is true." He reached in his pocket for his tape measure. "I'll meet you half way at 650 rupees."

Bhupat nodded his agreement and Kanu stretched his tape across my shoulders.

"Kanubhai, don't make a mistake. Ramesh leaves in a few days."

Kanu paused and stared at Bhupat. "You are *so* like your father."

***

We arrived home late in the afternoon and, with hardly a pause, I headed for Zaveri Bazaar. I found Jayant sober with a cigarette hanging from the corner of his mouth.

"You usually come in the evening," he said.

"I have news. Let's go for afternoon tea."

Jayant called Laxman to take over and we navigated our way through a bustling crowd to the corner teashop. I chose a seat in the shade and pulled a 5-rupee note from my pocket. "My turn to pay."

He raised an eyebrow, "So what's your news?"

I knew my reply would shock him, yet there was no way to soften the blow. "Jayant, I will be leaving for America in two weeks. Most likely, I won't be back for two to three years."

His jaw dropped, followed a fraction later by his shoulders. He motioned to say something, but no words came out. A tear formed and he rubbed it away with his sleeve. "Ramesh, if you leave…Laxman is thinking of returning to his village…you know I don't have anyone…"

More tears flowed. I leaned across the table and gripped his forearm. "Be strong, my friend."

A waiter brought our tea. I sipped from my cup while Jayant regained his composure. His eyes looked weak, the eyes of a man on the edge of despair.

"I will miss your visits in the evening," he said.

I hesitated for a moment. "Jayant, will you do something for me?"

"Of course."

"I want you to take better care of your health."

He looked away.

"You need to stop drinking. You're a nice person, but people are scared of you when you drink."

He reached for his cup and sipped some tea. "Ramesh, I want to stop drinking…but I get so depressed at night. I'm sleeping on the street and no one cares."

"Jayant, drink makes you angry and that drives people away. If you stop drinking, you will have many friends."

He snorted. "I've never had friends…only you."

I took another sip of tea. "Jayant, there's something else I want to say."

His eyes narrowed. "Go on."

"At GT Government Hospital, I treated many VD patients. They were pitiful men with terrible sores and blisters on their genitals. I hated to see it. Jayant, they got that from prostitutes. You're taking a big risk when you visit those girls."

"Ramesh…that's all the comfort I have."

I felt sad for him. What else could I say? We sat in silence until we finished our tea.

I didn't want that exchange to be our farewell. "Jayant, please come to the airport when I leave, to send me off."

He swayed his head in thought, and then nodded.

***

December 28 arrived. I dressed smartly, checked my document folder, and headed for the U.S. Embassy.

"I'll come with you," Bhupat said, "I have to deliver a radio to an office near there."

"Bhupat, the embassy will not let you inside."

He thought for a moment, "Then let's meet after your interview."

I liked that idea, "There's a café across from the embassy. Let's meet there for lunch."

At the embassy, I received a numbered token and joined a crowd of other applicants in an undersized waiting room. An attendant shouted numbers at a steady rate, but there were dozens ahead of me. I did some math and realized I had a long wait.

It seemed like the hands on the clock on the wall slowed to a standstill as the morning progressed. I wanted to be at the café when Bhupat arrived, but as midday approached, the flow of applicants to the interview rooms slowed to a snail's pace. I guessed the agents were taking their own lunch breaks. I had no way of contacting Bhupat.

Finally, an agent called my number and I was escorted to a cubicle where a big-framed, middle-aged white man with receding hair and spectacles sat at the desk. He signaled me to sit down and introduced himself as Mr. Smith. I presumed he was American. I felt so nervous that I just shook my head. My palms felt sweaty.

Mr. Smith reviewed my file. "Mr. Shah, what do you plan to study in Atlanta?"

"I plan to study for a diploma at the pathology lab at St. Joseph's Infirmary in Atlanta."

He nodded. "When do you plan to leave for the U.S.A.?"

I wiped my palms on my trousers. For some reason it felt more like an interrogation than an interview. "I leave on December 30."

Mr. Smith glanced at his watch and raised an eyebrow. Without asking another question, he stamped two places on my visa application document and one page in my passport. It must have been time for his lunch break.

"Good luck," he said, handing me my passport and one copy of the visa form. I glanced at the stamp in my passport and wanted to shout for joy. It read: *Non-Immigrant VISA, Issued December 28, 1966.*

***

I found Bhupat waiting at the embassy door and showed him the stamp in my passport. He grinned and slapped me on the back. "Nothing can stop you now."

We strolled to the café and ordered food. In the bright sunlight, I noticed how tired Bhupat looked. His business demanded many late nights to keep customers happy.

Bhupat asked about my interview and we chatted until our food and tea arrived. I bit hungrily into a spicy cucumber-and-tomato-chutney sandwich. It tasted delicious. For the first time in months, I felt relaxed.

"Bhupat, what's new with your business," I said.

His eyes came to life. "I'm going to buy a scooter."

The thought of Bhupat weaving through Bombay traffic on a scooter with a radio under his arm almost made me choke. "Where will you keep it? It will get stolen on the street and you can't bring it up three flights of stairs."

"It's not for me."

His reply didn't make sense and I gave him a questioning look.

"You know Bansi Lal who is working for me?"

"Yes. You hired him a few weeks ago. He's a radio repair technician."

Bhupat sipped his tea. "He's often late for work and I'm falling behind with my customers."

"Will you fire him and find someone else?"

"No! He is very skilled. He repairs a radio as fast as I can diagnose what's wrong with the next one. When we are together, we do three times the work I can do on my own."

I bit into my sandwich, "That's good money."

He nodded, "Money I lose when he's late. He lives far away, near Malad Train Station, and is often delayed."

My jaw dropped, "You're giving *him* the scooter?"

Bhupat grinned, "Then he'll get to work on time."

"Are you crazy?"

He leaned across the table, "Ramesh, it's the perfect solution. He'll get to work on time and won't have to ride crowded trains. He'll never want to leave me and work for someone else."

It sounded bizarre. "Where will you get the money?"

"Ishwarbhai has loaned me the money. I do plenty of repair work for him. He says I can deduct the payments from his bill, so no need for cash."

I shook my head, "So you'll walk to work while your employee rides a scooter that you've paid for?"

Bhupat shrugged, "I've no problem with that." He leaned forward, "Ramesh, when I walk home, I'll have more money in my pocket. That's all that matters."

I couldn't fault his logic. "Does Hasubhai know?"

He grinned. "Not yet."

***

That evening the whole family celebrated my success. I had stopped at the bazaar to invite Jayant along and we all had a good time.

"Let's go and see a movie," Jayant suggested. "We must do something together before our friendship is separated."

I agreed, and we headed to the Eros Cinema near Churchgate to see the latest English movie, *Solomon and Sheba.*

The movie had been playing about half an hour when I felt an unexpected sharp pain in my abdomen like someone had stabbed me with a hot knife. I doubled up in my seat to control the pain.

"What is it?" Jayant said.

Another wave of pain hit me, "I don't know. A bad pain below my stomach."

People seated in the row behind hissed at us to stop talking. Jayant rose from his seat and glared at them. They stopped.

"Is it very bad?" he said.

I nodded.

He reached for my chin and turned my face so he could see my eyes. "We must leave and visit Dr. Malkan."

Jayant supported me while I struggled to my feet, "I hope he's still there."

We reached the street and the pain eased slightly as I walked.

"Shall I run ahead and let him know?" Jayant asked.

I shook my head, "No, stay with me."

We reached Dr. Malkan's office and Jayant helped me up the steps. I told Dr. Malkan about the pain and he pointed to the examination table. "Lie down."

I climbed onto the examination table with Jayant's help and Dr. Malkan examined my abdomen. "Ramesh, you have appendicitis. You need surgery."

"But Doctor, my flight to America…"

Dr. Malkan raised his voice, "Listen to me, Ramesh. Untreated, this could kill you. Go to the free ward at GT Government Hospital early in the morning for surgery. Dr. Dufftary will help you get admitted." He walked to the dispensing desk. "I'll give you a painkiller to get you through the night."

15

Surgery

None of us slept much that night. I lay in the fetal position with Ma and Bhabhi doing what they could to make me comfortable. They fought a losing battle. If the painkiller helped, it didn't feel like it.

Whenever the pain eased, mental anguish took over. We had everything in place, now all was lost. I would not be in Atlanta for the first day of class. We had spent big money for an airfare that could not be refunded and on clothes I would not wear.

I've let down my family. It would be best to die now. Let it all end here. Bhagwan Mahavir, where are you? What are you doing to me?

***

Somehow I made it through the night. Hasubhai left the apartment shortly after dawn to hail a taxi. When he returned, he helped me down the three flights of stairs and into the vehicle. We arrived at GT Government Hospital shortly after 7:30 a.m. and went straight to Dr. Dufftary's office. He took one look and leapt from his chair, "Ramesh, what is it?"

"I have appendicitis. Dr. Malkan says I need surgery."

Dr. Dufftary took over, and I thanked Bhagwan Mahavir that I knew someone with influence when it mattered most. In a whirlwind of activity he had me admitted to the free ward and insisted on surgery later that morning.

I ended up on a makeshift gurney waiting with other patients on the crowded ward. Some patients were lying on the floor and in the hallways. From my horizontal position, I could see paint peeling from the ceiling. One light bulb lit the room.

I knew that the free ward ranked low on the hospital's priority list. Funding came from charitable donations and was never enough. Two nurses staffed the ward, although the workload demanded six. They ran from one patient to the next, prepping them for surgery with no time to think.

Weeks earlier, when I first saw the ward, I had wondered how many mistakes they made. Now I feared that I would be one of them.

Hasubhai and Ma stayed with me until a nurse came to prep me.

***

I awoke after surgery with a headache. My mind seemed to float around the room. I vaguely remembered an anesthetist, but not a surgeon. A patient next to me screamed every few seconds. Another shouted for a nurse.

I could tell I was in the recovery area and lifted the flimsy gown that covered my naked body to take a look at my wound. Metal clips held together a five-inch incision that carved its way across my lower abdomen. I touched the skin near the wound and winced with pain. My whole abdomen felt like a raging fire. Turning on my side or sitting up were impossible.

"Ramesh, how are you?"

I recognized Hasubhai's voice.

"Ramesh, how do you feel?"

He and Ma were standing beside me. Their presence comforted me.

"I feel groggy."

Hasubhai squeezed my arm. "I spoke with the doctor. The surgery went well, no complications. We can take you home. They need the bed."

"I can't move."

"Bhupat has gone to the travel agent to rearrange your flight. As it's a medical emergency, we don't have to pay extra. The clips must stay on for four or five days."

My mind worked slowly through the residual anesthesia. Could I still make it to America? Would St. Joseph's Infirmary hold my place? "We must send a telex…"

"First, we must get you home." Hasubhai reached under my armpits from behind and slid me off the gurney. I yelled with pain. Ma helped me into some loose fitting clothes. Then the two of them, supporting me on either side, guided me out of the hospital into a waiting taxi.

At 64-D, neighbors appeared from nowhere to help me up the stairs. Bhabhi waited in the apartment with a glass of orange juice that Hasubhai had purchased from a street vendor. When I had finished drinking, they laid me on a bed to rest.

The following morning, Hasubhai sent a telex to Dr. Godwin giving details of my emergency operation and stating that my new arrival date would be Sunday, January 8, 1967. The time zone difference meant that it was already late evening on Friday, December 30 in America. Most likely, Dr. Godwin had already left work and would not see the telex until after the weekend.

***

The next few days were a blur. We received no reply from Dr. Godwin and assumed he had no issues with my late arrival and that he would send someone to pick me up at Atlanta airport as originally planned. I had my suture clips removed and started to move about more freely as the days progressed. I still felt sharp pain with any movement that stretched my stomach muscles, but I tried to hide this from my mom.

When January 7 arrived, my new departure date, Ma and Bhabhi packed two suitcases and a large shoulder bag for carry-on. They filled one suitcase with clothes and the other with a variety of spicy Indian snacks they had made for me. Most were dried or fried so they would last several months. The weight of the two suitcases seemed like more than my body weight.

That afternoon, Ma changed the dressing on my wound for the last time. "Son, how do you feel?"

I smiled the best I could, "It's better than yesterday. I'll take it easy for the first few days."

In reality, I should have rested longer. It was not a good time to leave on an adventure with two overweight suitcases, but I had no option. My flight was scheduled to depart at 2 a.m. If the journey went as planned, I would land in Atlanta at 10 p.m. local time after thirty hours of travel, with stops in Cairo, Geneva, London, and New York. I would change aircrafts in London and change airlines in New York.

As evening approached, friends and relatives arrived at the apartment to say farewell. I was pleased to see Dr. Freitus from St. Xavier College. She brought best wishes from everyone in the department and made a point of speaking to my mother.

"I'm the one who suggested America," she confessed, speaking in English. Ma did not understand what she had said. When I translated, Ma gave her a stern look and everyone laughed.

The presence of all these people helped me realize the trailblazing nature of my trip. This was a first not only for my family, but also for the apartment block. After a while, the scene became too much for Ma and she began to cry.

"Son, don't leave us. We will be fine if you stay."

A lump formed in my throat and I hugged her. "Ma, you know I have to go. I'll be back soon."

"But you are not well. Who will take care of you?" Her tears became sobs. "I'm afraid I may not be here when you come back."

Emotion overcame me and I also began to cry. Soon every member of the family was in tears. It was a sad and touching moment that I never forgot.

***

At 9 p.m., I slipped into the kitchen and put on my new suit and leather shoes. Everyone cheered when I emerged.

"You look very smart," Dr. Freitus said.

My younger sister Pratibha, now a teenager, placed dried coconut in my palms, made a small circle of red dye on my forehead, and tossed a few grains of rice over me. These were to protect me from bad omens. My older sister, Damuben, presented me with a small box, about one inch cubed. It had a hinged lid with a small ivory figurine of Bhagwan Mahavir inside. "Carry this with you for protection," she said before hugging me.

I thanked her and slipped the cube carefully into my jacket pocket.

Hasubhai gave me a small photograph of Mom and Dad to take with me.

It was almost time to leave. Hasubhai had hired a minibus to transport people to the airport so people who wanted to give me a send-off could come along.

The minibus arrived around 10 p.m. and friends carried my suitcases down the stairs. I turned to the framed photographs on the wall and prayed my usual prayer, unaware that I would never step foot in the apartment again. With tears in my eyes, I asked for strength, courage, and a special blessing as I faced the unknowns of my journey.

The ride to the airport in the Bombay suburb of Santa Cruz took about an hour through mostly empty streets, and we arrived about three hours before departure time. On the journey, I sat next to Ma and she held my arm. "Son, write letters to me. Tell me all about your health and your studies, and about the people you meet."

"I will. And you must tell me all the family news."

Her voice cracked. "If you don't like it in America, come home and look for a job here."

I nodded my head, knowing I could never consider that option. We had borrowed 12,000 rupees for my studies in America. I had to get my diploma, find a job, and pay off the loan. An early return would leave Hasubhai and Bhupat with all the payments and no additional income. That would bring my family to a level of poverty we had never known, not to mention the taboo of failure it would bring to our family name. I carried my family's future on my shoulders.

At the airport, Bhupat signaled a uniformed coolie to unload my suitcases and bring them into the terminal. Ma interrupted him to retrieve my winter coat and gloves. "You may need these on the journey," she said to me.

Bhupat made a joke. "That's right, Ramesh, we don't want you getting cold on the aircraft."

Ma ignored him and placed my winter clothes with my carryon bag. Then we entered the crowded and chaotic departure lounge. For each flying passenger, there must have been fifty supporters. My entourage was small compared to most.

Only ticketed passengers were allowed past a set of glass doors. I hugged Ma and told her I would see her soon. She cried and refused to let go of me. Hasubhai had to intervene to separate us.

I embraced Bhupat and told him to take care of his health. Then I said farewell to my other siblings and my friends who had joined me. I told Jayant to remember our conversation and to look after himself. The farewells took a toll on me, and I felt a sense of relief when I finally passed through the glass doors. The coolie accompanied me, carrying my suitcases on his headgear. I turned and waved goodbye for the final time.

At the economy class check-in counter, I joined a waiting line of people. As the line shuffled forward, I kept peeking for a final glimpse of my family.

I reached the desk. "Destination?" the attendant asked.

"Atlanta."

She checked my bags to New York. "That's your port of entry. You must collect your bags and pass through customs there before you fly to Atlanta."

After check-in, I moved to the departure lounge until boarding time and occupied an empty seat before they were all taken. My abdominal wound throbbed with pain. Most passengers were Indian nationals with a sprinkling of Europeans and Americans. Outside on the tarmac, an Air India Boeing 707 waited for us to board. In the moonlight, it looked an unbelievable piece of engineering. I felt excited and scared at the same time. My adventure had started.

***

Flight attendants dressed in smart Indian saris arrived, and boarding started soon after. As I entered the plane, I began to feel nervous about my first flight. An attendant guided me to my designated window seat in the middle section of the plane and helped me place my jacket and carry-on bag in the overhead compartment.

The seat was narrow but comfortable, and I watched in amazement as two hundred people with carry-on baggage streamed onto the aircraft and settled in such a small space. I felt lucky to have a window seat.

A young student sat next to me and he looked tense. I introduced myself.

"I'm Ashok," he responded. "Where are you flying to?"

"America. To study."

His face relaxed. "Me too. I'm going to Columbus, Ohio. To study engineering."

"Atlanta, Georgia. Medical technology."

We discovered we both came from Gujarat and slipped into our native tongue.

Soon, the intercom sounded. "Ladies and gentlemen, we are ready for takeoff."

I listened to the safety announcements and mentally prepared myself for my first flight. When we moved down the runway for takeoff, I gripped the arms of my chair and noticed that Ashok did the same. A few seats away, a baby screamed. The young mother tried to sooth the child without success.

During the night, I found it difficult to sleep in a seated position with my wound throbbing, and Ashok and I exchanged many dialogues. Dr. Malkan's painkillers did not seem to help.

After stops in Cairo and Geneva, the plane landed at London's Heathrow Airport. Here we had to change aircraft. Inside the terminal, I listened to the loudspeaker announcements. They were given in English and another language I didn't recognize. I nudged Ashok. "Do you understand the announcements?"

He shrugged. "A little. The accent makes it difficult."

I listened to another announcement and wondered if the problem was the accent or my lack of vocabulary. Maybe my grasp of English was not as good as I thought. That could be a problem.

Working together, we found our next departure gate and I prayed a silent thank-you that I had a companion for the first leg of my adventure. "Let's see if we can sit together on the next flight," I said.

With boarding passes in hand, we approached the Air India counter attended by an Indian lady. "May I help you?" she said with a strong English accent.

I responded in Hindi, thinking she would understand. "We'd like to sit together on our flight to New York."

She gave us a blank look and it took me a moment to realize she did not understand. I was shocked that a woman of Indian descent did not speak the most common of Indian languages. "Sit together," I said in English, pointing to Ashok and myself.

She nodded and took our boarding passes. I glanced at Ashok with a raised eyebrow while the lady busied herself behind the counter. Seconds later, she handed us two new boarding passes. I smiled and thanked her. She smiled back.

While we waited, we exchanged our American addresses. I looked at the piece of paper Ashok handed me. "Ashok, you have the wrong zip code. The ZIP code for America is 30303."

He frowned. "That's not the number they gave me."

"Your number is wrong unless America has more than one ZIP code. I think each country has only one."

After some persuasion, Ashok wrote down the number I gave him.

***

The flight from London to New York was the longest segment of the journey and seemed to take forever. Although I'd hardly slept for twenty hours, my body refused to rest. I sat thinking of Ma and my siblings going about their daily chores, and wishing I was with them. My eyes welled with tears. I had not yet arrived at my destination and already I felt homesick. Eventually, I dozed off.

I woke to the pilot's voice on the intercom announcing we would soon begin our descent into JFK airport. I tapped Ashok's arm to wake him and lifted the window shade to look outside. The light dazzled me and it took several seconds for my eyes to adjust. We were flying just above fluffy white clouds that looked like cotton wool. I had never seen anything like it. Moments later, the plane descended into the clouds and the cotton wool turned to gray-white nothingness.

A flight attendant announced the local time to be just after 4 p.m. My body clock disagreed, insisting it was nighttime. I rubbed my eyes and looked out the window again. The aircraft had dropped below cloud cover and I could see a white winter landscape as far as the eye could see. I sat mesmerized. "Ashok, take a look at this."

He leaned over and looked out the window. Neither of us had ever seen snow before.

"Amazing," he said. "The black lines must be roads."

The plane continued its descent. Soon I could see individual rooftops, each with its own accumulation of snow. I picked out a big machine clearing snow from the streets. It was remarkable to see how fast it worked. If it ever snowed in Bombay, an army of shovels would do this job. Here it took one man and a machine.

We approached the landing strip and I braced myself for touchdown in my new world. The airplane hit the ground with a bump that made several passengers gasp. I hoped it was not an omen for my new world adventure.

16

Welcome to America

A biting wind blew across the tarmac as I descended the airplane steps and walked to a waiting bus. I had put on my winter coat and gloves in the aircraft and silently thanked Ma for moving them to my carry-on bag in the stifling heat of Bombay.

It took several minutes for the bus to fill and, while I waited, I began to shiver; a sensation new to me. It felt similar to cold water touching my spine in the shower. My ear started to throb and I feared I had picked up an infection on the flight. Finally, the bus moved and we were on our way to the terminal.

Inside the terminal, warmth enveloped me and I began to feel better. Ashok and I followed other passengers to Immigration Control, a large and brightly lit room with a floor that looked like polished marble. Uniformed staff gave directions and people followed their instructions, waiting in line without pushing or complaining.

"People are polite here," I whispered to Ashok. "I like it."

We joined the line for non-citizens and I removed my passport and visa papers from my bag, praying that the immigration officer would speak slowly so I could understand.

When my turn came, an officer waved me forward, examined my visa papers, checked the photo in my passport, and stamped the entry date on a blank page in my passport without asking a single question. "Welcome to the U.S.A." he said.

"Thank you, sir," I said, taking my papers and moving to a location where I could wait for Ashok to join me.

Next, we had to collect our luggage. We watched other passengers collect a cart, check a monitor, and then move to one of the conveyor belts that delivered luggage. We followed their example and soon spotted our suitcases. Ashok retrieved them all so I didn't strain my abdominal wound.

At the line to get through customs, I watched closely to see if passengers were tipping the officials to let them pass without delay. The process of giving small bribes to help things go smoothly was endemic among government officials in India and Hasubhai had heard nightmare stories of foreign visitors coming through customs in Bombay.

I saw nothing suspicious but pulled a $10 bill from my pocket just in case. The customs officer made no eye contact or gesture as I approached that suggested he expected a bribe. "Open your bags please," he said.

I quickly pocketed the $10 bill and unlocked my cases.

The officer inspected the case containing clothes and then lifted the lid of the case with food. I knew that unprocessed fruit and vegetables were not allowed but everything in my case was dried or processed.

"What are these?"

"Indian snacks and spices."

The officer picked a container. "Open it."

I opened the container and watched his grimace when he sniffed the contents. He returned the container to me and placed "inspected" stickers on my two suitcases. I pulled them to one side and repacked them.

Outside the customs area, I met up with Ashok again and we entered the main terminal; a spectacular, brightly lit building with a spotless floor and decorative art pieces hanging on the walls. Through tall glass windows, we could see snow falling and settling on people's clothing. Exhaled breaths looked like puffs of white smoke. I remembered how cold it had been outside, yet inside it was comfortably warm. The whole building had to be heated. *Oh my Lord, how much did this cost?*

We studied our tickets and the monitors hanging from the ceiling and concluded we had to go in different directions. After wishing each other well, we parted company.

I took another look around the vast terminal and suddenly felt very much alone.

***

My flight to Atlanta was with Eastern Airlines and I followed directional arrows to their check-in desk until an arrow pointed up to the next level. Ahead of me, I saw a big rolling staircase that moved constantly. People stood still on it but they were moving. I had never seen such a thing.

A sign said "No Carts." Up to that point, I'd not had to carry my suitcases. I put my carryon bag round my neck, grabbed one case in each hand, and lifted them from the cart. Pain shot through my abdomen. I grimaced, but had to continue. At the moving staircase, I stepped on and started to climb but the staircase would not work for me. Each time I took a step up, the mover brought me back down. I stood there feeling helpless until I felt a tap on my shoulder.

"Hey fella, you need help?"

I turned to see an oversize African American porter. He looked three times my size. I nodded my head, "I need upstairs desk."

His face remained blank, so I put down my suitcases, showed him my ticket and pointed upstairs. He nodded and lifted my bags as if they were featherweight. "Follow me."

I followed him to the rear of the moving staircase where the conveyor went up, not down, and we reached the second floor with ease. Fromm there he led me to the Eastern Airline desk. I thanked him and gave him the $10 bill I had pocketed at customs.

The check-in agent looked disinterested as I handed her my ticket.

"Miss, I go to Atlanta."

She glanced at the ticket. "Window or aisle seat?"

I smiled.

Her eyes narrowed and she repeated her question speaking louder and with a momentary pause between each word. "Window—seat—or—aisle—seat?"

I smirked. "Window seat."

Without another word, she checked my luggage, prepared my boarding pass, circled the departure gate, and pointed in the direction I had to go. I thanked her and followed signs to the departure gate. After twenty-four hours of traveling, my abdomen ached and my body wanted sleep. Everything around me seemed different and I felt vulnerable and utterly alone.

At the gate, I stayed standing so I wouldn't doze off and miss the flight. While I waited, another fear began to bother me—what if no one was waiting for me in Atlanta? I had not received a confirmation telex from Dr. Godwin, and had assumed everything would be fine. Now I had my doubts. I checked my papers to make sure I had the hospital address.

The Eastern Airline aircraft was much smaller than the others I had flown on and the boarding process went quickly. I settled in my seat and looked around the cabin. The passengers were mostly white with a few African Americans. Only I had brown skin. I felt like a jigsaw puzzle piece in the wrong box.

An attractive young flight attendant approached me. "May I get you something to drink?"

"Tea, please."

"Milk and sugar?"

I nodded.

A minute later she returned with a cup of hot water, a small bag of tea, two small white sachets, a container of milk, and a tiny spoon. She handed me the tray and I studied the items and read the labels. My mom had never served tea like this. The white sachets were sugar. I tore open the small bag of tea, poured the contents into the hot water, and added some sugar. The water changed color and I began to feel better. Now I needed a filter to remove the tea leaves and wondered if the young attendant had forgotten it. When she passed by, I got her attention, "Miss, I need filter."

She paused for a moment, gave me an odd look, and then removed my tray with everything on it. *Had she misunderstood me?* My feeling of isolation grew and I stared out the window at airport workers dressed in thick winter clothes transferring luggage into the belly of the plane. I searched for my bags but did not see them.

"Sir, here is your tea."

I looked up at the attendant. She carried a tray bearing a cup of tea and nothing else. I thanked her and took a sip of tea. She had already added milk and sugar. It tasted nothing like Ma's or Bhabhi's ginger masala preparation, but I did not grumble.

The attendant returned a minute later to shut the overhead compartment and collect the tray. "We'll be taking off shortly."

"We go Atlanta, Georgia?"

She smiled. "Yes, we're going to Atlanta. It's a two-hour flight and we'll be serving dinner. Relax and enjoy the flight."

I leaned back and closed my eyes—I do not remember takeoff.

I woke to the stewardess tapping my shoulder. "Mr. Shah, here is your dinner. It's a turkey and ham sandwich."

I didn't recognize the words she used but I could tell it was not vegetarian. I pushed it away, "No thank you."

A puzzled look crossed her face.

"Vegetarian."

She removed the sandwich, "Let me see if I can find you some fruit."

I stared out the window. Stars sparkled in the evening sky. They seemed brighter here than from the apartment window in Bombay. I checked my watch: one hour to go. Fears resurfaced in my mind. *What if no one's there to meet me? How far is the hospital? Do I have enough money for a taxi?*

I reached in my pocket for the Mahavir idol that Damuben had given me, but it was in my jacket in the overhead compartment. I prayed anyway.

"Sir, here is your fruit plate. I also found a bread roll and butter." The attendant handed me a tray.

"You are very nice. Thank you."

She smiled.

The arrangement of cut fruits looked attractive. I recognized apple, orange, and grapes, but there were other items new to me. It didn't matter. I finished the plate and enjoyed every mouthful.

When we landed and exited the aircraft, the temperature felt warmer, though I still needed my winter coat. I followed other passengers into the terminal and saw an area where people held placards with names written on them. Some wore chauffeur uniforms.

I held my breath and scanned the names. An Indian man in his late twenties held a sheet of paper bearing my name. "*Mahavir, you are awesome,*" I whispered.

I approached the man, "I'm Ramesh Shah."

He spoke Hindi, "I'm Dr. Kumar. Welcome to Atlanta. Dr. Godwin sent me to receive you."

We moved to the designated conveyor belt to collect my luggage. One by one, people I recognized from my flight collected their bags and departed. I began to worry my luggage had not arrived. Soon, we were the only two remaining and the conveyor belt stopped. I wanted to cry. I had nothing but the clothes I wore, the contents of my carry-on bag, and an aching abdomen.

Somehow, losing my suitcases felt like a link with my family had been severed. I reached in my pocket for the small wooden box that Damuben had given me and forced myself to stay strong. I turned to Dr. Kumar, "What do we do now?"

He shrugged, "We go to the Eastern Airlines desk."

He led the way and helped me fill out a lost luggage claim form. The Eastern Airlines clerk offered me a utility kit. I looked inside and saw a toothbrush and a Wilkinson razor. I thanked her and followed Dr. Kumar to the outdoor parking lot.

"Ramesh, don't worry. They will deliver your suitcases in a day or two. They will find them."

Walking through the parking lot, I felt even more thankful that Ma had taken my winter coat from my suitcase in Bombay.

***

Dr. Kumar started his car, turned the heater to full blast, and showed me how to use the seatbelt. "It will take about an hour," he said.

"Thank you for picking me up."

"I'm glad you got here. Mrs. Kay was concerned when you didn't arrive last week. She's your lab supervisor. I'll introduce you tomorrow. You'll spend most of the day with her."

"Didn't she get my message—about my surgery?"

He glanced at me. "She said nothing about surgery…just that you would be arriving late."

"I had appendicitis."

He slowed the car. "Are you okay? I thought you look drained."

"It's been a long journey, but I'll be okay. Are you a student at the hospital too?"

"I'm in my final year of residency…in the pathology lab under Dr. Godwin."

When the car had warmed, Dr. Kumar adjusted the heater controls and the noisy fan quieted. I studied the dashboard. It looked modern and I wondered how a student could afford such a nice vehicle. It even had a radio.

Soon we were on the highway and Dr. Kumar accelerated across the smooth road surface that was so much better than the potholed roads of Bombay. We seemed to be moving very quickly and I tilted my head to see the speedometer.

"I thought we were traveling faster than 75," I said.

Dr. Kumar smiled, "Ramesh, you're thinking in kilometers. This is 75 miles per hour. That's 120 kilometers per hour."

"Wow."

"Nice, isn't it? You can't do this on the Bombay highways."

I asked Dr. Kumar about the large signs that edged the highway.

"They're billboards. Companies pay to advertise on them. It's like ads you see in the newspaper, only bigger. The lighting is called neon lighting."

It seemed like a dream world. I'd never seen so many colorful lights and could hardly take it all in.

"What does your father do?" Dr. Kumar asked.

"My father died when I was young."

His voice softened, "I'm sorry to hear that. Do you have brothers and sisters?"

"There are nine of us: five brothers and four sisters. My oldest brother is an accountant and my next brother runs his own business."

"Impressive. My father is an officer in the Indian Army. I have one sister."

From his tone, I could tell that Dr. Kumar was proud of his father. We drove on, talking in Hindi about family and the politics of the Indian subcontinent.

Dr. Kumar exited the highway, "We're almost there." A minute later, he slowed and pointed to an attractive three-story red brick building, "That's the hospital. I'm taking you to the physicians' quarters, one block away. You'll stay there until you find an apartment."

We turned into a parking lot and found an empty space near the entrance. Dr. Kumar led the way into the building and stopped halfway down a corridor. He pulled a key from his pocket and handed it to me, "This is your room."

I opened the door and turned on the light. A bed and a study desk occupied part of the room. Beyond that, I saw a window and a small kitchen area. A fan hung from the ceiling.

Dr. Kumar stepped in and pointed to the kitchen, "You have a stove and a fridge. Toilets and showers are at the end of the corridor." He paused. "Ramesh, it's 11:30 p.m. and I'm sure you're tired. I'll give you a brief tour and then I'll see you at the hospital café at 7:30 in the morning. Is that okay?"

I nodded. "That is very good."

He showed me the toilets, showers, and emergency exit on the ground floor, and then led me upstairs to a lounge area with a black-and-white television, coffee maker, and a payphone. "Over there is where mail gets delivered." He pointed to a wooden cabinet with numbered partitions mounted to the wall, "The spaces are called pigeonholes. You put outgoing mail in the large space at the end. There's a place you can buy stamps at the hospital."

I followed him to the door and thanked him for his help.

"I'll wait for you tomorrow morning outside the café. You can walk to the hospital in ten minutes."

I waited until he pulled away and then rushed to the bathroom.

17

Welcome to America (cont.)

Despite my lack of sleep, my internal clock read midmorning, not 11 p.m. I returned to my room and began to explore. It had similar floor space to the apartment back home where eleven of us lived. Was it possible I had this room to myself? A neat pile of towels rested on the end of the countertop with a small bar of soap and some toiletries. I felt the rich texture of the towel. *How wonderful…a luxury towel that no one else will use.*

The bed had a base that supported the mattress at sitting height. I had not seen that before. I sat on the bed and opened my carry-on bag to munch some of Ma's namkin (salty, spicy snack). The mattress felt firm, and I lay back to rest for a few moments before exploring further. My abdomen felt sore and I could feel it throbbing, but considering the long journey, it was not too painful.

On the bedside table, I noticed a small radio. It had dials and knobs and a thin trailing cable similar to radios that Bhupat had brought home. I pushed a knob and music blasted from it. How can it be so small, I wondered?

I turned off the music and moved to the kitchen area where I noticed the sink had two faucets with the letters H and C marked on them. I turned one of the handles and water flowed. *Wow, no more fetching water every morning.*

I turned the other handle. A few seconds later, hot water flowed and it dawned on me what the letters H and C stood for. *This is amazing.*

The stove that Dr. Kumar had pointed to had metal spiral rings on the top and circular knobs at the front. It didn't look like it used charcoal and I wondered how it worked. I turned one of the knobs but nothing happened. Several seconds later, one of the metal rings began to glow and I could smell heat. *Incredible. It must be electric. This makes cooking so easy.*

I opened the refrigerator door and a light went on. I had seen a refrigerator before at Bachukaka's home. I put my hand inside and felt the cool air. *What a luxury. We dreamed of this at home.*

I moved to the window and peered out into the darkness. My room overlooked the parking lot. How lucky was I to be staying here until I found an apartment? With all these modern appliances, this had to be a special room for a very important person.

I returned to exploring my room. The ceiling fan had a light attachment in the middle and two small chains that hung down to a level I could reach. I pulled one of the chains and the light got brighter. I pulled it again and the light went out. A third pull and the light returned to its original brightness. *How wonderful.* I tried pulling the other chain and discovered it controlled the speed of the fan blades. *What an amazing country. I must describe all of this to my family.*

A noise from the corridor caught my attention and seconds later a voice rang out, "Hi, Doc. Welcome."

My heart missed a beat. A naked man stood in my open doorway. I felt scared and wondered what to do. In my culture, one rarely saw a completely naked man. People kept their bodies very private. *Oh Lord, is this normal in America?*

He spoke as if we were having a casual conversation. "Are you joining the pathology department?"

I remained frozen…speechless.

"I'm Dr. Pearson. Third-year resident. I work with Dr. Kumar."

I swallowed hard. "I…I am student in pathology lab. My name is Ramesh Shah."

He smiled, "How was your flight? I know it's a long trip. I'm from Athens, Greece."

I did not want him to enter my room, "Thirty hours. I'm very tired."

He took the hint. "Let me know if you need help. I'm two doors down on the left." He turned toward the shower room and moved away.

I took a deep breath and locked my door. *Had I come to a land where people walked around naked? Would they expect me to do the same?* The thought horrified me.

***

Fatigue finally came at 1 a.m. and I prepared for bed. For the first time I could remember, I would sleep in a room on my own. As my eyes closed, it dawned on me that no one would not be there to wake me in the morning. With jetlag I might sleep till noon and I had to meet Dr. Kumar at 7:30 a.m. What could I do?

I remembered that the radio had the word ALARM on it and took another look. I found the instruction booklet in the drawer and soon had the alarm set for 6.00 a.m. I sank back onto the bed and fell asleep.

Five hours later, I leapt from the bed to a loud buzzing noise and fumbled with the radio until the noise stopped. I felt totally disoriented. Where was I? Where were my siblings? Slowly, reality came into focus. *Ramesh, you're in America.*

Thoughts of the naked man made me hesitate about taking a shower. I did not want to meet him again, and the thought of showering in the same room as him scared me. I opened my door a fraction and checked the corridor. All seemed quiet, so I gathered my clothes, a towel, and the toiletries and tiptoed to the shower room where I listened at the door. Silence. I entered and hung my towel on a hook by one of the shower stalls. The stall had a curtain on a rail to provide privacy, another new detail I would describe to my family.

Inside the shower, I studied the faucet. I had never seen one like it before, and when I turned it, nothing happened. It would not rotate more than half a turn. I was about to move to another stall when I pulled on the handle. It moved and cold water gushed over me. I jumped to one side and pushed on the handle. The water stopped.

I looked closer, and noticed the letters H and C on either side of the handle. Within seconds I was enjoying a wonderful warm shower with all the water I wanted. As I dried myself with the thick, plush towel, I thought of the concrete plinth back home and the damp, threadbare towel I had used for so many years. Life in America felt good.

I got dressed and ventured to the toilet. The stalls were brightly lit, and I was pleased to glimpse no roaches or earthworms. Mentally I felt *so* good. I had seen Western-style toilets on the aircraft, but had not sat on one. They were so different from the toilets I knew.

Back in my room, I pulled Damuben's gift from my jacket pocket and prayed my usual prayer before I left for the hospital.

***

In daylight, the streets looked different. I could see office skyscrapers, shops, and residential buildings all mixed together. The wide roads felt airy, not claustrophobic, and looked so clean compared to Old Hanuman Lane. I saw no piles of garbage anywhere and detected no foul smells. Traffic moved in regular patterns and without the incessant beeping of horns.

Everyone I saw looked well dressed and well fed. No one appeared poor. I wondered if it was true that everyone in America was rich and drove a big car, including the janitor. It appeared that way.

At the hospital, a sign directed me to the café. As I approached, a variety of aromas teased my nostrils, many of them new to me. My stomach growled.

Dr. Kumar stood near the entrance. We exchanged greetings and he led the way inside, where he handed me a tray and raised his voice above the clamor of conversation and kitchen noise. "Ramesh, there are many choices of food. You serve yourself whatever you want, and then pay for it over there." He pointed to the checkout. "On this counter, you'll find eggs, bacon, sausage, and pancakes. Over there are cereals and other items. Drinks are near the checkout."

"I am vegetarian."

He chuckled, "You are a minority here. Can you eat eggs?"

I shook my head. "No."

"Then it's fruit and cereal. Over there."

I followed his direction and ended up with a bowl of cereal he called cornflakes, a banana, a cup of hot water, and a small bag of tea. At the checkout, Dr. Kumar paid for my food.

When we sat down, I described what happened on the flight, and asked him how I should prepare the tea.

"Did you tear the bag?"

I nodded, "How do you know?"

"Many Indians make that mistake. You should dip the tea bag in the hot water and leave it there for three or four minutes. Then remove the tea bag with a spoon."

"Do I dip the sugar packets the same way?"

He laughed, "No, Ramesh. You tear them open and pour in the amount you want."

I followed his instructions and sat thinking about how to ask my next question.

"Did you sleep well?" he said.

I nodded. "Dr. Kumar, last night a doctor from Greece came to my door. He was naked. Is that normal?"

Dr. Kumar smiled, "You mean Dr. Pearson. No, people generally don't walk around naked. He won't bother you. He's a nice man."

***

After breakfast, Dr. Kumar showed me the lab where he worked and then introduced me to Mrs. Kay Turner, the pathology lab supervisor. She had short brunette hair and wore a white lab jacket with her name sewn in red on the lapel. We shook hands.

"Ramesh, I'm glad you're here," she said in a Southern accent. "We thought you weren't coming. I heard about your telex on Friday." She smiled and pulled me gently by the hand, "Let me introduce you to your classmates and other members of staff."

We approached a group of students congregated in the hematology laboratory. Mrs. Turner leaned in close, "What do you want us to call you?"

The question confused me. "My name is Ramesh."

Mrs. Turner nodded. "Please call me Mrs. Kay."

In comparison to the pathology lab at GT Government Hospital, this laboratory looked brand new. Modern analytical equipment lined the bench tops and all the work surfaces sparkled under bright fluorescent lights.

***

Around midmorning, Mrs. Kay rushed from her office. "Ramesh, there's a call from India."

I followed her and she handed me the phone. The line crackled constantly but I recognized Hasubhai's voice. He sounded panicked.

"Ramesh, are you all right? Did you see…hello, hello…Are you there…hello?"

"Hasubhai, slow down," I said in Gujarat. "Why are you worried? Is Ma okay?"

Mrs. Kay stepped outside and closed her office door.

Hasubhai continued, "We received a letter when we got home from the airport…"

In the background I heard Ma sobbing and Bhupat trying to calm her.

"Hello, hello, Hasubhai can you hear me? Hello…" I kept shouting for a few more seconds, but the call was lost. Why had Hasubhai sounded so scared, I wondered?

Mrs. Kay returned to her office and asked if everything was okay.

"My brothers call. Line cut off."

The phone rang again. Mrs. Kay answered and handed me the receiver.

"Hello, Hasubhai…Yes, I can hear you."

"Ramesh, we received a letter from Dr. Godwin saying your admission has been cancelled."

"Hasubhai, what are you talking about? I am in school. I have no problem."

I heard him give Ma and Bhupat that information. "Ma wants to talk to you," he said.

"Son, how are you? What are you going to do?"

"Ma, I'm fine. I'm in school. I don't know what Hasubhai is saying."

"Son, come back home."

"I'm fine, Ma. Let me talk to Hasubhai."

The operator's voice interrupted, "Three minutes are over."

"Operator, please continue," Hasubhai said.

"Hasubhai, everything is fine here. They are nice people. I will write a letter tonight. I am okay. Don't worry."

The line went silent.

Mrs. Kay raised an eyebrow, "Is there a problem?"

I shook my head, "No, everything is okay."

***

Hasubhai's phone call bothered me for the rest of the day, so I asked Dr. Kumar how to make an international call from the pay phone in the doctors' quarters.

That evening, I called the operator and requested an international call to India. The operator transferred me to an international operator and I gave details of Hasubhai's work number and requested a call at ten o'clock when Hasubhai would be at work. The call would cost more than three dollars per minute so I wanted to be sure he would be there to receive the call. I had a pocketful of quarters.

"And what is your number?"

I gave the number written on the payphone.

While I waited, I pondered the situation. Dr. Godwin must have sent the letter cancelling my admission before he read my telex. It dawned on me that if the letter had arrived a day earlier, I would not have flown to America.

At the appointed time, I waited by the phone. When it rang, I fed a handful of quarters into the phone and the operator made the connection.

"Hasubhai, can you hear me?"

"Yes. What is it?" There was static on the line but we could understand each other.

"Hasubhai, the letter from Dr. Godwin, what date was it sent?"

"January 3. It took six days to get here."

"Hasubhai, it's a miracle. Bhagwan Mahavir held up that letter until I left India."

"I thought that, too," he said with a chuckle. "You can't believe how worried we were. Ma was beside herself."

I imagined the scene of Ma anguishing over a lost child, thinking of me begging on the streets of Atlanta for money to fly home. "Is Ma all right now?"

"Everyone is fine. Write soon."

We hung up and I shouted out loud, "Thank you Bhagwan Mahavir. You are great."

***

Back in my room, I sat down and wrote a long letter about my journey to America, the stove and refrigerator in my room, and other wonderful things I had experienced in my adventure. I laughed and cried as I wrote, and didn't stop until my hand tired.

18

Surrogate Mother

That night, jetlag once again kept me awake into the early hours of the morning. I lay thinking about my first day in America and all the people I had met. Mrs. Kay seemed like a nice person, and the other staff members seemed friendly and knowledgeable, although sometimes their Southern accents made it difficult for me to understand them. Apparently the English I had learned at K.C. College in Bombay had been Indian English and I had to go through the learning process again.

There were ten other foreign students from Europe and South America, and while I struggled, they all spoke good English and blended easily with the Americans. Physically, I was the smallest by a long way and the only one with brown skin. I had felt like the midget of the class in more ways than one.

I made a mental list of things I had to do: pick up textbooks, register with the Immigration and Naturalization

Services (INS), and find a Jain or Hindu temple. It seemed like ages before sleep finally came.

The next morning, I found a note in my pigeonhole saying my luggage had arrived at the hospital front desk…a good start to the day. I got ready for classes and ventured to the café for breakfast. This time, I studied the array of foods more closely and realized that I couldn't name many of them. I played it safe and selected the same items I had eaten the day before.

At the beverage counter, I noticed a carton labeled chocolate milk. I had heard of chocolate, but not chocolate milk, and wondered what it would taste like. I decided to be adventurous and added a carton to my tray.

The cashier lady at the checkout was a middle-aged white American wearing a white hospital uniform and a hairnet. She gave me a smile as I approached. Her nametag said Mrs. Chandler.

As a foreign student, I received a free lunch, but I had to pay for my breakfast. While she totaled the amount I owed, I pulled from my pocket some of the quarters I had left over from my phone call. For some reason, my mind went blank when I tried to calculate how many coins to give her and she leaned over and helped me.

I smiled to thank her and wanted to comment on all the wonderful food and how clean the café looked, but I didn't feel confident with my broken English, so I said nothing.

I sat down at an empty table and opened the carton of chocolate milk. The brown color did not look appetizing. I took a small sip and the liquid tasted so rich and flavorful. I took a bigger mouthful and let the silky fluid glide down my throat. Delicious. I spent a few moments thinking of words I could use to describe this wonderful new flavor to my family. If only they were here with me to try it.

A newspaper on a nearby empty table caught my interest. It had headlines about the war in Vietnam. When several minutes passed and no one returned to collect it, I gathered my tray and moved to that table.

Looking around to make sure no one was watching me, I picked up the paper and thumbed through the articles. I could understand some of them where there were pictures to help, but my lack of vocabulary was a real problem. I turned to the sports pages and searched for information about international cricket matches but found nothing.

Looking around, I noticed that most of the black hospital workers were congregated at one end of the room. Before I left India, Dr. Freitus had warned me about discrimination in America and how people were treated differently because of their skin color. She compared it to the Hindu practice of treating untouchables differently because they were of a lower caste.

I wondered if the black students had to sit at that end of the room and if there were restrictions on what they could study, just like untouchables in India were restricted to certain jobs.

The thought made me conscious of my own skin color. What about brown people? Was there a place for them to sit? Once again, I looked around to make sure no one was staring at me.

A group of white students got up from a nearby table and emptied a large amount of uneaten food into a trash container on their way out. My jaw dropped. I couldn't believe the waste. Why had these people taken more than they needed? At home, we never threw food away.

On my way out I checked the waste container. It grieved me that so many people in my country could be fed from this one container, yet they would go hungry.

***

The rest of the day passed uneventfully. I understood the lecturers a little better than the day before and found time to pick up my textbooks. When classes ended, I located Dr. Kumar and he agreed to help me transport my suitcases to the physicians' quarters. On the way, I asked him where I could find the nearest Jain or Hindu temple.

"Ramesh, I don't think there are any Indian temples in Atlanta. You could look in the yellow pages."

"Yellow pages?"

He smiled. "In the phone book that hangs by the payphone there's a section with yellow pages. Sometimes it's a separate book. That's where businesses and organizations are listed."

We arrived at the physicians' quarters and Dr. Kumar helped me carry my suitcases to my room. "Ramesh," he said, "My schedule is about to change. I'll be working all hours and will not be available to you." He paused. "Leave a message for me if you need assistance. Maybe we will cross paths in the café."

I thanked him for his help and went upstairs to the lounge area to check the yellow pages. I searched for several minutes but found nothing. Dr. Kumar was correct. There was no Jain or Hindu temple in all of Atlanta.

I continued my search, this time in the white pages, looking for people with Indian surnames. I found none. A lump formed in my throat; I was on my own. No one in Atlanta shared my religion. My only resource was the tiny image of Bhagwan Mahavir that Damuben had given me. Before returning to my room, I looked for the address of the INS office in Atlanta.

For the rest of the evening, I studied my new textbooks, reading the chapters we had covered in class and looking up every word I did not understand.

Then I wrote a letter to my family. I wrote about taking a hot shower with as much water as I wanted, about the abundance of food in the café, and that I could drink water from any faucet without having to worry about worms. I didn't tell them that Atlanta had no temples.

***

At break time the following day, I spoke with Mrs. Kay about visiting the INS office. She gave me permission to miss classes one morning and explained that I could get there by bus. I would have to make one change in the center of town.

The next day, I followed her directions and boarded a bus outside the hospital, choosing a window seat so I could take in the details of this new city. The bus had luxury seating compared to buses in Bombay, and it made far less noise.

It amazed me that traffic stayed in neat lanes without endless beeping of horns, and that every vehicle stopped when stoplights turned red. The driver made rapid progress and I enjoyed the ride, arriving at the INS office feeling good about my first use of public transportation in Atlanta.

My high spirits evaporated when I saw the long line of people waiting inside the building. I joined the line of other newcomers to the country and waited almost an hour for a clerk to give me a number and a form to fill out. I moved to a crowded waiting area that reminded me of the U.S. Embassy in Bombay.

When my turn finally came, I moved to the designated booth and waited for a silver-haired white man sitting behind a desk to give me a signal to enter. He beckoned me in and I handed him my papers.

He studied the form without making eye contact and pointed to a box I had inadvertently left blank. "Fill this in and join the end of the line," he said, gesturing with a wave of his hand to the seating area I had just come from. His voice was sharp and insulting. It would have taken two seconds to insert the missing information.

By chance, after waiting in line again, I ended up with the same agent. He did not recognize me. This time, he looked over the form and thumbed through my passport to find my visa stamp. "When do you finish your studies?" he said, his voice still edged with aggression and insult.

"December."

"When will you go home?"

I knew the answer he wanted. "December."

He stamped my form, tore off the bottom copy, inserted it roughly inside my passport, and pushed the documents across the table, once more without making eye contact.

I took my passport and left the building, shocked by his attitude. No government employee in India would treat a foreign guest that way. I mulled this over on the journey back to St. Joseph's. The visit had left a bad taste in my mouth about the Immigration Office. I had also missed a full day of study.

***

The weekend arrived and I spent two days in my room studying and staring out the window. The initial euphoria of my arrival in America had turned to loneliness and despair. I checked my pigeonhole for a letter from home, but nothing had arrived. A deep sense of isolation enveloped me.

I watched a family with several children walk past the parking lot and thought about Ma, Bhabhi, and the smiling faces of my siblings. My hardships were small compared to theirs, but I could not shake the melancholy feelings that filled my mind.

I could have gone out and explored the city, but I had no desire to do that. Inertia held me back. In reality, my heart had never left 64-D. I longed to be with my family and to communicate with them in my mother tongue. The hugs I needed were more than eight thousand miles away.

My only solace was to write to them. I imagined the scene in the apartment when the letter arrived; the excited shouts of my younger siblings when Hasubhai shared my news of the people I had met and of my bus ride through Atlanta.

My letter expressed how much I missed them, but not the anguish I felt in my soul. It did not mention my feelings of loneliness and isolation, or my struggles with English, or that I would be on the first flight home if I had money to buy a ticket.

Perhaps Ma had known I would feel this way and had given me permission to come home. But I couldn't do that. I couldn't let down my brothers.

Over and over, I repeated my father's words: *Tomorrow will be a better day.* At times, his spirit seemed to be in the room with me and I felt strengthened. I had to persist. I had to continue his journey. I could not give up.

Bhagwan Mahavir, give me strength to make it here in America.

***

Monday came. Things seemed quieter than normal when I woke. I peered out the window and saw a blanket of white covering the landscape. It looked magical; the most peaceful city landscape I'd ever seen. Every few seconds, a gust of wind threw up a puff of snow from a car in the parking lot. I quickly got dressed and put on my winter coat.

When I opened the door to the parking lot, a blast of cold air slapped my face. I ignored the cold sensation and left a trail of footprints in the snow as I ran to the middle of the parking lot.

My breath billowed like a cloud in front of my face and I felt exhilarated. I lifted handfuls of snow from parked cars and squeezed it through my fingers and threw it in the air.

Soon my fingers numbed, and I wished I had worn my gloves. Snow inside my shoes began to melt, leaving my feet cold and damp. Wind gusts carved through my Indian winter coat as if Tailor Kanu had cheated on the amount of padding he used.

I returned to the warmth of the building and stood shivering in the foyer while my brain absorbed this new sensory information. The tips of my ears were cold to touch yet felt like they burned. My fingers tingled with pain in a way I'd never experienced. I had learned in school about hot and cold climates. Now I understood them.

I went to my room, changed my socks, and put on two more undershirts before setting out for my classes. This time I wore my hat and gloves, but I soon realized they were designed for a cold spell in Bombay, not the freezing temperatures that had gripped Atlanta. My hat did not cover my ears, and my gloves did not insulate my fingers.

Soon I could feel my appendectomy scar tightening, and my left ear began to throb with its familiar ache. I tried holding my textbooks under my armpits so my hands were free to cover my ears, but one of my books slipped and fell to the ground, half buried in snow.

I picked up the book and made it to the corner of a building that provided shelter from the wind. The pain in my ear eased a little. Ahead of me, someone had cleared the sidewalk and only a thin layer of snow covered the ground. I quickened my pace and, within a few steps, I fell on my butt. It felt like bruises formed before my books hit the ground.

Pedestrians around me paid little attention, all of them preoccupied with their own battle against the elements. I got up, collected my books, and focused on my balance. It seemed like I had no control on the slippery surface.

Half a block farther, I fell again. Looking around, I noticed that others were walking comfortably. I wondered if my lightweight body was the problem.

Finally, I made it to St. Joseph's.

***

In the café, I chose a window seat and gazed out at the winter scene while I ate breakfast. My body hurt from the falls. I was musing about how I would explain the new sensations that came with winter weather to my family when my thoughts were interrupted by a strong Southern accent.

"May I sit with you?"

I looked up to see Mrs. Chandler, the cashier lady with her white coat and hairnet, holding a breakfast tray. I glanced at the cash register. Another lady had taken her place. I moved my tray to make room, "Yes, please."

She sat down and stirred sugar into her coffee. "Are you the student at the doctors' quarters? I work there in the afternoon when I finish here."

I had to concentrate to understand her accent. "Yes," I nodded.

She smiled and sipped her coffee, "Where are you from?"

"India."

I watched her take a bite from a circular, bread-like item she later told me was a bagel.

"Do you have brothers and sisters?"

I nodded and held up four fingers, "Four brothers and four sisters." My eyes moistened. She was the first person to take an interest in me since the naked man came to my door the night I arrived.

"Are you the oldest?"

I shook my head, "I am middle. Number five."

"Five," she said, stressing the "V" sound that I found so difficult because it did not exist in the two languages I had learned as a child. I followed her lead and repeated the word, forcing my bottom lip to do what it didn't want to do to close out the word. "Five."

Mrs. Chandler smiled, "Would you like me to help you with your English?"

I nodded enthusiastically. "Very much yes."

Her smile widened. "Tell me about your mother and father."

I paused for a moment to compose a sentence. When I spoke, I concentrated on making the right sounds. "Mother is live. Father dead, five years before."

She stifled a laugh and reached out to give my arm a gentle squeeze. "I'm sorry to hear about your father." Then she corrected me. "My father died five years ago."

Memories of high school English classes about verb tenses stirred in my brain. "My father died five years ago," I repeated. "Oldest brother, Hasubhai, is top of family."

"Head of the family."

I nodded, "Head of the family."

She sat back in her chair and finished her coffee and bagel. "It's been nice meeting you. I have to return to work now. I'll see you at lunchtime." She pushed her chair back and stood. I stood with her, a common courtesy in India, and reached for her hand. Tears welled in my eyes; her kindness had lifted my spirits. "Thank you so much."

Her lip quivered, "You're welcome."

I watched her return to the cash register where she exchanged a glance with the lady who had taken her place.

***

In the subsequent days and weeks, Mrs. Chandler and I conversed each time I visited the cafeteria. She took time to introduce other students to me, and sometimes had them join our conversation. We continued to have trouble understanding each other, but with persistence, we managed to share family tales and discuss different aspects of culture and religion. With her patience and diligence, my vocabulary and grammar improved. Over time, I even mastered the V, W, S, and Sh sounds.

Mrs. Chandler often voiced her concern about my undernourished frame. Many times, when I arrived at the cash register with bread, butter, and cheese on my tray, she would nag me to eat more and I would add fruit and vegetables.

When I complained that the food had no spices and tasted bland, she introduced me to new food selections such as asparagus, broccoli and Brussels sprouts. Sometimes at lunch, she would load up my plate so I could take food home at no cost. Her interest in my well-being amazed me, and I often thanked Bhagwan Mahavir that we had met.

In the classroom, I continued to work hard. At break time, while other students laughed and joked, I studied the textbook, trying to keep up with the class.

I got to know some of my classmates and looked forward to laboratory classes when we could talk and interact. But when they went out in the evening, I returned to the doctors' quarters to study and write a letter home.

I knew my self-imposed isolation was not good for me, yet I felt unable to change. My daily routine was somewhere between survival and despair. At bedtime, I would wash my shirt and underwear with soap and hot water and hang them over the sink to dry. In the morning, I would head to the canteen to eat. I had everything I had dreamed of: a comfortable place to sleep, clean air, no leaky roof, and ample supplies of food and drink. These were blessings that millions in my home country did not enjoy, yet somehow my mind refused to celebrate them.

The highlight of my day came if I saw a blue airmail envelope in my pigeonhole. Sometimes there would be three or four letters that had been mailed on different days. I would revel in their content, reading each one several times over. Other days there would be nothing, and I would trudge to my room and sulk for the rest of the evening.

Newspapers contained very little information about India, and I heard nothing on the radio. The best source I had for news from home was the black-and-white television in the lounge at the doctors' quarters. I tried to be there at 6 p.m. each evening for the news broadcast.

On weekends, I had time to venture into the city or at least walk the neighborhood. Instead, I sat alone in my room, staring out the window with tears wetting my eyes and waiting for Monday to come. Even when I felt hungry, I had no desire to eat. I was falling into depression.

One Friday, I returned from classes and found no letters in my mailbox. I opened the door to my room with a sense of foreboding and gloom for the weekend to come. Late in the evening, I opened the refrigerator to get a drink of milk.

To my surprise, it had been stocked with milk, bread, orange juice, cheese, jams and jellies. A container on the top shelf had a note attached: *Son, eat well. Mrs. Chandler.*

Tears flooded my eyes. This lady, with no family relationship, cared for me. I thanked Bhagwan Mahavir for placing Mrs. Chandler in my life and sat down to write my mother a letter telling her some news I knew she wanted to hear: *I have found a surrogate mother in America who is treating me like her son, just like you.*

19

Making a Contribution

About ten weeks had passed at St. Joseph's Infirmary, and I needed to vacate my room at the doctors' quarters. I didn't know if my $90 per month stipend would pay for rent and buy food, so I decided to look for a part-time job to supplement my income. A job might also help me overcome my depression by keeping me busy and forcing me to meet other people. I wanted to move forward.

The INS regulations required people with a student visa to seek permission prior to looking for employment. I decided to skip that step because of my bad experience at the INS office.

A classmate told me that Crawford W. Long Memorial Hospital (CWL) had placed newspaper ads seeking lab technicians for night and weekend work. I had trained as a lab technician in Bombay and felt confident I could do the job. My biggest obstacle would be my language skills.

I decided my best approach would be to say as little as possible and use good English when I did speak. With that in mind, I sat down and wrote a script. After practicing, I headed to CWL with my lab technician certificate and the newspaper ad in hand.

At the front desk, I pointed at the ad, "I would like this job." The attendant looked at the ad and directed me to the pathology department. I followed signs to a locked door labeled pathology lab.

Through a sliding-glass window adjacent to the door, I could see a lab lined with modern analytical equipment. At the far end, a lady in a white lab coat leaned over an instrument. I tapped on the glass and she came to the window. Her eyebrows narrowed when she saw me.

I pointed to the ad, "I would like this job. I have lab technician certificate. I can work nighttime."

Her expression changed, "Wait there. I'll let you in."

A few minutes later, she walked me to the HR department and asked the HR manager to interview me for the phlebotomist/lab technician vacancy. In that role, I would visit patients in the hospital wards to draw blood samples and then perform standard lab tests on the samples.

The HR manager, a woman with gray-speckled hair, had me fill out a form and asked me some additional questions, but asked nothing about my visa status. Her assistant typed my information onto a standard contract form.

The manager checked the information and then turned to me. "The job pays $1.30 an hour for twenty hours a week on weekends and midweek nights. Your supervisor will tell you when you are on duty, and he will sign your timecard."

I nodded my understanding.

She handed me the contract, "Please read this. It includes details of our right to terminate the job at any time. Sign at the bottom if you agree. You start this weekend."

A big smile creased my face. Inside, I felt exhilarated. I had a paying job for the first time in my life. I read the form as quickly as I could and signed above my name.

The manager took the form and added her signature then pointed to a blank space. "You have not given an address. We mail paychecks weekly."

"I have to find an apartment. Can you help me? I want something with low cost."

The two ladies glanced at each other. "The studio on the top floor is empty," the assistant said.

The manager turned to me, "It's very basic."

"What is the rent?"

"$40 per month."

I could afford it. Very basic did not bother me.

An hour later, I left the hospital with the apartment key in my pocket. The one-room studio apartment had no windows and stood at the top of a concrete stairway used for maintenance access to the roof. No one else lived anywhere near it. Although less plush than my room at the doctors' quarters, it was still luxury accommodation compared to 64-D, Old Hanuman Lane, Bombay. It had bunk beds, a small round table, a kitchen area with a stove and a refrigerator, plus an en-suite bathroom. It even had its own access door to the roof.

Joy filled my heart as I boarded a bus back to St. Joseph's.

***

On my first weekend of work, I met four dental interns from Emory University named Robert (Bob) Boe, Bruce Jennings, Harold Peacock, and Wayne Bradley. They were my age and they worked weekends to help pay for their education. Very quickly, I bonded with Bob Boe. He was from Florida and stood six-foot-two inches tall, with a slim build and white skin—very different from my five-foot-six frame, ultra-slim build, and brown skin. We received many glances as we walked the hospital wards together.

One weekend, we started a conversation about the war in Vietnam and, when our shift ended, he came to my room to continue the discussion. My broken English did not seem to bother him and we talked late into the night about Vietnam, India, our families, music, and life in general.

That night, Bob slept on my spare bunk instead of driving back to his room at the university. The arrangement worked well, and we made it permanent. Bob saved time and gas money, and I had company on the weekends.

Bob soon realized how little I interacted with other people and invited me to tag along when he went out with his friends. "We're going for pizza," he said one evening, "Want to join us?"

"What's a pizza?" I asked.

He gave me a strange look. "Are you serious? You don't know?"

I shook my head.

He rubbed his chin for a moment. "It's like a large crusty flatbread covered with melted cheese and tomato sauce. You can add whatever toppings you want."

It sounded delicious, so I agreed to join them.

At the restaurant, the aroma coming from the kitchen made my mouth water. "This is making me hungry," I said as a hostess led us to a booth.

"Let's get one large pizza," Harold said, "It's cheaper."

Wayne nodded, "Good idea. Sausage or pepperoni?"

I knew that sausage was meat, but had not heard of pepperoni. I guessed the pizza would be covered in peppers. "Pepperoni for me," I said. "No sausage."

A server came and Bob ordered a pitcher of beer and a large pepperoni pizza.

"Water for me, please," I said.

Wayne looked at me, "No beer?"

I shook my head, "I don't drink alcohol."

He shrugged, "All the more for us."

We were talking about Vietnam, the Cold War, and international relations when our food arrived. I noticed the pizza had circles of meat all over it and not a pepper in sight. I sat motionless while Bob and his friends took a slice and started to eat.

"Go ahead, take a slice," Bob said.

I shook my head, "I thought pepperoni meant it would have peppers."

Wayne laughed, "Try it, you'll like it."

"I can't. It's meat."

The four of them paused mid-bite and stared at me.

"So?" Bob said.

"I am Jain. We are vegetarians."

"You don't eat meat?"

"Never."

"Why not?" Bruce said.

"You kill animal. Bad karma. We believe in non-violence to all creatures."

Bob gestured to my skinny frame, "That's why you're so thin. You need meat to make you strong. You could die in this winter weather."

"No," I said, "No meat."

Wayne reached over and scraped the pepperoni from one slice of pizza onto another with his plastic fork. He moved the extra-pepperoni slice to his own plate and placed the cheese slice on my plate. "How's that for international relations."

We all laughed and our conversation continued.

***

That night at the apartment, Bob asked me more about the Jain principle of non-violence and I explained the best I could with my limited English vocabulary.

"What about cockroaches? Do you kill them?"

I shook my head and brushed my hand across my forearm as if shooing away an unwanted insect. "We brush them away. Not kill them."

He leaned back in his chair and rubbed his chin. "What if an alligator was about to eat you? Would you kill it?"

I shook my head, "Better to die. Come back as better person in next life."

His eyes closed for a second. "You mean reincarnation?"

I nodded, "Good karma for not killing alligator."

"Is that the same as Buddhism?"

"No, different. Little bit same. Jain religion is older."

He rubbed his chin again. "So who were you in your previous life?"

"No one knows that." I reflected on my humble start in life and all of the difficulties I had experienced. "Maybe alligator."

Bob shook his head from side to side and got up from his chair. "I'll sleep on that."

***

A day or so later, a winter storm brought more snow and ice to Atlanta. By chance, I met Bob near the parking lot where he had parked his car. He saw me taking very small steps in the icy conditions. "Why are you walking like that?"

"I don't want to fall. I have trouble keeping my balance."

He took hold of my arm and reached down to lift my foot off the ground. "Your shoes have leather soles. They have no grip." He let go of my leg and felt the thickness of my coat, "Is that the best coat you've got?"

"It's my only coat."

He shook his head. "Follow me."

I followed him to his car, dropping farther behind with each step. By the time I reached the parking lot, he had his 1964 Pontiac Catalina running and the door open for me.

"Where are we going?" I asked.

"Richie's Department Store."

The name meant nothing to me so I sat back and let him drive to the store. When we entered, my eyes popped. I had never seen an array of clothes with so many choices. The brightly lit sales floor gleamed, and row upon row of racks displayed merchandise of all types and colors.

An attractive sales lady approached us with a big smile. "May I help you?"

Bob pointed to me, "My friend here needs winter boots and a warm coat."

She nodded and led us to the men's department where she pulled coats and jackets from various racks for me to try. Every one of them looked like an aircraft hangar on my small frame. Finally, the assistant whispered something to Bob.

He laughed. "Ramesh, how much do you weigh?"

"Ninety-two pounds."

They exchanged a glance. "This way," she said, heading to the rear of the store.

Bob waited for me to catch up. "We're going to the kids section. You're lucky—everything will be cheaper there." We both smiled.

On the young-teenager racks, we found clothing that fit perfectly and I ended up buying an insulated jacket, gloves, socks, boots, and scarf. I'd never had such colorful clothing. The deal got even better when we arrived at the checkout and learned that prices had been further reduced in an end-of-season sale.

This is amazing. They lower prices before you ask so there's no need to negotiate.

Before we left the store, I put on the boots and coat and walked to the car without slipping or shivering.

In the following weeks, my friendship with Bob grew and my English improved rapidly. The efforts of Mrs. Chandler during the week and long conversations with Bob on weekends were more effective than any English class I could have taken. This led to better understanding in class and at last I was able to keep pace.

Even so, my limited vocabulary left us in fits of laughter at times. Once, Bob and I were in a corner drug store purchasing school supplies when a young female sales assistant asked if she could help me.

"I'm looking for rubbers," I said.

She blushed and I didn't know why. Bob came to the rescue, "He means erasers."

Outside the store, he explained what the young girl thought I wanted. We walked home in hysterics.

***

One weekend, Bob and were waiting by the hospital elevators when an elevator door opened and a well-dressed man stepped out, extended his hands to me, and asked me in a strong voice how I was doing. I shook his hand and spoke with him for about thirty seconds.

When he moved on, Bob stared at me. "Do you know who that man was?"

"No," I replied.

"That was Lester Maddox, the Governor of Georgia."

I felt excited to have shaken hands with an important politician. In India, that was something to talk about. "I must write and tell my mom that I've shaken hands with the State Governor," I said.

Bob lowered his voice, "Ramesh, you need to scrub your hands."

"Why?"

"He's a racist. He hates colored people."

My eyes widened, "I didn't know that."

"He's a big friend of George Wallace. When the Civil Rights Act passed, he closed his family store rather than serve blacks."

I wiped my hand on my white smock. I had heard of George Wallace, but didn't know about Maddox. "Why did he shake my hand?"

"I've no idea. It wasn't a photo-op; there was no one with a camera." Bob pushed the button to call the elevator. "Perhaps he'd never touched brown skin before."

"Brown, black, or white; they all feel the same, my friend."

***

Later that evening over dinner in my apartment, we continued our civil rights discussion. Bob explained some basics about slavery and the Civil War before telling me about Martin Luther King and the Civil Rights Act of 1964, a law passed just three years earlier that was still very divisive. He explained the significance of recent segregation battles in the Southern states. I was shocked to hear how black people were treated in America.

"You must have seen the Whites Only signs."

I shook my head. "I haven't seen them. I've had other things on my mind." I thought of my visits to the INS and wondered if prejudice was the reason I felt so unwelcome there. "What about brown skin?" I asked, "What do people think about me?"

Bob smiled, "It varies. For some people, it's just blacks. For others, it's anyone not pure white." He looked me up and down. "You're so lightweight—you're a curiosity not a threat," he said and burst into laughter.

I thought about prejudice in my own country. "It's good that this debate takes place in public," I said. "In India, all these bad things are hidden under the carpet."

"You have black people?"

I shook my head, "We have untouchables. Many upper-caste Hindus treat them very badly…like they're less than human."

He raised an eyebrow, "Why are they called that?"

"They are considered unclean because they do dirty jobs like cleaning toilets and sweeping streets." I remembered an incident from my youth and decided to share it. "Once, as a young boy in Jamnagar, I went to temple with my maternal uncle to perform ritual puja at the temple. I had a small plate with a garland of flowers to decorate Jain idols."

Bob raised a hand to stop me. "What's a puja?"

"It's a special form of worship where we touch the idol with fingertip. Prior to touching the idol, we clean our body and put on clean clothes. On the way to the temple, we were very careful walking on the streets. In Jamnagar, the streets are narrow and spotted with excrement."

"You mean dog poop?"

"From all sorts—cows, camels, dogs, sometimes humans."

His eyes widened. "Humans?"

I nodded, "Bob, the street people have nowhere to go. You must keep eyes on the ground to make sure you don't step in it. Many locals walk with their nostrils covered because of the smells."

Bob thought for a moment. "Were there elephants?"

I smiled, "No. No big elephant piles."

"Go on," Bob said.

"Untouchables were sweeping the streets and raising dust. Near the temple, one of the sweeper ladies brushed against my uncle as she was doing her work. He got mad as hell at her." I leaned forward and brushed my hand lightly against Bob's arm to show how they had touched.

"I was shocked. I had never seen my uncle so angry. 'Ramesh,' he said, 'we need to shower again in the temple washrooms before we do puja.' It hurt me that my uncle had insulted another human like that. It breaks the rule of non-violence. She was only doing her job."

Bob leaned back in his chair. "What about Gandhi? Did he oppose the caste system?"

I was impressed that Bob new about Mr. Mohandas Gandhi. "My dad called Gandhi the most peace-loving person in the world," I said. "Do you know his teaching on non-violence called satyagraha?"

Bob shook his head, "Go on."

"Satyagraha is peaceful protest for just cause. He taught that passive resistance is a sign of strength not weakness. He used it to gain independence for India. Thousands of people would stop work and sit in the streets. When authorities came and told them to move, they would move. The next day they would sit somewhere else. If they were thrown in prison, they did not resist. Gandhi said that satyagraha is something that bullies cannot shake and bullets cannot kill."

"That's a good slogan."

I nodded, "The turning point for independence came when a British Brigadier ordered his troops to open fire with machine guns on a crowd of unarmed civilians—more than 15,000 people. His troops fired every bullet they had and hundreds died. Everyone in India wanted violent retaliation, but Gandhi refused. He insisted on satyagraha. The British knew they had done a terrible thing and could no longer to justify their rule with violence. They had to agree a path to independence."

"Martin Luther King preaches the same thing—peaceful protest."

"Then he will succeed."

Bob gave a wry smile. "Time will tell. Gandhi had one advantage."

"What's that?"

"His skin wasn't black."

***

Almost a month after starting work at CWL, I still hadn't received a paycheck, even though I had been told I would be paid weekly. I mentioned this to Bob one afternoon in the lab.

"Have you checked with the accounting department?"

I shook my head.

"Why not?"

"I don't know anyone there."

He looked up from his microscope, "Does that matter?"

"Yes. I don't want to ask a stranger for money."

"Why not? It's your money." He put the slide from his lab test away and pointed to the door. "Let's find out."

A few minutes later, we stood in the accounting department talking with a clerk about my paychecks. I stood behind Bob feeling uneasy and hoping the clerk did not think we were questioning his competence or his honesty.

"I'll check," the clerk said, and disappeared behind a row of file cabinets.

He returned with three envelopes and handed them to Bob. "We have no address on file."

Bob passed me the envelopes and gave the clerk my address. The clerk seemed pleased with the outcome. I opened one of the envelopes and saw a check with my name on it. After tax deductions, I had earned $21.06. I wanted to dance down the hallway.

***

That evening, I did some calculations: $21 a week times four is $84 a month. Adding my $90 stipend from St. Joseph's, and subtracting $40 for rent and another $40 for food, I could save…$94 a month! At an exchange rate of four rupees to a dollar, that was 375 rupees a month. I multiplied by twelve. Wow—4,510 rupees a year. I was earning almost as much as Bhupat did as a full-time radio repair technician. For the first time in my life, I felt rich.

I took a clean sheet of paper and wrote a letter to my family telling them I would be sending lots of money home to ease the family debt. At last I could make a contribution.

Silently, I thanked Bhagwan Mahavir for all his help. Things were moving in the right direction. Perhaps my father's dream of tomorrow being a better day could become reality. I signed the letter with tears running down my cheeks.

20
Tragedy Back Home

On another occasion, Bob and his dental intern friends decided to visit the Varsity drive-in restaurant, a popular gathering place for students. I joined them and sat in the front passenger seat while the other three sat in the back of the car. As we approached the restaurant, I noticed a long line of cars. Bob surprised me by passing them all and parking near the entrance.

"Can you go in front of everyone?" I asked.

The guys in the back seat laughed. Harold leaned forward, "Ramesh, they're in the drive-through."

Bob grinned and drove back around the parking lot so I could see. He pointed to a large menu board and then at two canopied windows at the side of the restaurant. "There's the menu. You order and pay at the first window, and pick up your food at the second."

I was mesmerized by the huge menu board, which I could read easily from twenty yards away. It seemed such a crazy idea, but it worked. "How do they cook the food so quickly?"

"It's a slick operation. Lots of employees each do a simple job."

"That's why it's called fast food," Wayne added from the back seat.

We parked and went inside. The restaurant had many separate eating areas, and each eating area had a large television screen that anyone could watch without paying a fee. The service counters alone were longer than my home in Bombay. All the furnishings were clean. Nothing looked broken.

"This is a great concept," I said.

Bob nodded. "There are some restaurants where you park in the parking lot and they serve you on roller skates."

I couldn't imagine what he meant, but I didn't want to show my ignorance.

A hostess seated us and I studied the menu for something vegetarian. Everything contained meat. I decided not to eat and asked Bob to order me a chocolate milkshake while I went to the restroom. When I returned several minutes later, I saw a hamburger with onions, ketchup, mustard, and French fries waiting for me. I looked at Bob, "I can't eat this."

"Ramesh, you're malnourished. You need to eat meat." He pointed out the window. "I've told you before, this weather could kill you. That's not going to happen on my watch."

His friends murmured their agreement and I got the impression it had been a group decision to get me the burger. I shook my head and pushed the plate away.

Bob reached across the table and picked up the burger. "Ramesh, you're in America. You need to eat American food to survive." He squeezed the edges of the bun together so the meat was no longer visible and offered it to me. "Do you see meat?"

I shook my head, "No."

"Then eat it."

My conscience wavered. With four sets of eyes watching me, I took a bite. To my surprise, it tasted good. Different sensations swirled in my mouth as unknown textures and flavors combined like the sounds of different instruments in an orchestra. With lots of hesitation, I took another mouthful. Bob and his friends cheered me on and took bites from their own food. I finished every last bite and had to agree that I enjoyed the meal.

Later that night, alone in bed, my conscience troubled me. An animal had died for my moment of pleasure. I felt I had drifted from my Jain values and done something terribly wrong. What would my father think?

The next day at break time, I talked to Bob and the others about this, but they gave me very little sympathy. Harold looked me in the eye, "Ramesh, you are in Atlanta, not Bombay. To survive and be successful, you must live like the natives."

Wayne nodded. "You can't live like an Eskimo at the equator."

Bob rested his arm on my shoulder, "Ramesh, if we went to India, we would change our diet and eat vegetables."

"Would you change your religion?" I said.

He thought for a moment. "My religion is what I believe, not what I eat. You can be peace-loving and non-violent in Atlanta, but do it the American way."

I didn't like their answers, although I had to concede Wayne's point that if an Eskimo lived at the equator, some things would have to change. Would those changes make him less of an Eskimo?

That night, I lay pondering that question. These guys were the only friends I had, and I did not want to lose them and return to spending the weekends alone in my apartment battling depression. Bob had gone out of his way to befriend me…and to clothe me. Now his concern had turned to feeding me in the only way he knew.

On another occasion, we returned to the first pizza restaurant we visited. This time, I ordered a cheese pizza for myself and sprinkled it with crushed red chili peppers.

"Whoa," Harold said, "Not too many."

I sprinkled on some more chili and offered him a slice, "Try eating like an Indian, Harold."

The others urged him to accept the challenge, but he declined. Instead, he picked up the pitcher of beer. "Ramesh, try the beer. See if you like it."

I let him pour a small amount in my glass. It tasted bitter and they laughed at the face I made. I returned to my food, which tasted delicious, and surprised them all by eating every mouthful of the twelve-inch pizza. I tried other beers at other locations, but never to my liking, and decided to stick with soft drinks or milk. My American friends seemed content that I had tried.

None of these decisions made it to the letters I wrote home at least twice a week. My family had no way to comprehend the vast differences between the life they knew and life in America. I could explain those differences no better than I could explain cold weather or the taste of chocolate milk. I did not want to upset them or make them feel bad for sending me here, or responsible for the decisions I made. Right or wrong, those decisions were mine.

Despite the good times I had with Bob and his friends, my greatest joy remained reading the letters I received from Ma and my siblings. I loved hearing the news from home and never lost the thrill of seeing a blue airmail envelope in my pigeonhole. Often, each family member would write one or two paragraphs on thin airmail paper, and all the pages would be folded together in the envelope. Hasubhai wrote in detail about the situation at home and included scores from cricket matches. Bhupat told me about his business, and Bhabhi gave family news. Ma wrote short notes, often expressing concern about my health. She begged me to come home as soon as I finished my year of study.

***

By mid-March, the weather had turned warm and my health started to improve. I stopped coughing, forgot I ever had allergies, started to sleep better, and my appendectomy healed to the point where I no longer felt pain. Each time my bank balance reached $300 or $400, I sent a check to Hasubhai. The knowledge that my efforts were making things better for my family in Bombay buoyed me every day.

I met Dr. Kumar in the cafeteria one day and he told me there were two or three other Indian students living in the area. I made contact with them by phone, but with busy schedules and living far apart, we found it impossible to meet on a regular basis.

***

One evening, after a long day of laboratory classes, I returned to my apartment to find an airmail letter in my pigeonhole. I had been on my feet all day, so I made tea and sat down at my kitchen table to read the news from home.

My Dear Son,

I have bad news. The apartment block at 64-D Old Hanuman Lane has been condemned by the Bombay Municipality. Everyone has been evacuated from the building. Many of our belongings are still there and we cannot retrieve them. Bhupat has a friend who helped us find a two-room rental apartment in a suburb named Borivali West. It is about 25 miles away, in the middle of nowhere. We have no family or friends near us. The streets are undeveloped and there is no vegetable market or milk shop nearby. Hasubhai and Bhupat leave very early each morning to catch the train for Bombay and don't come home until after dark. I am busy finding schools for the siblings.

Bhupat is having a phone installed in our new home. I will send you the number when we have it. I am worried about him. He is working very hard and his spinal cord is bending more. He complains constantly about severe pain in his leg. I pray your brother will be okay. We don't know any doctors in this area and they won't see Bhupat unless we pay in advance. Son, I hope your health is better.

I love you so much. Come home soon.

Ma

The news shocked me. My heart yearned to be with my family—to give Ma a hug and make Bhupat smile—yet I could do nothing to help. I sipped my tea, but it had gone cold. Bhupat had worked so hard to help me get through college and give me this opportunity. Now he was in pain and I was in America. It didn't seem right.

A few weeks later, in the first week of July 1967, I arrived home and found an envelope with Hasubhai's handwriting. A spell of beautiful weather had settled on Atlanta, so I made a sandwich and walked to a nearby park to enjoy the weather and read his news. Puffy white clouds dotted the sky.

Ramesh,

Our old home at 64-D Old Hanuman Lane collapsed yesterday evening during a heavy monsoon rain. All our household possessions, including pots, pans, the two stainless steel storage cabinets, your old study table and all other household items were destroyed. Some belongings are hanging loosely in the wreckage of the third floor, but the municipality will not let us salvage anything because the wreckage is unsafe. The whole building had been cordoned off and all access is denied.

Your brother,

Hasmukh

A cloud cast a shadow where I sat. Losing our possessions was a financial blow, but more than that, it felt like a piece of my childhood had been stolen. I would never again visit the apartment, sit by my window, or listen to drips from the leaking roof.

I wondered how Ma and my younger siblings had taken the news and decided I had to talk to them, regardless of the expense. Scattering the remains of my sandwich for the birds, I ran to the payphone at CWL and arranged a call to the phone Bhupat had installed. While I waited for the international operator to place the call, I read the letter over and over with tears rolling down my cheeks. The wait seemed to take forever and I felt helpless and hurt.

At last the phone rang and Ma was on the line.

"How is everyone?" I asked.

"Son, we're all okay. I want you to come home."

I could hear her sobbing. "Ma, please don't worry. Everything will be fine. Remember what Dad used to say? Tomorrow will be a better day."

She gave no reply. All I could hear were her tears.

"How are Hasubhai and Bhupat holding up?"

"They're working hard. Bhupat's leg is still hurting him."

"And the younger ones?"

"Kirit and Sadhana cry a lot. They don't like it here. They have no one to play with." Her voice dropped to a whisper. "They want to go back to 64-D."

"Ma, don't cry. I promise you, we will be fine."

She did not respond.

I had nothing else to say.

***

One evening in mid-August, little more than a month later, worse news arrived. I sat studying at the kitchen table late one evening when a co-worker knocked on my door, "There's a telephone call for you downstairs. It's your brother."

My heart thumped as I ran to the pay phone. Why would Hasubhai call this number without letting me know in advance? I grabbed the receiver, "Hasubhai, what is it?"

"Ramesh, I have tragic news. Our mother passed away last evening in the hospital."

My jaw dropped. It couldn't be true. She was not yet fifty years old.

"Are you there?" Hasubhai said.

My voice faltered. "Yes, I'm here…what happened?"

"Two days ago, Ma insisted on visiting our old home, 64-D. When she saw the destruction and our tangled belongings, she cried hysterically. We tried to console her, but she wouldn't stop. 'We've lost everything,' she howled."

I could hear Hasubhai sniffling, holding back tears.

"A few minutes later, she collapsed with a massive heart attack. Dr. Malkan came to our rescue, but she died a day later in the hospital."

The news crushed my spirit. I felt numb from head to toe, unprepared for such news. We tried to continue the conversation but neither of us could stop crying. I told Hasubhai I would call him the next day when I got back from school.

That night, I had no desire to live.

***

The next morning, my eyes were bloodshot and my whole face looked tired. Mrs. Chandler noticed when I approached her at the café checkout, "Are you okay?" she asked.

I shook my head, barely able to hold back tears, "My mother died yesterday." For a moment, the world seemed to stop. I couldn't believe my own words. In what seemed like slow motion, Mrs. Chandler stepped from behind the counter and gave me a hug, rubbing her hand on my shoulder like a mother comforting a small child. I held on to her and couldn't let go. It felt so soothing to have someone share my pain. She called someone to replace her at the cash register and led me to an empty table.

"Drink some tea. Then tell me what happened."

I did as she said and wiped my eyes before telling her everything Hasubhai had told me.

"Will you go back for the funeral?"

I shook my head even though I longed to be there. The $350 in my bank account was not enough for an airfare. "Our custom is to cremate very quickly. Besides, I can't afford…"

More tears flowed, and Mrs. Chandler reached out to comfort me. "If there's any way I can help you…"

***

In the lab, I couldn't concentrate. I prayed silently, asking many questions without any satisfaction. *Who will care for my younger siblings who have no father and no mother? Can Bhabhi take on that role—four children aged 8 to 13?* I hoped she could. She had been a member of our family for five years now and had shown her caring and unselfish nature many times.

I remember nothing more of that day until my phone call with Hasubhai. I told him I couldn't afford to return home, and that leaving the country could affect my student visa status. I said I'd send him $300 the following morning. Then I spoke with each of my siblings. Mostly we cried. Hasubhai, Bhabhi, and Bhupat assured me they would care for the younger siblings. In adversity, our family stood as solid as a rock.

When I hung up, I cried out to Bhagwan Mahavir, "*Why are you doing this to us? Our troubles are getting deeper.*" I pulled out the photograph of Dad that I kept in my wallet and asked him the same question. Amidst the tears and turmoil in my soul, I felt him speak to me, "Son, you will be fine. Better days are coming." Even his photograph gave me strength.

The weeks that followed proved how important Bhabhi was to our family. She looked after my siblings like they were her own children and never let them feel like orphans. Her dedication and kindness were a wonderful example of Jain philosophy at work. How I wished my dad could have known her.

21

Celebrating Thanksgiving

One Friday afternoon in late August, I was looking at hematology slides in the pathology lab at CWL when Bob entered with sweat trickling down his forehead. A spell of hot and humid weather had descended on Georgia. He dabbed his face with a paper towel and put on his white smock, "How do you like this weather, Ramesh?"

I gave him a big smile, "I like it very much. It reminds me of home."

"Trust you to be different. We call these the dog days of summer."

"Why? Don't you like dogs?"

He glanced at me. "You're sharp today. Something good must have happened."

I smiled. "I know how I can stay in America when I graduate." For weeks, I had been struggling with the dilemma of finding a company that would sponsor my application for a work visa. No American company would hire me based on a certificate from GT Government Hospital in Bombay, so I needed my medical technology diploma from St. Joseph's Infirmary before I could apply. But by then it would be too late, because I had to leave the country by December 31. Earlier that day, I had learned of an alternative.

"Tell me," he said

I gestured to the microscope on the bench in front of me. "First look at this slide. How many platelets do you see?"

He looked through the eyepiece at a blood sample magnified forty times. One of our duties was to count the number or white cells, red cells, and platelets in each blood sample. Based on our information, doctors would make patient diagnoses.

"I see twelve platelets."

I took another look and recorded the count.

"So what's your plan to stay in America?" he said.

"I can extend my student visa for two to three years if I'm accepted for another course of study. I'm going to look for a graduate school that specializes in microbiology."

He rubbed his chin. "Grad school is expensive. How will you pay for it?"

"I should be able to get a job with better pay once I have my medical technology diploma. And you know I can live very cheap."

He nodded, "You may have to cut back on those veggie pizzas."

I knew he was joking, but I took it seriously. "If I have to, I will."

"I believe you." He rubbed his chin again. "Take a look at University of Georgia in Athens, about seventy miles from here. It has a good science program, and the campus is beautiful."

I wrote the information down in my notebook and returned to the hematology slides until break time when we walked to the hospital cafeteria for drinks and donuts.

"I discovered something else today," I said as we sat down. "My grandmother had hemophilia."

Bob raised an eyebrow. "How do you know?"

"I worked it out in my hematology class. We were discussing the danger of transmitting disease via blood transfusions. Mrs. Kay used hemophilia as example. When she described the symptoms, they matched perfectly with what happened in Ma's family. For years I'd been told it was a curse or black magic. Now I know it was science."

"Black magic?"

I took a bite of my donut; "My mother had seven or eight brothers who all bled to death as young boys playing in the streets. People blamed it on a family curse, but it had to be hemophilia. Their blood didn't clot."

"But you don't have it."

"No. Ma had a fifty percent chance of being a carrier. But none of her children have had a problem, so our family got lucky."

***

Following Bob's advice, I sent a letter to the University of Georgia requesting information. A big brochure and an application form arrived a few days later. I read it through: the bacteriology department had a suitable program that would start in January 1968. I had all my original transcripts from Bombay University with me and Mrs. Kay Turner supported my application with a letter of recommendation. I mailed my application in mid-September.

Weeks passed with no response and I became nervous. Some of my American classmates voiced their support.

"You study harder than anyone. Why would they throw you out of the country?"

"Don't leave until they deport you."

In mid-November, two months after I mailed my application, Mrs. Kay pulled me to one side, "Ramesh, I have good news for you. Dr. Godwin has approved a three-month training period for you that will run from January 1 to March 31."

I had some breathing room.

***

Thanksgiving approached and I heard my classmates planning trips home. I wished I could do the same, but it was not possible. Bob told me that he planned to work the weekend before Thanksgiving and leave for his home in Pahokee, Florida, the next day. The prospect of a long week alone in my apartment loomed and my heart grew heavy.

When Bob arrived at my apartment that weekend, he surprised me by asking if I'd like to join him on his trip to Florida. "Mom says you're welcome. Harold is also coming, and one of you will have to sleep on a spare mattress on the floor of my room."

I couldn't hold back a broad grin. "Bob, I'd love to come. Sleeping on the floor is no problem to me."

We set off in Bob's Pontiac around 5 a.m. the following Monday morning. Harold sat in the front passenger seat, while I made myself comfortable in the rear. Once we were out of town and the likelihood of speed traps decreased, Bob accelerated. This was the first time I'd traveled a long distance by car, and I watched the needle of his speedometer climb to 90 miles an hour. Other cars around us were traveling just as fast, or even faster, in the pre-dawn hours.

I felt scared, "Bob, please slow down."

He showed no interest in listening to me. "Ramesh, what's the problem?" Harold said.

"We would surely die if we drove this fast in India."

"Why is that?"

"We would hit a big pothole or a cow would wander onto the road."

"Not here," Bob said, "We keep cows in the fields."

I closed my eyes and lay down on the back seat. Soon, I fell asleep.

When I woke, it was daylight and Bob had tuned the car radio to NPR, national public radio. We were traveling much slower, approaching a small town. I looked around and saw no slums or any visible air pollution. The road was smooth with a beautiful median and clear directional signs, yet this was not a special town. No wonder the world talked about America's beauty.

The radio aired a debate between two reporters about America's involvement in the Vietnam War. Both reporters were passionate in their opposing points of view.

"Do you believe in this war?" I asked.

"I have doubts," Harold said.

Bob glanced at his friend, "Don't know if it's right or wrong, but my brother Billy's in 'Nam, so I want us to win. I volunteered for the Navy Reserve. I'll do two years' active duty when I finish dental school."

Harold looked surprised, "Why did you volunteer?"

"The government started drafting younger students, so I decided to be proactive. That way, I had some control."

"Why the Navy?" I asked.

"My father was in the Navy. He started as a cook with the Coast Guard."

I noticed Bob had a smile on his face.

"He traveled lots of places. Told us lots of stories. He even made it to India."

I raised an eyebrow. "Where?"

"Calcutta."

I wondered if that was why Bob had accepted me as a friend so easily. "What's he doing now?"

"He died five years ago. 1962."

"In action?"

"No. Failing health."

Bob seemed to respect his dad as much as I did mine. They had died in the same year. I wondered if he had felt the same turmoil as I had, but decided to wait until we were alone for that discussion.

The debate on the radio grew heated and Bob returned my question, "What do you think of the war?"

"I'm confused by it," I said. "Jains believe in non-violence, so any conflict is bad. India has had three wars with Pakistan since 1947, and thousands have died on both sides. Nothing good has come from them. War is never a solution."

"Doesn't sound like you're confused," Harold said.

"I'm confused why the U.S. has to be there. Russia has abandoned the Vietnam conflict."

"Communism is still there."

"Communism is a philosophy and you can't fight a philosophy with bullets."

"We have napalm," Harold said.

"I worry about Billy," Bob said.

We fell silent, and Bob tuned the radio to country music.

***

We reached the Florida border after eight or nine hours of driving along U.S. Route 41, the predecessor to Interstate I-75. I was amazed at how quickly we had travelled such a long distance. After crossing the border, we stopped at McDonald's for lunch. The sign outside the restaurant said: Two Billion Hamburgers Served. I turned to Bob in disbelief, "That's a lot of hamburgers!"

He laughed. "It's the whole chain, not just this restaurant. There are McDonald's everywhere."

"Are they all the same?"

Harold nodded. "They have identical menus and prepare food in the exactly same way."

This business concept was another piece of new thinking for me.

***

We reached Pahokee late that evening, a small town with less than a thousand people nestled on the eastern shore of huge Lake Okeechobee. All the houses looked beautiful in the moonlight, and I wondered if only rich people lived there.

We pulled into Bob's driveway and stopped in front of a single-level house in a secluded setting of tall palm trees and a neatly cut lawn. Small bushes framed the front entrance. Mrs. Boe came out to greet us. She looked attractive with curly, brunette hair that was cut in a short style and wearing a printed dress that suited her slim five-foot-four frame. Bob embraced his mom while Harold and I stretched our legs.

Mrs. Boe approached with her hand extended, "You must be Ramesh." As we shook hands, she grasped my forearm, "Bob told me about your mother's death. I'm so sorry for you."

"It's kind of you to invite me to your home."

"Not at all. I want to hear all about India."

We walked inside to a family room tastefully decorated with artwork, family photographs, and knickknacks. Country-style couches and rocking chairs surrounded a coffee table. The dining room was big enough to seat eight people, and reminded me of Grandpa Tribhovandas' dining room in Jamnagar.

***

The next morning, Bob, Harold, and I went for a walk, and Bob introduced us to some of his neighbors and old school friends. From the way they stared at me, I guessed they had never seen or met a young man from India before. "Did you go to school on an elephant?" one of them asked. For the rest of the day, we hung out by the lake.

Other members of Bob's family arrived on Wednesday, and the house filled with activity. In the evening, I played board games with Harold, Bob, and two of his cousins, reveling in the relaxed family atmosphere, something that had been missing from my life for almost a year.

On Thanksgiving morning, activity in the kitchen started early with Mrs. Boe directing an orchestra of helpers. When mealtime came, ten of us squeezed around the dining room table.

"Ramesh, sit on this end," Mrs. Boe said, "I have some questions for you."

There were many vegetable dishes alongside the ham, turkey, and stuffing. Most people didn't notice my vegetarian choices.

"Do you have a Thanksgiving meal like this in India?" Mrs. Boe asked.

"No, Mrs. Boe. We are thankful at every meal."

She smiled and I continued. "We don't have Thanksgiving Day. Nearest thing is family gathering to celebrate a wedding. Those can last four days, with three or four hundred people."

Her eyes widened, "You have big families! Who pays for that?"

"Families share the expense. For Hasubhai, my oldest brother, the bride's father paid most of the wedding cost. Very generous."

"Was it an arranged marriage?"

"Yes. All marriages are arranged by parents. We have very few exceptions. I have two older brothers and two older sisters. All arranged marriages."

I noticed that others around the table were listening to the conversation.

"Did your brothers and sisters know the person they married?" Mrs. Boe asked.

I shook my head. "Someone in our extended family made a suggestion, and both sets of parents liked it. So the parents met to negotiate. For both my brothers, the girl came from the Jain community in Jamnagar where my parents grew up. We live in Bombay."

"What is Jain?" someone asked.

"That's his religion," Bob said. "There's Jain and Hindu and Buddhism and several others."

"Do they call those castes?"

"No, that's different. That's about what jobs people do," said Bob.

I was impressed by how much Bob remembered.

"Time for dessert," Mrs. Boe announced.

Plates and dishes were cleared from the table and replaced with dishes of apple pie and ice cream, my favorite part of the meal.

"When does the couple first meet?" Mrs. Boe asked.

I smiled. Her interest intrigued me. "My mother and father met on their wedding day. Dad lifted the veil and saw his bride for the first time. For my brother, our parents arranged a meeting as part of negotiation."

"Could your brother say 'No,' when he met the girl?"

"In our family, it's okay to say 'No'. Other families may be different."

"Were they alone when they met?"

"No, never alone. Some family member stays. A brother or sister."

"Do they hold hands or kiss?"

"Oh no. No touching during meeting, and kissing is absolutely forbidden."

Bob and Harold listened intently. "Tell them how old your mother was," Bob said.

"She was young. Thirteen, fourteen. Father was sixteen, seventeen."

Mrs. Boe raised an eyebrow, "When did they start living together?"

"After the ceremony. It is custom for the bride to move in with the boy's family in joint family living."

The questions continued for some time.

"What about you," Mrs. Boe said. "Will you let others choose your bride?"

Bob and Harold leaned closer. I thought of when I first met Mina at our apartment and wondered if she was still available. "I'm not sure. If they choose the right girl…"

***

After dinner, the ladies cleared the table and washed dishes while the men gathered around a black-and-white television in the family room to watch football. Bob tried to explain the rules of the game to me, but I didn't understand.

That night, I thanked Bhagwan Mahavir for this opportunity to share family life with Bob and his family. If Mrs. Chandler was my surrogate mother, in Bob I had a surrogate brother.

We left early the following morning, arriving in Atlanta around midnight. A letter with a University of Georgia crest nestled in my pigeonhole. I tore it open. I had been accepted into the graduate school program.

Mrs. Kay, the lab staff, and all my classmates at St. Joseph's were happy for me. On the day the class graduated, they gave me a small cake-cutting celebration to send me on my way.

Bob volunteered to drive me to Athens, and on December 30, I entered the graduate school dormitory with my original two suitcases, plus one additional midsize box. On the journey, Bob and I reflected on our relationship and the things we had done together. Because of his friendship and help, I had no fear of meeting and communicating with my new colleagues.

The graduate dormitory stood near the center of the campus and was surrounded by landscaped lawns with winding, tree-lined paths. The rooms were small, although still spacious compared to what I had known in India. They had two single beds, two small study desks, and a small sink with running water. Bob helped me bring my luggage to my room.

"Thank you for all you have taught me," I said, "From how to write a check to letting me drive your car."

He laughed, "I will miss you, my little Indian friend."

"Bob, we will keep in touch. You know how many letters I write."

He laughed, "You could splurge and make a phone call."

"You think I'm stingy?"

He shook his head, "I don't think that, I know it."

"Bob, I have to pay off my debts. Besides, an Indian would not agree with you. I spend more than most Indians. Americans don't know how the rest of the world lives."

"I do. I've watched you."

We laughed.

"My friend, I will call you regularly. You will not forget me."

His voice faltered, "I don't want to forget. You have also taught me things."

His words surprised me, "What have I taught you?"

"The importance of family. Your lack of aggression."

Emotion welled inside me, "You have a nice family. I liked your mother."

He nodded, "She liked you."

His words cheered me more than I could imagine. "Bob, our friendship will never die."

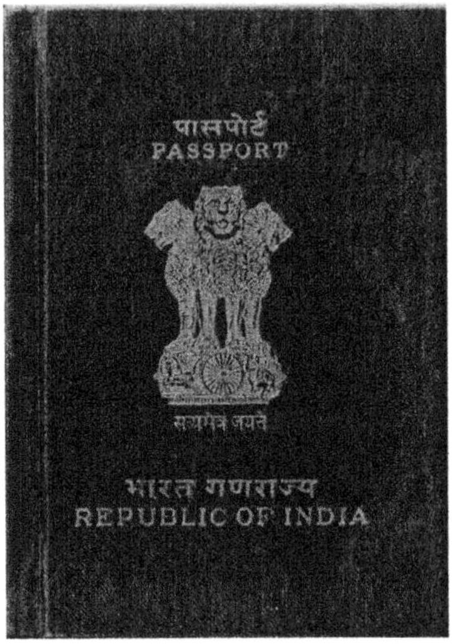

My Indian passport, issued December 1966

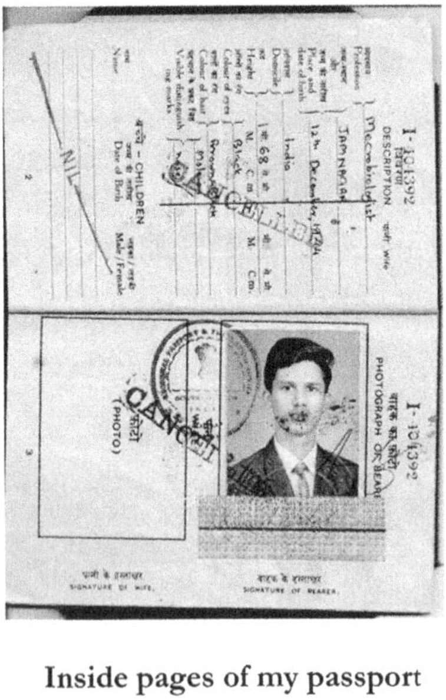

Inside pages of my passport

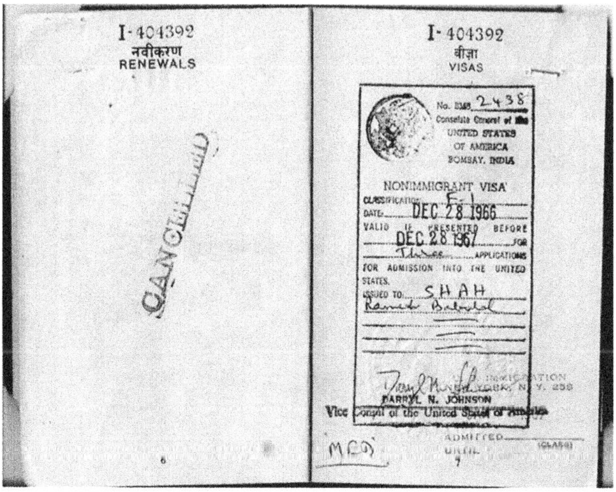

Student visa issued by the United States of America, December 28, 1966

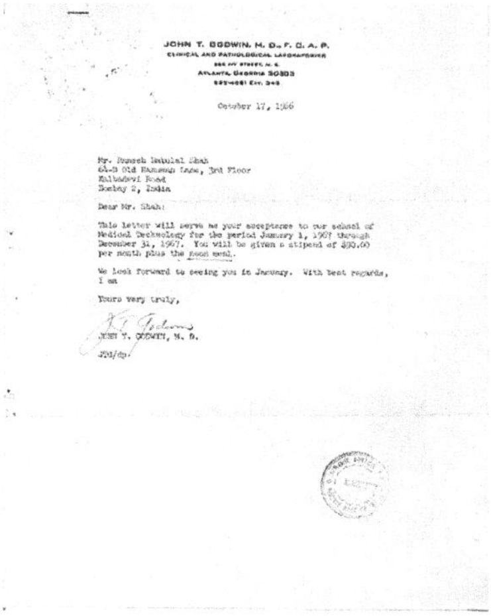

JOHN T. GODWIN, M. D., F. C. A. P.
CLINICAL AND PATHOLOGICAL LABORATORIES
ATLANTA, GEORGIA 30303

October 17, 1966

Mr. Ramesh Babulal Shah
61-B Old Hanuman Lane, 3rd Floor
Kalbadevi Road
Bombay 2, India

Dear Mr. Shah:

This letter will serve as your acceptance to our school of Medical Technology for the period January 1, 1967 through December 31, 1967. You will be given a stipend of $90.00 per month plus the noon meal.

We look forward to seeing you in January. With best regards, I am

Yours very truly,

JOHN T. GODWIN, M. D.

JTG/dp

Acceptance letter from Saint Joseph Infirmary.

April, 1967, the Author on the terrace of the C. W. Long Hospital, Atlanta GA.

Robert Boe, dental intern at C. W. Long Hospital.

22
Grad School

When I had unpacked, I went for a walk around campus. Winter had not yet come to Georgia, and the temperature was still pleasantly mild. Bob had been right about its beauty, and I felt excited to continue my schooling here. Back at the dorm, my roommate had arrived. I extended my hand, "Hello, my name is Ramesh Shah. I'm from India."

He shook my hand. "Nice to meet you. I'm Joe Leach, from Atlanta."

Joe was tall and slender, with blond hair and a quiet nature. We didn't talk much while he unpacked and we never really bonded.

Within a few days, I met three other Indian students living in a dorm just one block away. Two of them, Ravi and Dhanesh, were engineering students from Gujarat. The third, Das Gupta, was a graduate student in Chemistry. I enjoyed having new friends to talk with in my native tongue.

My first week also included a visit to the university clinic for a medical exam that was given to all incoming students. The doctor paused during this routine exam to listen carefully to my heart. "You have a murmur," he said, "Any history of heart problems in your family?"

I told him about my dad.

"Do you tire easily?"

I nodded, "Sometimes."

He listened to my heart again and frowned.

"Doctor, what is it?"

"It's difficult to say. There's definitely a murmur. That's normally associated with heart valve leakage. You should have a regular checkup. If the fatigue gets worse, come and see me."

I left with something else to worry about in addition to my finances.

Once I felt settled in my new environment, I called the local hospital and spoke with the pathology lab supervisor about job opportunities. I told him about my previous work experience and my new diploma from St. Joseph's Infirmary in Atlanta.

"When can you start?" he said.

"I can come in this afternoon."

For the second time, I walked into an American hospital for an interview and walked out with a part-time job. *This truly is a land of opportunity.*

***

The laundry room on the lower level of the dormitory contained several coin-operated machines. One evening, I had loaded my clothes into the washer and was about to insert coins when I heard a voice, "Wait, my Indian friend. You don't need money."

I recognized the student although we had never spoken. He introduced himself, "I'm Wayne Ferguson, room 109. You're Ramesh, right?"

I nodded.

"There's a trick. You don't need money to turn on the machine." He reached for the top of the doorframe and retrieved a small device the size of a movie ticket, constructed from a piece of index card and scotch tape.

He inserted the card into the money slot on the machine and wiggled it until the internal circuit clicked and the machine started. Then he carefully withdrew the device and offered me a high five. We both giggled.

"We call it The Connector," he said, returning the device to the top of the doorframe. "It works for the dryer too."

I didn't know what to say. I was not comfortable with cheating, but the conversation I'd had with Bob and his friends about an Eskimo living at the equator had made an impact. I decided to play along with the local rules.

The Connector lasted about a month before the owner of the laundry equipment found out and removed the machines. I returned to hand-washing my clothes.

***

My new job started smoothly and I received my first paycheck from the hospital on schedule. Once again, I was able to build my savings and soon reached the point where I could send money home to my brother.

One night, asleep in my dorm room, an irritated student knocked on the door, "There's a phone call for you."

It had to be Hasubhai. No one else would call me in the early hours of the morning. The last time he made an unexpected call was to tell me that Ma had died, and I wondered what had happened this time. I ran to the pay phone in the dorm lobby that was used by all students to stay connected with family and friends.

"Hello, hello…Hasubhai…Is everyone okay?" We had a poor connection, and I had to shout for him to hear.

"Everyone is doing well." He sounded calm and I relaxed. "How is your study?" he said, "Did you get the parcel of khakhara and papads Bhabhi made?"

I could barely hear him, and continued yelling in the darkness of the lobby. "My studies are fine. I have not received a parcel."

"Bachukaka contacted me. He's in London. Can you send him $500 from the loan? He wants the money there. I'll send you his London address by telex."

"Yes," I shouted, "I'll send it straight away."

"Shut the G—damn phone off, we can't sleep," a student shouted from the other side of the lobby. He stood glaring at me with a handful of others.

I dare not say another word and hung up the receiver. "Sorry."

I walked calmly back to my room and lay in bed worrying about how I had disturbed the other students. Fortunately, no one said anything in the morning.

***

The workload in graduate school was much greater than I'd experienced in my prior studies. In just ten weeks, we covered the biochemistry textbook that took a complete year at St. Xavier College, and I had three other classes in that same time period.

In addition, the semester system was new to me and I didn't understand the grading system. I was used to a grading system that focused on end-of-year exams, so I gave the Friday quizzes little attention, not realizing that they accounted for sixty percent of the course credit. That error, coupled with frequently working nights at my hospital job, resulted in poor grades and a summons to the office of Dr. Payne, head of the Microbiology Department.

Dr. Payne was a well-known and well-respected academic, and the thought of getting kicked out of the program kept me from sleeping. I arrived at his office at the appointed time and knocked on his door. My hands shook.

"Come."

The door creaked its displeasure as I opened it, and a lump formed in my throat.

Dr. Payne looked up from his dark mahogany desk and directed me to a chair. Behind him, two matching bookcases were lined with neatly arranged books interspersed with pictures of what I guessed were his immediate family. He had no smile on his face and I knew I was in trouble.

"Ramesh, I've reviewed your grades. They are not good."

"Sir, I'm sorry. I did not understand the semester and quiz system. I thought these courses were for the full year. With my job at the hospital, I couldn't keep up with homework for four courses plus the quizzes."

He frowned, "You work at the local hospital?"

"Yes sir, to pay for my education."

He breathed deeply through his nose and shifted in his chair, "How do you plan to improve your grade?"

"Sir, I will take only ten or twelve credit hours next semester and cut my hours at the hospital so I can study more. My grades will improve, I promise you." I felt myself posturing like a panhandler pleading his case on the corner of Kalbadevi Road.

"Graduate school requires complete dedication. If your grades don't improve, you will be in trouble with the University."

"Sir, I will study very hard."

Dr. Payne leaned back in his chair. "I believe you." He paused for few seconds, "Why don't you talk to Dr. Norvel McClung. He may have a job in his lab. He's a good man. I'll talk to him."

"Thank you Dr. Payne. I'll see Dr. McClung very soon."

I left his office, relieved to have a second chance…but I knew a hard road lay ahead of me.

The next day, I visited the laboratory run by Dr. McClung, an expert in Mycology (study of yeast and mold). I knocked on his half-open door, "May I come in, sir?"

"You must be Ramesh. Dr. Payne told me about your conversation. Please sit down."

The single visitor chair was laden with papers.

"Let me move those," he said, getting up and transferring the papers to a desk already cluttered with other scientific papers. The only clearly visible item was a framed photograph of a very pretty woman. The rest of his room looked equally chaotic. His bookcases were packed so tight with reference books that it had to be impossible to find anything in a short period of time.

His personal appearance gave complete contrast. His shirt had a brand logo, and he wore a matching tie and silver-framed spectacles that complemented his groomed, whitish-gray hair and long, thick sideburns. His smile relaxed me.

"Ramesh, Dr. Payne informed me of your semester grades and asked me to help. I'm prepared to have you as one of my graduate students and be your advisor on one condition: that you show desire to improve your academic standing."

"Yes sir, I will work very hard."

He nodded, "I can also offer you a few hours of laboratory work so you don't have to work off-campus at night. You will prepare microbiological media plates and test tubes for my teaching classes and also be responsible for washing all glassware and for keeping lab countertops clean and in good order."

"Thank you, sir. I will not disappoint you."

After the meeting, I visited the Admin Building to reduce my course workload to ten hours, and then walked to the hospital to quit my job. In the weeks that followed, I was able to work a similar number of hours, yet study much harder than before. I met regularly with Dr. McClung, and with his guidance my grades improved.

One afternoon, at the end of a study session, he surprised me. "Ramesh, you're invited to my home for dinner this evening. My wife would like to meet you."

"It would be an honor. Thank you, Dr. McClung."

"Finish cleaning the lab. We'll leave in ten minutes."

Half an hour later, we drove into a new subdivision of single-family homes. He pulled into the driveway of a ranch-style home with stucco walls, set among a neat array of palm trees, native grasses, and clipped flower beds. Later on, I learned that Dr. McClung did all his own landscaping.

Mrs. McClung greeted me at the door with a big smile. She was heavyset and had a walking disability, and looked nothing like the attractive young lady pictured on Dr. McClung's desk. I wondered what could have happened. Over dinner, we exchanged family stories and I learned that a car accident a few years earlier had caused her disability.

In the following weeks, I developed a special bond with Dr. and Mrs. McClung, and I felt blessed to have met such a caring advisor and his spouse. One evening I learned that Dr. McClung participated in the University theatrical society and that he had played several roles on stage. *Yes,* I thought, *he does look like an actor.*

***

One day, out of nowhere, I received a letter from George Lopez, an old classmate from St. Xavier College. He came from a Christian family living in Goa, an ex-Portuguese territory on the west coast of India, south of Bombay. I learned that he was studying medical technology at Raleigh-Durham Hospital in North Carolina. After exchanging some phone conversations, George invited me to visit him for a weekend in October 1968. I made arrangements to travel by Greyhound bus.

The air-conditioned ride took about six hours and every passenger had a seat—so different from the buses I had ridden in India, where passengers filled every space and even hung onto the sides. I sat in a comfortable window seat and took naps when I wasn't enjoying the lush farmland scenery.

When the bus stopped in Raleigh, George greeted me. We embraced and slapped each other on the back. "George, I'm so happy to see you. How are your studies going?"

"Very well. I like it here. There are several Indian students in the Raleigh area. We meet at weekends and help each other."

"You're lucky. There are only a handful of Indian students at Athens."

We climbed into a taxi and continued talking about our lives in America. At his dorm, our discussions continued late into the evening. Our experiences were different, yet filled with the same themes of loneliness and friendship, challenges and achievements. As an Indian Christian, his transition had been easier. He had found a local church to attend and benefitted from the friendship and fellowship of others who shared his beliefs. Without a doubt, he had a much better network of friends to keep homesickness and depression at a distance.

The next day, we visited the labs where he studied, looked around the campus, and met some of his Indian friends. At his dorm, George introduced me to one of his American Christian friends. "Ramesh, we go to a local Catholic Church on Sunday morning. Why don't you come with us? I'll take you back to the bus station after the service."

"Sure," I said, "That would be nice." Jain philosophy accepted other religions as equals so I had no problem with his request. "You are lucky to have a church to go to. I wish there was a Jain or Hindu temple in Athens."

After the church service, George introduced me to Father Murphy and some other parishioners, "Father, this is Ramesh Shah, my friend from St. Xavier College in Bombay. We were classmates."

Father Murphy shook my hand, "George mentioned he had a friend coming to visit. I'm so glad you joined us for mass. A few of the parishioners stay and have lunch here. Why don't you join us for sandwiches before you leave?"

I glanced at George and we agreed to stay. I was pleased to see George relaxed and happy. He seemed accepted by the entire congregation.

Over lunch, I talked with Father Murphy about politics, Jain religion, and my family. "Ramesh, do you plan to become a citizen like George?" he asked.

I had not really thought about it. "First I have to get a work visa and pay off my debts," I said with a chuckle.

Father Murphy smiled, "It came as a shock to hear that Hindus in India discriminate so badly against Christians. I hope George gets the asylum he's asked for."

His comment surprised me. In my experience, the different religious groups in India lived together peacefully—other than some conflict between fanatic Muslims and hardliner Hindus, which was more political than religious. I turned to my friend, "George, what are you talking about?"

George squirmed and tried to change the subject but I wouldn't let him, "George, what have you told them?"

"We've talked about the discrimination against my family and other Christians in Goa. I've asked for asylum."

"George, I'm sorry you feel that way, but you never mentioned this at St. Xavier."

Father Murphy intervened and changed the topic, "India's a big country, just like America. Have you had chance to travel, Ramesh?"

We finished our lunch and George dropped me at the bus station.

On the ride home, I thought at length about citizenship. Would I want to live in America permanently? I could understand George wanting to stay, but his way of achieving that goal disappointed me. Our friendship was never the same again.

***

One Saturday morning, I arrived at the lab to prepare microbiological media plates for Dr. McClung's classes and noticed him typing at his desk. He looked at me over half-moon spectacles, "Hi Ramesh."

"Hi sir. How is Mrs. McClung? I heard she was sick."

He smiled, "She'll be fine. Thanks for asking." He hesitated a moment, then got up and lifted the papers from the chair in front of his desk, "Come in and sit down. I need to talk to you."

I wondered what he had to say "Is Dr. Payne unhappy with my progress?"

"No, he's very pleased. This is something else."

I sat quietly and waited for him to continue.

"Ramesh, I have taken a position as Head of Bacteriology at the University of South Florida (USF) in Tampa. I start there in January."

I didn't know what to say. Was he telling me my job would go away?

He moved his chair closer and rested his arm on my shoulder, "You have a choice. You can stay here in Athens, or you can transfer with me to USF and continue your graduate studies there."

Just when my life had settled, another big decision loomed.

"Most of your graduate credits will transfer, and I will have financial grants to give you part-time work, just like here. I'd like you to think about it." He sat back in his chair, "Mrs. McClung would like you to move with us."

"I don't know what to say."

"Ramesh, we can talk more next week, after you've had time to think about it."

I left his office feeling confused. Should I stay in Athens, or move to Tampa? Dr. and Mrs. McClung had been genuinely kind to me, and I felt confident they would help me in Tampa. Financially I was okay, with a few hundred dollars in the bank.

After a weekend of mental gymnastics, I told Dr. McClung that I was willing to transfer.

"That's excellent," he said, "Mrs. McClung will be very pleased."

23
Job Hunting (Again)

I moved to Tampa during the Christmas break of 1968 and soon settled into a new routine of study and preparing lab samples for Dr. McClung. With homesickness now a minor issue and my English more fluent, I found it much easier to mingle and make friends with other graduate students. I felt relaxed and energized with this new group of friends, and I even joined them in eating meat and consuming alcohol at social gatherings, although I avoided marijuana parties that were commonplace at that time. A police raid and a drug-related arrest could result in deportation of foreign students without a hearing.

One Friday, as I prepared lab samples, one of my new friends approached me. His six-foot-four-inch, 250-pound frame cast a shadow across the lab bench. He had blue eyes, a beard, and hair down to his shoulder blades. I looked up at his friendly face, "Hi, Joe."

"Ramesh, we're having a party tonight and then joining the war protest tomorrow. You're welcome to join us."

"Joe, you know foreign students are barred from involvement in American politics, and that includes protests. And you guys will be smoking weed tonight. I have to avoid those things."

He smiled, "Then come early. We're ordering pizza. The pot will come out later."

"Okay, I'll come for pizza."

The campus had seen its share of protest activity, including intentional fires and bomb threats. Just a week earlier, a protest that had started peacefully turned ugly, and students had been injured. My heart cried out to join non-violent demonstrations, but I couldn't risk my future.

When I arrived at the party, a group of Joe's friends were planning the protest rally. A television in the corner of the room provided background noise. Everyone quieted when the evening news came on with a lead story about the Vietnam War. One or two jeered when pictures of dead soldiers in body bags filled the screen. The next scenes were of student protests across the country and cheers rang out. *Why does this human suffering have to continue?*

"Ramesh, will you join us tomorrow?" one of Joe's friends asked.

"I'd like to, but I can't…"

"Yeah, we could take your photo. It would show that opposition is worldwide."

I shook my head, "No photographs. You know my situation."

It took me several minutes to convince them that I had to stay on the sidelines, despite a burning desire to participate.

***

I became good friends with two other graduate students from India, Ravi and Dhanesh, and together we rented an apartment about four miles from campus. The bus timetable for that location did not match my late work hours, so I decided it was time to buy a car.

Dr. McClung advised me to look at the school bulletin board, and a few days later I saw an ad for a Volkswagen Beetle. I called the student who wanted to sell it, and we agreed to meet at a campus parking lot.

The beige bodywork of the car looked in good shape, with only one or two minor dings. He opened the door for me to look inside, "It runs on regular gas and the tire treads are good."

I had no idea what he meant by regular gas and tire treads, but I didn't want to embarrass myself by asking questions. I climbed into the driver's seat and saw that the car had a radio. Everything looked clean and the seat felt comfortable. I got out the car, "How much?"

"Eight hundred dollars. Cash only."

I shuffled my feet and tried to look disinterested, "I'll give you seven."

"Seven fifty," he countered.

I looked at the car and shook my head.

He hesitated for a second, "Okay, we have deal. Seven hundred cash."

We exchanged the money and the car title, and he handed me the key.

"Can you drive me to my apartment," I asked. "I don't have a driver's license yet."

He rolled his eyes. "Fine. Get in. I'll take you to your apartment."

I got in the passenger seat, proud to own a car. This would generate a lot of excitement back home.

At the apartment, my roommates checked out my new purchase. Ravi already had a car. "You know you have to register the vehicle and get a provisional license before you can drive? Then you have to take a driving test."

I nodded. Bob Boe had given me a few driving lessons in his car, so I felt confident that I could pass the test and get my license. "Where do I register it?"

Ravi explained how to get to the DMV. "When you're ready, I'll drive with you so you can practice. The driving test is easy."

***

With many students focused on protests and drugs, much of campus life seemed unproductive. I found it difficult to concentrate on my research thesis and had to force myself to study. As my final year progressed, the mood on campus darkened further with news of a weakening economy. Inflation and rising unemployment made job prospects very slim.

I heard rumors that very few corporations had contacted the University. In good years, major corporations visited the campus for recruitment drives and student interviews, and smaller companies sent in job descriptions. I kept a close eye on the notice boards where job opportunities were posted, and searched local and regional newspapers for openings, but no microbiologist jobs were on offer. It seemed like the only way I could stay in America would be to continue my studies. That would mean a Ph.D., and only Dr. McClung could arrange that.

He and his wife continued to take a keen interest in my progress and regularly invited me for dinner at their newly constructed ranch home; a home even more elegant than the one in Georgia. One evening, I sat in their beautiful sunroom while Mrs. McClung finished preparing dinner.

"Time to eat," she said, directing me to a chair when I entered the dining room, "I hope you like it."

She had prepared a typical American dinner with turkey, ham, mashed potatoes, and bean casserole. Dr. McClung offered a glass of California Merlot and I truly enjoyed everything from the table.

"How's your thesis coming along?" Dr. McClung asked.

"It's almost done. I have to list my references and then get it typed."

He gave a wry smile, "I wish all my students worked as hard as you."

"Do you have a job lined up?" Mrs. McClung asked.

I shook my head, "I've been looking, but there's nothing."

Was this the time to ask Dr. McClung about a Ph.D., or would that be pushing our friendship too far? If I said something and he had to say no, it would hurt his feelings. *If Bhagwan Mahavir wants me to stay in America, Dr. McClung will raise the subject. He knows my situation.*

Dr. McClung sat bolt upright, "I just remembered something." He rose from his chair, fetched his briefcase, and rummaged through the contents until he found a letter. "This came today from a company I've never heard of. I didn't have time to post it on the notice board." He read the letter, "They want a Research Assistant—a microbiologist whose main activity will be preparing culture media." He handed it to me. "You're the perfect fit."

Goosebumps danced up my spine. I glanced at the letterhead. The company, Microlife Technics, was located in Sarasota, Florida, a coastal town less than an hour's drive. I read on; it was a small, private company that prepared microbial cultures for the food industry.

The next day, I sent off my résumé.

***

Driving to Sarasota for my interview, I felt confident, yet full of nerves. On the passenger seat, an envelope containing a letter of recommendation from Dr. McClung rested on top of my new suit jacket.

I found the street and drove slowly, looking for a sign bearing the company name. I reached the end of the street and turned around. On my second pass, I checked the building numbers and found my destination—a single-level, cement-block building in an industrial park alongside several other small manufacturing companies.

Inside, a receptionist named Ms. Marlene Wood welcomed me and gave me an application form. Her smile helped me relax, "Please take a seat and complete this. Mr. Glendenning, President of the company, will be interviewing you."

I filled out the application form and handed it back. My nerves were still on edge, and I silently repeated one of my father's mantras while I waited.

"Ramesh, Mr. Glendenning will see you now."

I took a deep breath and entered a large office with an oak-paneled desk set in front of a floor-to-ceiling window. Four or five leather visitor chairs were arranged in an arc in front of the desk, with small corner tables between each chair. A tall, slender man stood to shake my hand, "Hello Ramesh, I'm Larry Glendenning, President of this company."

"Pleased to meet you." I wished my hand was less sweaty.

He pointed to one of the chairs, "Have a seat. My brother John, V.P. of Operations, and Mr. Al Gryczka, Research & Development Director, will join us."

I sat quietly until the two gentlemen entered the room. We shook hands, sat down, and Larry Glendenning started the interview: "Ramesh, tell us about yourself and why you think you are a good fit for this job."

I told them about my studies in India and that I expected to graduate from USF with a Master's Degree in Microbiology, and that I had spent three years preparing microbial growth culture media for undergraduate lectures given by Dr. McClung, the department head. I opened the envelope and handed the letter to Mr. Glendenning, "Dr. McClung has written this letter for me."

Larry Glendenning read the letter and passed it to his brother John. It gave me a moment to gather my thoughts.

More detailed questions followed concerning my technical knowledge and practical laboratory skills. Everything seemed to be going well.

"Ramesh, I have one concern," Mr. Glendenning said, "If we offer you the job, how long do you plan to stay here?"

I had asked myself this question and didn't know the answer. I gave them an answer I thought they wanted to hear, "Sir, I would like to work here for five or six years, maybe longer. Once you hire me, the Immigration Office will give me a work visa. You will have no problem with my work."

The interview ended and I drove away with a good feeling, although I continued to look for other jobs while I waited for a reply.

My continued search resulted in an offer from the Pathology Department at Tampa General Hospital to do the type of work I had done in Atlanta and Athens. To keep my options open, I asked if I could work weekends only and they quickly agreed.

Two weeks later, I received an offer letter from Microlife Technics that I immediately accepted. My salary would be $8,400, with two weeks paid vacation after I had worked for a year. The next day, I applied to the INS office in Miami for a work visa. Two months later, I received an approval letter to stay in America provided I maintained employment.

For the first time in four and half years, I could start planning a trip to India to see my family. I could even tell Hasubhai to set the wheels in motion to find a marriage partner. Secretly, I wondered if Mina had remained single during my years in America, and whether I had climbed the social ladder far enough for her father to consider me a suitable candidate. How far would "educated in America" take me?

***

A newspaper ad for a duplex apartment in Bradenton, on the north side of Sarasota, caught my attention. I needed a place where I would be close to my new employer, yet within reasonable distance of my weekend job at Tampa General Hospital. I called the landlord, and a few minutes later I was on my way to view the apartment.

An elderly white American man with round, gold-rimmed spectacles opened the door.

"Mr. Himebaugh? My name is Ramesh Shah. We spoke a few minutes ago."

He eyed me for a moment, "Come in. What was your name again?"

"My name is Ramesh. I'm from India."

He nodded, "I'm Evert. Where do you work?"

"In Sarasota."

He handed me a pen and writing pad, "Give me the name, address, and phone number of your workplace."

I did as he asked.

He read the information, "Let me show you the apartment. It's the other half of this duplex."

The apartment had about seven hundred square feet of living space and a carport outside. It matched what I wanted, "Sir, when can I move in?"

He hesitated, "I have to check with my wife. Let me call you back in a couple of days."

His response surprised me, and when three or four days passed with no telephone call, I visited Mr. Himebaugh to check out the status.

"Mr. Himebaugh, have you made a decision?" I asked when he came to the door.

"Come in," he said, "I'm glad you're here. My wife and I have agreed to rent you the apartment for one year. We require a one-month deposit."

I relaxed, "I got nervous when you didn't call."

He smiled, "I had to check that none of my neighbors would object to us renting the apartment to a darker-skinned person. I explained that you were from India."

My whole body tensed, "You had to get your neighbors' permission?"

"Well, not really. I just wanted assurance there would be no trouble for you."

I thought about walking away—I didn't want to live in a neighborhood where my light brown skin barely passed the whiteness test. But I was tired of commuting from Tampa every day and needed somewhere to live. I smiled, "That's very kind of you."

***

In my job as Research Assistant, I supported research in the study of microorganisms and their role in food fermentation. For practical reasons, I worked directly for Al Gryczka. He taught me the laboratory techniques and production processes used to start fermentations, cultivate the growth of desirable microorganisms, and then harvest those microorganisms for later use by companies that manufactured fermented meat and dairy products such as pepperoni, salami, sausage, and yogurt.

I learned that the precise control of cleanliness, fermentation temperature, media addition, pH control, and airflow were critical. A small error on my part could result in a lost batch and lost revenue. My natural attention to detail worked in my favor, and I found myself enjoying the work.

In Bradenton, I met a family from New Delhi named Kailash and Mona Jain. They had a cute ten-year-old daughter, Anila. Mrs. Jain was an excellent cook, and they often invited me for delicious Indian dinners. As time passed, we became close friends.

At home, I cooked a few simple Indian dishes based on okra, potatoes and cauliflower. I didn't know how to cook Indian chapattis or paratha, but found that American Wonder Bread made a perfect substitute.

One evening, I prepared a pound of spicy okra curry, pulled a cold Budweiser from the fridge, and made myself comfortable at my wobbly kitchen table. I had purchased the table and three chairs at an auction for $10. The CBS Evening News with anchorman Walter Cronkite played on my small TV. As usual, the news focused on the Vietnam War.

I had taken my first mouthful when the doorbell rang. I got up and found Kailash and Mona standing at the door. "Come in," I greeted them, "Join me for my homemade dinner."

Kailash smiled, "We just had pizza and thought we'd drop by."

"How about a beer, Kailashbhai? Monaji, can I get you a glass of orange juice?"

They agreed and sat down at my wobbly table while I ate my curry. Mona laughed at my Wonder Bread chapattis and her eyes widened as I finished all twenty slices. "Ramesh, I can't believe you stay so skinny."

I wiped the last crumb from my mouth. "I'm proud of my meal."

Kailash touched his wife's arm. "We must think twice before inviting Ramesh for dinner. He's a garbage disposal!"

We all laughed.

***

With good friends at work and at home, a job I enjoyed, and bouts of depression a thing of the past, I felt very content with life in Sarasota. The thought of living here permanently seemed attractive and I investigated the possibility of citizenship.

First, I needed to obtain a permanent resident visa, known as a green card. Then, after three years of living within the law, I could apply for citizenship. What excited me most was that once I became a citizen, I could sponsor other family members to come to America. What would Hasubhai and Bhupat think of that?

A green card also brought the obligation to serve in the U.S. military, if called upon. I respected that requirement and, for the long-term well-being of my family, I decided to pursue the opportunity.

Obtaining a green card had two important conditions: First, my employer had to sponsor my application and effectively guarantee my employment, and second, my employer had to provide evidence that it could not find an equally qualified American to do the job. I shared this information with Al Gryczka, and he passed it on to Larry and John Glendenning.

After several weeks of employment, Larry's secretary arranged a meeting where Larry, John, Al, and I discussed the matter. Larry opened the discussion, "Ramesh, we are pleased with your progress and have decided to sponsor your green card application."

I bowed my head and tears came to my eyes, "Thank you so much. I will work hard for you."

Larry continued, "To provide the evidence we need, Al will post an ad for your job in the local Sarasota newspaper. The ad will run for a month, as required by law, and will state that candidates must have a master's degree in microbiology and experience in microbial fermentation. They are the required qualifications."

"What if someone has those qualifications?" I asked.

"We would continue to employ you for the duration of your current work visa, but we would not be able to sponsor you for a green card."

Each day for a month, the tension built. Whenever I saw Al Gryczka, he shook his head in answer to my unasked question. Finally, in November 1970, after a month with no qualified applicants, he completed the INS paperwork and wrote a sponsoring letter, and I submitted my application for permanent residency.

During this time, I continued to work weekends at Tampa General Hospital to earn extra money. Hasubhai and Bhupat were also doing well in their careers and, together, we made good progress in paying off our debts. Bhabhi urged me to come home to find a suitable partner, but leaving the country while my green card application was under review created complications. I also had several months to go before I could take vacation from work. I decided to wait until all these things fell into place.

Six weeks later, I came home from work and found an official-looking envelope in my mailbox. I ran inside with my heart pounding, read the letter, and did a little dance. My application had been accepted. "Yes," I said, punching the air. I still had to go for an interview and have fingerprints taken, but after those formalities, my green card would be sent to me.

I sat down and thought hard about my future life. Now I could get married and bring my wife to America. In time, I could apply for American citizenship and sponsor other family members. The thought excited me.

The downside would be giving up my Indian citizenship. I pondered whether that would make me less Indian…less Jain. What would my father say? Surely this was in line with his dream. He didn't move his family to Old Hanuman Lane to stay there, but as a stepping-stone to a better future. And what better future than life in America for my brothers and sisters?

I called home to tell Hasubhai about my green card, but did not mention citizenship and sponsorship of other family members. I wanted to sit face-to-face with him for that conversation.

***

In February 1971, I received a registered notification from the U.S. Selective Service instructing me to attend their office in Bradenton, Florida. This was not unexpected, but I was shaken and very afraid. The appointment would be for a physical exam that would determine my involvement in the armed forces. Failure to show up would guarantee my deportation.

The odds were high that I would be sent to Vietnam. I could only hope that my skills in medical microbiology would take me to a medical unit treating wounded soldiers. I had not killed anything in my entire life, and wanted no involvement with the front line.

I did not tell my family about the appointment or the draft requirement because I knew they would worry. Hasubhai would tell me to come home to India, and I would have the dilemma of disregarding my oldest brother and head of family, or disregarding the United States government.

On the day of my appointment, I arrived at the Selective Service office in Bradenton and signed a register at the front desk. A soldier handed me an application form to complete while I waited for my call. I entered a waiting room with a dozen young men with faces the color of stone.

In the section that requested education details, I listed all my medical experience and reached in my pocket for the small cube that Damuben had given me when I left India. *Bhagwan Mahavir, make my medical experience count.*

When my turn came, a soldier directed me to a cubicle where a uniformed officer seated behind a small desk pointed to an empty chair, "Please sit down."

I wiped my palms and tried to control my nerves. "Thank you, sir."

The office was small, with framed photographs of President Richard Nixon and Secretary of Defense Robert McNamara hanging on the wall.

The officer looked through my paperwork, "What do you do at present?"

"I work as a microbiologist in Sarasota, Florida."

"Tell me about your experience as a med tech."

"Sir, I worked in a hospital in Bombay for six months before coming to America to study medical technology at St. Joseph's Infirmary in Atlanta. I graduated in 1968, and then studied microbiology in graduate school." I reached for my pocket-handkerchief to dab away beads of sweat from my forehead. My mouth felt dry.

The officer made notes on my application, but I could not read them upside-down. His face had no expression. "Okay. I'm going to take you next door where a nurse will take a blood sample and give you a physical."

I followed him from the room.

***

After the physical exam, I drove to my workplace full of anxiety. Larry Glendenning approached me as I put on my white lab jacket, "Hi Ramesh, how did it go?"

I shrugged, "They'll let me know their decision in six to eight weeks."

He reached out and shook my hand, "John and I are so proud of you. We hope everything goes well."

That evening, I arrived home to find Mr. Himebaugh relaxing in a rattan chair on the duplex driveway. I shared my news with him and we chatted for a few minutes.

For the next few weeks, my mind never seemed to rest. There was nothing I could do other than continue my daily routine. I thought about buying a plane ticket to India several times, but in my heart I knew the best thing for me and my family was to stay in America and follow the calling from Bhagwan Mahavir, whatever that might be.

The registered-mail envelope finally arrived. My nerves were on edge as I pulled it from the mailbox. I did not know what to expect. I walked to my apartment, repeating a mantra from my father's teaching, "Whatever Lord Mahavir does, it has better meaning."

Inside, I laid the envelope carefully on my wobbly kitchen table and wondered if I should prepare dinner or just open the envelope. I chose to open the envelope and find the truth.

Dear Mr. Shah,

It is the pleasure of the Selective Services of the United States of America to let you know that you have been classified under the category of I-Y classification (Unclassified for duty except in time of declared war or national emergency). The Selective Services will contact you further in the future if your service will be needed for the Armed Forces.

Selective Services

I read the letter several times to make sure I understood it correctly, then ran next door to confirm with Mr. Himebaugh what I-Y classification meant.

He read the letter and laughed. "You're too old."

"Too old at twenty-six?"

He nodded, "You won't hear from them again."

I jumped up and down with delight.

Dr. Norvel McClung, my mentor and professor.

My first car, a VW Beetle, Tampa, FL 1969

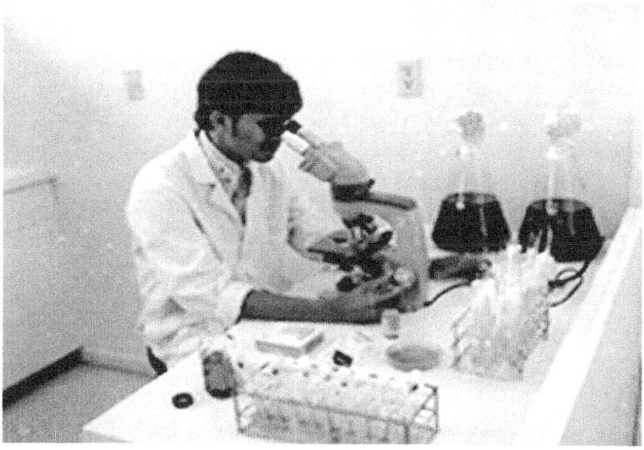

At work as a microbiologist, Microlife Technique, 1970

24

Finding a Soul Mate

"Ramesh, take a seat. You've been with us a year and we have good news for you."

I glanced from Larry Glendenning to his brother to Al Gryczka. All had smiles on their faces, and so did I.

"As you know," Larry continued, "your contract includes a salary review after twelve months. Both John and Al are pleased with your attendance and work habits, and we've agreed to raise your salary by $1,200 a year. Your new salary will be $9,600 a year, effective tomorrow."

I did a mental calculation…almost a fifteen percent raise. "Thank you so much."

I owed these men a huge debt of gratitude. They had helped me beyond my wildest expectation, and this was my opportunity to say something. "Without your sponsorship, I would not have my work permit. Thank you for your trust. I will work hard."

Al Gryczka nodded, "We're pleased to have you, Ramesh. You keep the lab spotless."

I hesitated for a moment. "I need to ask another favor."

"What is it?" Larry said.

"I haven't seen my family for almost five years. I'd like to visit India for a month."

"A month?" John said, "That's a long vacation."

I paused for a second, "My family wants me to marry."

Larry raised an eyebrow, "You have a fiancée?"

I didn't want to go into details of arranged marriages, "Not quite a fiancée…"

"Aha," Al said with a broad grin, "He needs time to persuade the girl of his dreams."

I smiled. He was very close to the truth.

Larry looked at Al, "Can we cope for a month?"

Al nodded and Larry consented to the request. That evening, I called home and announced I would be visiting.

"That's wonderful," Hasubhai said. Squeals erupted in the background when he told the rest of the family.

"Tell him we need two weeks to prepare for marriage negotiation," I heard Bhabhi say.

It was a joyful phone call, made better when Hasubhai announced we had paid off all our loans and would soon be out of debt with people like Dr. Malkan. I felt on top of the world.

The next day, I booked a flight to India, and for the rest of the week I enjoyed buying gifts for my siblings, sisters-in-law, and friends. I packed two big suitcases with clothing, perfumes, candies, and household items such as a toaster, blender, kitchen knife sets, and dinnerware sets. I also took money for wedding expenses and jewelry for my future bride, in case that endeavor succeeded.

By Indian standards, I had progressed well in a short period of time. I had a nice apartment, a Volkswagen Beetle in the driveway, and $3,500 in my savings account, equivalent to around 27,000 rupees. My dad would be impressed.

***

My arrival at Bombay airport came as a wakeup call. During my time in America, I had grown accustomed to clean streets and gleaming public buildings. Now, in my home country, I saw dirt and disorganization that shocked me. Three aircraft had landed at the same time, and the arrivals area was ill equipped to handle that number of people.

The ceiling fans in the immigration and customs area made little impact on the stuffy, humid air even at 2 o'clock in the morning. My shirt became wet with perspiration while I waited. Finally, an immigration officer inspected my visa forms and stamped my passport.

I moved to the baggage claim and customs area and searched for a luggage cart. The one I found had its own mind regarding the direction it wanted to go. Other people around me had the same problem. Many of them pushed more weight than they could control, their carts piled high with gifts for loved ones.

I collected my bags and approached the chaotic crowd waiting for customs clearance. Everyone was pushing for the shortest line. I knew that an unofficial bribe was expected, but had resolved not to pay one, since I was not smuggling any illegal items.

After a long wait, I faced a disgruntled customs officer who raised his voice to show he was boss in this situation, "What did you bring in these suitcases?"

I made no motion to bribe him, "Gift items for family members."

"Any gold?" he sneered.

"No sir."

"Open the bags."

While I unlocked my suitcases, an airport porter channeled other passengers ahead of me. The porter handed their passports to the officer and I saw the exchange of a small envelope. The officer signaled the porter to proceed and retuned his attention to my suitcases. "Stand back," he ordered in a crude manner.

I watched him run his fingers through my neatly packed belongings. When he found nothing, he became disinterested and told me to move on.

I repacked and locked my cases, and then pushed my cart to street level, where hundreds of people waited between barricades under dim streetlights. I heard my name called and turned to see Hasubhai and Bhupat waving from the crowd. A warm, wonderful feeling enveloped me, melting away my fatigue. I waved back and maneuvered my cart through the mass of people. My brothers pushed forward and we embraced at the barricades. Tears of happiness ran down our cheeks. I felt such joy that we were together again.

Bhupat took the handle of the luggage cart, "Come this way. A taxi is waiting."

We cleared the crowd and Hasubhai slapped me on the back, "Ramesh, you're looking good." His face had a few wrinkles I'd not seen before. "You've gained some weight. Ma would have been proud of you." He smiled and gripped my hand.

I remembered the conversation with Ma five years earlier, when she said I might never see her again. At the time, I had dismissed the idea, but her words had been true. Tears welled in my eyes.

We reached the taxi and loaded my suitcases. "How are Ramanbhabhi and Pravinabhabhi?" I asked.

"Very well," Bhupat said, "They are waiting at home." He climbed into the front seat with the driver while Hasubhai and I occupied the back seat.

"Tell me about Pratibha, Rashmi, Kirit, and Sadhana."

"They are getting taller. Kirit has long hair; you won't recognize him."

The taxi pulled away. At 4 a.m., the roads were quiet and the taxi sped through the streets leaving a cloud of dust behind. We entered an area with shanty huts on both sides of the road: tin-roof structures with no running water or toilets. Next, we passed through built-up suburbs with homeless people sleeping beside the road in every available spot. The sight disheartened me.

We entered another shantytown area. "This is Borivali West," Hasubhai said. "We'll be home soon."

We turned onto roads I did not know. "It looks really depressing," I said.

"We had no choice after our apartment at 64-D collapsed. We were lucky to find this. Bhupat's friend, Ishwarbhai, helped us."

Bhupat turned from the front seat, "It's better than you think. We have three rooms and a toilet, and it's only five minutes from Borivali railway station."

"And we have a telephone," Hasubhai said.

Bhupat laughed. "Yes, we have a telephone. The problem is it that the commute from here to Churchgate is an hour and a half, and the trains are very crowded."

The taxi stopped at a dusty, unpaved courtyard in the middle of five or six apartment buildings. Bhupat pointed to a small first-floor balcony on the right. "That's our apartment."

Bhabhi and Pratibha waved at us from the balcony. I got out of the car and waved back. Bhupat carried my hand luggage while Hasubhai and I carried the suitcases.

Pratibha, Rashmi, Kirit, and Sadhana leapt at me as soon as I entered the house. Damuben and Nimuben waited by the window to greet me. Nimuben had come all the way from Jamnagar to be there. Laughter filled the room as I greeted and hugged each one. Lastly, I hugged my two sisters-in-law. Tears ran down Bhabhi's cheeks. "Rameshbhai," she said, "tea is ready. I have your favorite gathia, chili peppers, and spicy puri on the table."

I removed my shoes and placed them at the entrance, then folded my hands in prayer in front of portraits of Bhagwan Mahavir, my ma, and my dad. My eyes welled at the thought of Ma not being with us.

"You must be tired," Nimuben said.

"A little. But I'm so glad to be home."

Bhabhi pointed to the kitchen, "Come and eat something and then take a rest."

"First we must open the suitcases. I have gifts for everyone."

The younger ones cheered and I handed my luggage keys to Pratibha so she could unlock the suitcases while I washed my hands and changed my shirt.

"Rameshbhai, eat first before opening the bags. Your tea will get cold."

The children objected. "Bhabhi, let's open the suitcases," Kirit said. The others agreed with him and Bhabhi shook her head slowly, knowing she was outvoted.

It was a joyous time, watching my siblings receive the gifts I had brought from America. I had not seen such jubilation in years.

We moved to the kitchen, and I ate some snacks while I shared photos of my duplex, my workplace, my car, and my American friends.

"We must talk about you seeing some girls while you are here," Bhabhi said. My younger siblings cheered.

I held my breath. "Bhabhi, is Mina married?"

She grinned. "No. Mina is single. We also have invitations from three other parents for_you to see their daughters."

I bit into a spicy puri. "Bhabhi, let's contact Mina's parents first and see if I can meet her. If that works, I really don't want to see anyone else."

Hasubhai slapped his fist on the table. "Good choice."

Everyone laughed.

"I'll talk to her grandma tomorrow," Hasubhai said. "Mina spends a lot of time there while her parents' apartment is being remodeled."

***

The next morning Hasubhai contacted Mina's grandma and made the request.

Do you think they'll agree?" I asked Hasubhai in a quiet moment. "Her parents have high standing."

"I think they will. Your studies overseas have improved our own standing in the Jamnagar Jain society."

Bhabhi joined us. "Her family is closely related to my family. We know them well."

"And we don't have to pretend about finances anymore," Bhupat added. "Our debts are gone."

"Do they know that?" I asked.

Hasubhai shook his head, "Not from our lips."

Bhupat grinned. "Word gets around."

Our conversation moved to my experiences in America, and I told them about my job and the wonderful people I had met there.

"Rameshbhai, you sound very happy," Bhabhi said.

"Yes, I like it in America. It's not crowded, and I don't need to wait in any lines to get food or milk or anything. The apartments are clean, with running water and private toilets. The roads are wide and there's no honking of horns. Everyone is far better off than here."

Her eyes sparkled, "It sounds wonderful."

I decided to share my thoughts. "Do you like it here in Borivali?"

Hasubhai shrugged, "It's like living in a small village. We are far from friends and relatives."

"And it's very dusty," Bhabhi said. "The roads are not paved. Luckily the Jain Temple is close by."

I took a deep breath. "I think we should all immigrate to America. Our life would be much better there."

Bhabhi stared at me, "Is that possible?"

I nodded, "Now that I have a permanent resident card, I can apply for citizenship after three years. Then I can sponsor other family members to come to America. There's a quota system. I don't know how long that takes, but it's possible." I glanced at Hasubhai to gauge his reaction.

"I like the idea," he said, "Life is tough here."

Bhabhi touched her husband's arm. "It would mean moving away from all our relatives. Do you want that? Rameshbhai says there are no Jain temples there."

"Let's not decide now," I said. "We can think about it. The immigration process takes a long time."

Hasubhai nodded his head slowly. "It's an opportunity very few people have. We should plant the seed."

***

Later that day, Mina's parents gave permission for a mid-afternoon meeting on the upcoming Saturday. Hasubhai and Bhabhi chose a restaurant popular with locals and foreigners called Gaylord, near Churchgate. They would accompany us as chaperones.

We arrived early and waited outside the restaurant for Mina's arrival. I felt nervous and kept rubbing my palms together. Bhabhi touched my arm, "Rameshbhai, don't be nervous. Mina needs to see that you have confidence."

A taxi stopped and Mina stepped out wearing a pink Punjabi suit known as a kurta kamiz (loose fitting pants with loose, patterned top) with matching sandals. We stepped forward and I noticed she had red lipstick. Her beauty took my breath away. Her dark eyes, braided black hair, and fair skin came alive when she smiled, and with her bright personality, she smiled a lot.

Bhabhi embraced Mina and immediately they settled into quick-fire conversation. Hasubhai and I waited. After a few moments, Bhabhi made the formal introductions.

"Rameshbhai, this is Mina. Mina, this is Rameshbhai."

My heart pumped double-time. She looked radiant. I bowed my head slightly and gave her my best smile. A whiff of her fruity perfume filled my nostrils.

Inside the restaurant, Hasubhai organized our seating. Mina and I occupied a corner booth, while Bhabhi and Hasubhai sat in another booth a few feet away, giving us some privacy while still fulfilling their chaperone duties.

Mina and I chatted about our various interests for a few minutes, switching between English and Gujarati. Her English was good. She asked me how long I had lived in America. I replied in English, "Almost five years. I arrived in January 1967, to study in Atlanta. Now I work in Sarasota, Florida."

"What did you study?"

"Medical technology for a year. Then I went to graduate school for a master's degree in microbiology."

A server brought our Coca Colas and Bombay Chat Masala, a spicy Indian snack. I sipped my Coke and asked her if she had graduated from college.

Her eyes lit up. "I graduated in June. I have a Bachelor of Arts in economics from St. Xavier College."

I smiled, "We have a lot in common. St. Xavier College is my alma mater. Do you know Dr. Freitus?"

"Not really. I'm in a different building."

We shared tales of St. Xavier, giggling frequently. "An economics major will get you a good job in the banking industry," I said. "You could even go to law school."

She laughed, "That's what I plan to do. I've been accepted at Bombay Law School."

Her ambition and future planning impressed me. Then it struck me: With that opportunity waiting for her, would she want to move to America?

Our conversation continued and I found it easy to talk with her. Two hours passed in what seemed like a few short minutes. She must have felt the same. When she looked at her watch, she gasped, "I need to go. I have some errands to run."

Hasubhai paid for our snacks and we exited the restaurant and said goodbye. Hasubhai hailed a taxi for Mina.

"How did it go?" Bhabhi asked as the taxi pulled away.

I wanted to say, "Like a dream," but I tempered my optimism. "I think we both had a good time. She's very attractive, and her English is excellent."

Hasubhai gripped my shoulder. "We have other girls you can meet. Shall I make calls to their parents?"

"Let me think about it. We can wait a day or two."

25

Mr. & Mrs. Shah

I woke early the next day, Sunday, to traffic noise, loud horns, and constant bell ringing from nearby temples. We had no plans, and the whole family relaxed over tea and breakfast. Radio music played in the background.

"How's your business?" I asked Bhupat.

His eyes lit up, "Very good. I have another person, named Bansilal, working for me in the shipyards."

"Why there?"

"Old ships come from all over the world to be dismantled and stop in Bombay while the deal is done. We remove radio and communication equipment before they go to the shipyards in Gujarat where the steel is recycled."

"How did you find out about this?"

Bhupat grinned, "Ishwarbhai knows someone at the docks. I tell Bansilal what to remove, and he removes it. The agents have no idea what the components are worth. I can pay ten rupees for something worth a hundred."

A news broadcast interrupted the music on the radio. The lead story described tension between India and Pakistan, and the prospect of war. I listened carefully, as I had heard nothing about this in America. The Pakistani government blamed India for inciting a separatist movement among the Hindus of East Pakistan (later to become Bangladesh), and was threatening retaliation. The Indian government denied any wrongdoing.

"It's serious," Hasubhai said. "There's no Gandhi to broker peace."

Before we could discuss the situation, the phone rang and Bhabhi answered it. Her face lit up and she rolled her eyes at me. "Rameshbhai, Mina wants to talk to you."

My pulse accelerated as I ran to the phone. "Hello, this is Ramesh."

"Hi, this is Mina. Would you like to go out and talk more?"

I felt giddy with excitement. "Of course. We can go somewhere for a brunch."

"That would be nice. I'm at my grandma's home."

"I'll pick you up." I hung up the phone and turned to see Bhabhi with a big smile on her face.

"Rameshbhai, get ready quickly. The journey will take some time." She gripped my hand. "I'm so pleased for you."

Mina's grandma lived on Princess Street, only a few blocks from our old 64-D apartment. I thought about taking a taxi so I could arrive looking my best, but the fare from Borivali to Kalbadevi Road would be expensive. I decided to risk taking the subway. The trains would not be busy on a Sunday morning.

While I changed into my suit in the other room, Hasubhai and Bhabhi thought about where I should take Mina. Hasubhai spoke loud enough for me to hear. "Ramesh, there's Hotel Sun-N-Sand at the Juhu Beach. The restaurant overlooks the Indian Ocean."

"Yes, make a reservation." If I saved the taxi fare, I could afford a nice restaurant.

I entered the living room dressed in my American suit, blue shirt, matching tie, and polished black shoes. Pratibha smiled at me, "Rameshbhai, you look very smart."

I returned her smile.

Hasubhai gripped my arm, "Good luck."

***

The journey to Kalbadevi Road took only one hour, so I decided I had time to visit the ruins of 64-D before picking up Mina. Very little had changed on the streets of my childhood, yet it felt very different walking them dressed in an American suit.

The site at 64-D looked very much like Hasubhai had first described it, with our old third-floor apartment nothing more than a hole near the top of the rubble pile. The local authorities had quarantined the side street, but had done little to clear the rubble. Hawkers and street vendors carried on business as usual, and the through street was as crowded and noisy as any Sunday I could remember.

"Hey, Rameshbhai. How are you?"

I turned to the familiar voice, "Shankarbhai, it's so nice to see you."

"Rameshbhai, I'm so sorry your mother passed away." He pointed to the spot in the road where Ma had collapsed.

"It happened so quickly—the moment she saw the building wreckage."

I gazed at the pile of rubble that held my childhood memories and sensed Ma's presence. I found it hard to look.

"Let me order tea for you."

I had to get to Princess Street and didn't have time for tea. I slipped off my jacket, "I just had tea, thank you. Can you press my jacket?"

He grinned and reached for his iron.

"Is your family okay?" I asked.

"They are fine…still living in the village. We have a new baby boy. I'm going home next week to see him. I haven't been home for eight months."

He returned my jacket. I gave him 10 rupees and asked if he knew where Mr. Vakil and our other neighbors had moved. He didn't know, so I shook his hand and moved on. The familiar sights and sounds reminded me of other friends, and I decided to return another day to visit Dr. Malkan, Pradip, and Jayant.

The route to Princess Street took me past the vegetable and grain shops, where I often hid my face on my way to school to avoid shouts about overdue accounts. This time I held my head high and looked around.

There were no familiar faces at the vegetable shop, but I saw Babu attending his stalls at the grain shop. He was the one we disliked most. I stopped to speak with him and he greeted me politely. "Ramesh, I hear you have a job in America and that Bhupat is doing well. It's good to see your family succeed."

I jokingly reminded him that he once chased me down the street.

He laughed. "Your father was a good man. I always knew your bills would be paid one day."

I shook his hand and moved on toward Princess Street, my pulse quickening as I approached the apartment. I paused at the side of the road and looked up at the third-floor window to see Mina peeking at the street below. We made eye contact and I waved.

"I'll be right there," she shouted.

I waited for her. When she arrived, we greeted by shaking hands. She wore a beautifully decorated Punjabi salwar kamiz. Her eyes sparkled and she gave me a big smile. Her perfect white teeth reminded me of the Colgate toothpaste commercial I had seen on American TV. I led the way to a place where I could hail a cab and instructed the driver to take us to Hotel Sun-N-Sand.

I had never taken a girl on a solo date before, and we sat in silence in the taxi for a couple of minutes before I finally spoke. "Ramanbhabhi tells me you are very close to your grandma."

"I've spent most of my time with her since my college days. Do you know my grandma is Raman's aunt?"

"I knew there was a close connection."

Mina smiled. "Raman talks very highly of you."

I chuckled, "She's a very generous person."

After a thirty-minute drive, we arrived at the hotel. A greeter led us to seats overlooking the ocean. I pointed at the beautiful view. "The beach in Sarasota is like this. It has soft white sand."

She smiled, "Do you live near the beach?"

"I drive there sometimes and walk in the sand. It's beautiful."

"You have a car?"

I nodded, "A Volkswagen Beetle. You can't get anywhere in Sarasota without a car."

A waiter came, and we ordered Coke and appetizers.

She brushed a strand of hair from her face. "Ramesh, what type of job do you have in America?"

"I'm a research microbiologist at a company called Microlife Technics."

"What do you do each day?"

I explained the details of my work.

"It sounds very interesting. How long will you stay there?"

I had anticipated this question and wished I knew what Mina wanted to hear. I didn't want to lie to her and I didn't want to scare her away. "Three- or four-years minimum, maybe more. I need to gain experience in America before I can find a really good job in India."

"When are you flying back?"

"I leave on October 21."

Her eyes widened, "You are sure in a hurry."

I smiled. A glint in her eye told me the rush of activity excited her rather than worried her. "I have to go back to my job. The people I work for have been good to me. I cannot let them down."

She nodded her understanding and looked thoughtful for several seconds. I sensed this was an important moment.

"Ramesh, my parents would like to meet you. When can you come?"

I wondered if I was dreaming. Could a boy from 64-D really be dining at a restaurant overlooking the Indian Ocean, telling a beautiful girl about his life as a research scientist in America? And did that girl say, in the language of arranged marriages, that she would spend the rest of her life with him if her father agreed? My pulse quickened. "I'm free any time."

She smiled, letting her eyes do the talking.

"Mina, would you like to come to America?"

Her eyes widened. "I…I need to talk to my dad."

I sensed that she felt she had already said too much. Yet there was no hint of dejection in her smile. In my heart, I felt good.

We both relaxed and had a wonderful time ordering dinner and chatting about family and friends, my experiences in America, life at St. Xavier College, and her favorite Hindi movies, which I had not seen. Three hours flashed by before we left the restaurant and took a cab back to her grandma's home. In the cab, I had enough courage to hold her hand and felt sensations in my heart I'd never felt before.

At Princess Street, I said I would ask Hasubhai to arrange a meeting with her father. She smiled and slipped inside the apartment, then paused for one last glance. I never knew eyes could say so much.

On the train to Borivali, I replayed the highlights of our meeting in my mind and prepared for the barrage of questions Bhabhi would have for me. I suspected she had been planning this day for many years.

***

Mina's father, Mr. Kanaklal Shah, welcomed us at the door, led us to the living room, and introduced his wife, Mrs. Jashwantiben. I felt less nervous than I thought I would. Mina stood by the open window, dressed smartly in a pinkish kurta kamiz. She gave me a wonderful smile. Street noise from the open window and the hum of fan blades filled her grandma's apartment. The meeting took place there because her parent's home was still being remodeled.

After the formal introductions, we all sat down and Mina's father, a wholesale cloth merchant, started the conversation. "Ramesh, we know your family through Hasubhai and Raman, and we've heard about your studies in America, so we feel like we already know you. However, I still have some questions for you." He spoke in a friendly manner and made notes of my answers. The others sat and listened.

"What is your income in America?" Mr. Kanaklal asked, a typical question from an Indian elder during marriage negotiations. I told him my latest salary in U.S. dollars, and then converted the number to rupees. His eyebrows rose.

"And do you have any debt?"

I glanced at Hasubhai, "No sir. I have no debt. I even paid cash for my car."

Mina's father continued with questions about my work, where I lived, and my future plans. I repeated what I had told Mina about staying in America for a few years and said nothing about the possibility of obtaining American citizenship.

"So, Mina will come to live in America?"

"Yes. As soon as she has her visa, she can come. The day after we are married, I will make the application at the American Embassy. It will take a few weeks. When she has her visa, she can fly to America and I will be waiting for her."

He exchanged a glance with his wife. Mina's mother whispered something about traveling alone, and I agreed to meet Mina in New York, where her Indian Airlines flight would terminate.

At the end of our meeting, Mina's parents formally agreed to our engagement, and we ended our time together with a festive lunch.

That evening, I reveled in thoughts of marrying the girl of my dreams. So much had happened to me since I first met Mina. Back then the events of today had seemed impossible, yet the stars had aligned. The hardships and struggles had all been worthwhile. I felt elated.

On my return to America, Al Gryczka informed me that Mina's father had called Microlife Technics to confirm my employment and salary, and to ask about my character. I was surprised at first, but appreciated her father's concern about sending his daughter to a far-away land with a young man he had known for only a few hours.

***

Planning for the wedding moved into high gear. Hasubhai and Bhabhi went with Mina's family to visit a jotish for an astrological consultation. The jotish proposed

Tuesday, October 5, for the engagement and Thursday, October 14, as an auspicious day for the wedding.

In less than a week, we sent out guest invitations, rented a hall, planned the reception, bought new outfits for all my siblings, and prepared a family gift of new saris and gold jewelry for my bride. Mina's parents wanted an elaborate wedding for their daughter, and invitations went out to four hundred guests. It was a most hectic week for both families.

We celebrated the engagement with a gala luncheon at our house in Borivali West with about twenty guests from Mina's family attending. We also had a celebratory luncheon for close relatives a few days before the wedding at the Malabar Hill residence of Mina's elder uncle, Mr. Jamnadas Bhai.

Mina's father wanted to pay all the wedding expenses, but Hasubhai and I insisted that we share the expense. After a lengthy but friendly discussion, Mina's father conceded. We knew that our parents would have liked this arrangement.

***

On one of those hectic days, I had arranged to pick up Mina and take her shopping at Zaveri Bazaar for gold jewelry she would wear at the wedding. Hasubhai and Bhabhi had agreed to meet us there.

I left early in the morning so I could catch up with Dr. Malkan before he got busy with patients, and then visit Pradip and Jayant before picking up Mina. I wanted to ask Pradip to be my best man, and hand-deliver wedding invitations to Dr. Malkan and Jayant.

"Hello, Dr. Malkan," I said, climbing the three steps to his office.

Dr. Malkan raised his head, "Ramesh! How are you?" He got up and extended his hand, "Come and sit down. Tell me what you're up to now."

We spoke for a few minutes about what I did as a microbiologist in America and the well-being of my family.

"That's excellent," he said.

I grinned, "There's something else. I'm getting married."

He was genuinely pleased for me, but unfortunately had another engagement on the day of the wedding that he couldn't change at such short notice. I thanked him for his guidance and generous help when the family was having financial trouble and left with a warm glow from the reception he gave me.

A few minutes later, I knocked on the door of Pradip's apartment, hoping he still lived there. His mother came to the door and quickly called Pradip who was not at work that day.

After we had greeted, I asked him if he had any plans for Thursday, October 14.

He gave me a puzzled look, "I'll be at work."

I shook my head. "I'd like you to be somewhere else."

"Where?"

I reached in my pocket for the invitation. "At my wedding."

His eyes lit up. "Congratulations."

Before he could embrace me, I held up my hand. "Pradip, there's more. I *need* you to be there. I'd like you to be Best Man."

His jaw dropped. "Me? That's such an honor."

"You were my best friend—you should be my best man."

We embraced and I told him about Mina, and how getting a degree from an American university made it possible for Hasubhai to approach her father.

He smiled. "Going to America has helped you!"

"It's helped me a lot. Pradip, there are so many opportunities there. You should consider it. You can apply to study there like I did, and if things go well, you can settle there."

He thought for a moment. "I couldn't do that, Ramesh. I have to look after my parents."

I understood his situation. As an only son, he had the responsibility of looking after his parents in their old age. Tradition dictated it.

We talked for few more minutes before I left and headed for the crowded streets of Zaveri Bazaar.

I weaved my way to Jayant's hair oil shop, where I found Jayant sitting on the side while Laxman attended a customer. They were both delighted to see me and we embraced.

It was mid-afternoon.

I was pleased to see Jayant sober, but his health did not look good.

"Have you returned from America?" he asked.

I shook my head, "I've come back to get married."

"Ha! Tell me about it."

We talked for a while about the marriage and my life in America while Laxman attended to customers and occasionally joined the conversation.

When he ran out of questions, I looked him in the eye, "How are you, Jayant?"

"I'm fine, Ramesh."

I could tell he wasn't fine. "Jayant, your health is not looking good since I left five years ago. Please tell me you are in control of your drinking."

"Ramesh, let's not talk about it. We should talk about your wedding."

"Jayant, we've talked about my wedding. Tell me you are controlling your drinking."

Laxman leaned toward me and whispered, "Rameshbhai, it's getting worse."

Jayant became agitated. "Ramesh, I am not able to control my drinking and I have no plan to change."

The sad conversation continued, but without any headway. I glanced at my watch; it was time to leave. I pulled a wedding invitation from my pocket. "Jayant, I have to go, but I want you to come to my wedding." I extended the invitation to him and he gracefully accepted it.

"I promise I'll be there," he said.

"Sober?"

He nodded.

I thanked him and moved on to pick up Mina for shopping.

***

On the morning of October 14, four hundred guests gathered for the Hindu wedding ceremony at a prestigious and popular venue in the Fort District of South Bombay. Mina wore a beautiful, elaborately embroidered red sari with a gold necklace, matching bangles, and earrings. I was dressed in a western style, custom-made two-piece suit. The wedding hall hummed with activity and Indian wedding music played in the background. A Hindu priest performed the traditional wedding ceremony. Joy and celebration filled the room.

The evening reception took place on the open-air terrace of the Bombay Chamber of Commerce. Colorful lights illuminated the terrace, and hundreds of flowers were woven into festive decorations that created a unique and wonderful atmosphere. For the reception, Mina wore a multicolored sari with a diamond necklace, diamond earrings, and diamond bracelets. She looked incredible, and her personality bubbled with joy and laughter all evening.

The vegetarian dinner menu included appetizers, soups, various entrées, tandoori breads, and rice, followed by fabulous desserts to finish the joyous occasion. In line with Jain tradition, no alcoholic drinks or wine were served.

Pradip did a nice job of orchestrating the speeches, and later, when the music played, I noticed Jayant in conversation with other guests. I hoped he would realize that an evening without alcohol could be enjoyable.

Toward the end of the evening, I stood with Hasubhai, gazing at the throng of people.

"Did you ever expect anything like this?" he said.

"Four hundred people…at the Chamber of Commerce?" I shook my head. "It's beyond my dreams."

"And mine. We've moved up in society."

I nodded, "Everything had to fall into place. I think Bhabhi has been at work."

Hasubhai smiled.

***

With my departure only a week away, we had no time for a honeymoon. Mina and I spent our first night together at home in Borivali West. Now a member of our family, she would stay there until she joined me in America.

The final week was as hectic as the week before the wedding. The first priority was applying for Mina's immigration visa. Delays at the embassy meant the process took longer than I had hoped. When Mina had the required passport-sized photograph taken, she presented me with a copy, "This is for you to carry with you."

I carefully put it in my wallet.

We also squeezed in a train trip to Jamnagar, my birthplace, to visit a special holy site for a blessing. That completed the final ritual of the religious wedding practices. We returned to Bombay just one day before my departure date.

Back in Borivali West, Mina became very anxious. Her eyes were filled with sadness. "Ramesh, I don't know how long before I will see you in America."

I reached for her hands and pulled her close. "I know it's difficult. I wish I could stay here with you." We hugged and tried to console each other. "Mina, time will go fast. We will write to each other. Every day when I get home from work, I'll be hoping there's a letter from you in my mailbox."

She nodded. "What worries me most is all the chatter about a war with Pakistan. Do you think it will happen? It could delay my visa."

I had the same fear, but tried to be optimistic. "We must hope everyone stays calm."

We hugged again and I felt her cling to me. I caressed her face, "Where's that courage of yours?"

She buried her head in my chest. "It's hiding."

"I know it's there somewhere," I said and gave her my biggest smile. "Come on, help me pack."

***

Family members from both sides came to the airport in the early hours of October 21 to wish me a safe journey. It was painful to say goodbye to my siblings, and even more painful to leave my bride of one week. I hugged Mina before boarding my flight. I wanted to kiss her, but tradition frowned on kissing your spouse in front of family elders. Mina knew this and behaved perfectly.

At the last moment, I led Mina to one side and took her hands in mine. "I have to go, but my heart stays here with you. I will wait for you in America."

Mina's eyes were wet.

"Stay on track with the visa process and let me know if the embassy needs any documents."

She nodded. "Write to me…every day."

***

In the air, I reflected on my visit. So much had happened in just four weeks. The dirt and grime of the arrival's hall at Bombay airport seemed a lifetime away. I was returning to

America married to the only girl I had ever wanted. I pulled her photo from my wallet and gazed at it.

I had also witnessed my family's new living quarters in Borivali West and how well Ramanbhabhi cared for my four younger siblings. My family's financial situation had been transformed. Best of all, Hasubhai liked my idea of all of us immigrating to America. It had been a wonderful trip. If only Mina could be on the flight with me.

I closed my eyes and whispered a prayer to my father: *You taught me that tomorrow would be a better day. I think that day is here.*

Mina (October 1971)

Our Wedding: October 14, 1971, Bombay, India

26

Back in the U.S.A.

I enjoyed showing the photograph of Mina to all my work colleagues. At break time, Marlene Wood and several others asked questions about my marriage. I explained how Hasubhai, as head of our family, had made the arrangements.

"He set up your first date and you had chaperones?"

"Yes."

"That wouldn't work in America."

"When did you first kiss?"

"After the engagement ceremony."

"That definitely wouldn't work in America."

When I left the break room, the conversation continued.

That evening, I wrote a letter to Mina telling her how much I loved her and missed her, and that I couldn't wait for her reply. I resisted the temptation to arrange a phone call, because neither of us would want to hang up, and long phone calls were expensive. After the expenses of my trip, I needed to rebuild my savings.

Six weeks crawled by. Then on December 3, 1971, a bombshell landed. For the first time, the India-Pakistan conflict made American TV. The morning news anchor announced that Pakistan had launched pre-emptive air strikes against a number of Indian Air Force bases, and the two countries were now at war.

I immediately arranged a call home and waited impatiently for the phone to ring.

Hasubhai answered and assured me that everyone was fine. Then he put Mina on the line. She sounded upset. "Ramesh, this could delay my visa."

"I don't think so. The U.S. government will carry on working. We are not waiting on the Indian Government." I had doubts about my words, but I tried to sound confident. "Stay safe. That's all that matters."

Her tone lightened. "Bhupatbhai says we are very safe here. The Pakistani bombers will not attack Borivali West."

I smiled. They lived so far from anywhere that even a wayward bomb would not hit them.

"When the air raid sirens sound, we have to put out the lights," Mina said. "The Pakistani pilots use lights to navigate. Hasubhai thinks that will cause delays for night flights. It could also make getting to the airport difficult."

"Please take care. I will wait for you."

Two more weeks dragged by before Mina called back.

"Ramesh, I have my visa. I've booked an Air India flight for December 14."

My heart jumped for joy. "I'll see you at Kennedy Airport in New York."

Later that day, I visited a travel agent to check flights to New York. The prices shocked me. This expense would send me back to square one in my efforts to rebuild my savings. I also wanted Mina to have a budget for turning my sparsely furnished apartment into our family home. Although I had promised Mina's father that I would meet her in New York, I decided not to go and wrote a letter to Mina to let her know my decision.

***

My excitement grew as the day of Mina's flight approached. I counted down the days and then the hours, and imagined the joyful sendoff she would be given. I drove home from work thinking: *She's in the air now. She will arrive tomorrow.*

I was preparing dinner when the phone rang. Mina sounded upset, "Ramesh, they canceled my flight. I have to try again tomorrow." Tears welled in my eyes.

Hasubhai came on the line. "Ramesh, it could happen again tomorrow. We will keep trying. There are only three flights a week. I will call you when her flight takes off."

I thanked him and finished preparing my meal, although I no longer felt hungry. When I ate it, the food seemed tasteless.

Two anxious days followed. Then Hasubhai called. The connection was bad. "Ramesh, she's…it was touch and go.

The air raid sirens…waiting at the airport. She had to board the aircraft in darkness with the sirens sounding."

"Did the plane take off?"

"Yes, but very late. The Air India agent couldn't say when…arrive in New York."

I thanked Hasubhai for all his efforts. At last, Mina was on her way. That night, I slept for a few hours and rose early to call the Air India desk at JFK Airport for a flight update. The agent couldn't say if Mina's flight would arrive in London in time for the connecting flight to New York. He suggested I call back later.

I made several calls as the day progressed, but without satisfaction. Finally, after midnight, an Air India desk attendant at JFK gave me some hard information: "The flight from London landed half an hour ago, sir."

"Was Mina Shah on the flight?"

"Can you spell that, sir?"

I did.

"I have that name. Please wait a moment." The knuckles on my hand went white while I waited for the desk attendant to come back on the line. "Sir, she landed in New York, but did not make her connecting flight to Sarasota."

My heart sank like a ship's anchor. I imagined Mina wandering JFK airport feeling scared and very vulnerable. I should have been there with a bouquet of roses to greet her on her arrival in America. Why didn't I go? Why was I penny pinching? There is a time to save and a time to spend, and I'd gotten it wrong.

The desk attendant came back on the line. "Passengers who missed their connecting flights were given hotel vouchers and transported to New York City."

My heart sunk further. Mina could be lost in New York. "Do you know which hotel?"

"One moment."

The wait seemed forever.

"I'm sorry, sir. I can't get that information."

I thanked him for his help and fell prostrate to the floor. *Bhagwan Mahavir, keep her safe.*

I continued chastising myself for not being there. Why had I reneged on my promise? My father had taught me to always keep my word, whatever the cost.

An hour later, maybe more, the phone rang. I grabbed the receiver.

"Ramesh?"

"Mina!" I'd never been so thankful to hear a person's voice. I tried to calm myself. "Mina, where are you?"

"In a hotel."

I could hear sniffles as she spoke. "Are you okay?"

"I'll be on a flight tomorrow morning."

"Do you know the flight number?"

Another sniffle. "I have it here."

She gave me details of a National Airlines flight leaving early in the morning.

"Mina, you're so brave. I'm proud of you. I'll be waiting for you. Sleep well."

***

I did not sleep well. I lay on my bed, hating myself. How could I be so uncaring? I had brought pain to the girl I'd promised to care for, the girl I loved more than anyone else. I wished there was a temple I could visit to seek peace. All I had was my small figurine of Bhagwan Mahavir. Over and over I prayed for Mina's safety.

Early the next morning, I called Kailash Jain and asked him to join me at Sarasota airport to greet Mina. He agreed, and I picked him up in my washed and polished VW Beetle. On the way, I stopped to buy roses.

At the airport, we waited by a window overlooking a large area of tarmac where aircrafts parked and passengers disembarked. When Mina's flight landed, I watched with mounting excitement as the ground crew wheeled a stairway into place and the aircraft door opened. Passengers started to disembark.

"There she is," I said when Mina appeared and began descending the stairs. She wore a light blue sari with a handbag slung over her shoulder. I recognized the sari as one I had bought her as a wedding gift. I waved to her as she walked toward the terminal.

"You are right, she is beautiful," Kailash whispered.

When Mina entered the meeting area, I hugged her and handed her the roses. A smile lit up her face, although her eyes looked tired.

"I'm so glad you are here," I said. "You look so beautiful."

"It was a long journey. I'm so glad to be out of the war zone. We must call Dad to let him know I arrived safely."

We hugged again and, after I had introduced Kailash, we walked hand in hand to the baggage claim area.

Back at my apartment in Bradenton, Mina unpacked her cases and then slept. The eleven-hour time difference made her tired. I gazed at her, thinking how wonderful life would be now that we were together.

***

For the first few days, life truly was wonderful. We had much to share and learn about each other, and conversation filled our days. When her jetlag eased, I took her to my workplace and my colleagues welcomed her. Each day after work, I took her to different places and delighted in her response to all things new. It reminded me of my own first days in America. We went to the beach, a shopping mall, and a cinema. Even a simple trip to the grocery store brought gasps of amazement at the array of fruits and vegetables.

As time moved on and homesickness set in, Mina fell into a depression. I recalled my own experience and waited patiently for this period to pass. "Mina, I felt the same in my early days," I told her, "You must work through it."

"I want to go home."

"Give it time. The pain will go away."

"I want to see my family."

"Mina, you are with me. This is your home. Let's go to the beach today."

"I want to go home."

"Mina, tomorrow will be a better day."

"No, I want my family."

When I fell into depression, I assumed the underlying cause was loneliness—facing my new environment with no one to talk to in my mother tongue and no one who understood my culture. Mina had me, yet she experienced similar symptoms of despair and could not express the overwhelming emptiness that engulfed her. The situation got worse by the day.

We had been raised not to discuss family difficulties with outsiders, especially anything that could be interpreted as mental anguish or mental disorder, so we hid the situation from Kailash and Mona, the couple closest to us. I prayed to my father and to Bhagwan Mahavir for strength on many occasions, but without success.

Some days were better than others. At times, Mina enjoyed arranging our apartment and preparing food, but I never knew what state she would be in when I arrived home from work. More than once, when Mina's anguish became unbearable, we spent the evening packing our bags, ready to return to India. I said I would call the travel agent the next day to arrange flights, hoping that the next day Mina would feel better and we could unpack.

One day, I left for work with Mina feeling the best she had for several days. At work, after more than an hour of meticulous preparation, I'd started a time-sensitive sanitation procedure when she called me.

"What is it, Mina?"

"I want you to come home."

"Mina, I can't come home now. I have to work."

"I have no one to talk to."

"Why don't you write a letter to your family? You know your ma and grandma love to hear from you."

"I called my ma this morning. I want you to come home."

"Mina, not now. I have to work."

I restarted the sanitation procedure, having lost valuable time. Minutes later, Mina called again. This disruption of my work went on throughout the day.

After several days of interruptions, Al Gryczka spoke to me. My situation at home was impacting the production schedule. I tried explaining this to Mina, but without success. Tensions rose. Then the phone bill arrived and I discovered that Mina had been calling India every day, sometimes multiple times. My monthly budget was out of control.

"Mina, you must not do this."

"Then take me home."

"This is our home."

"I don't want to live here."

"Mina, if we go back to India, we lose a big opportunity. The best long-term home for our family is in America. Going back would end that dream. We need to stay here."

Mina became frantic. To calm her, I agreed to call Air India, but after dialing the number, I secretly ended the call and went through the charade of a mock conversation with an Air India travel agent: "When is the next flight to Bombay? Tomorrow night is full? Nothing till next week? One moment please."

I put my hand over the receiver, "Mina, there are no seats for us this week."

***

We were in serious trouble. As a loving newlywed couple we had done everything we could, yet nothing relieved the deep feelings of sadness and dejection Mina felt. I could sympathize—I had been through the same upheaval—but that didn't stop my frustration. My hopes for a perfect life had been dashed. Finally, I spoke to Kailash.

"My friend, why didn't you tell me sooner?" he said.

"It's not something we can talk about."

He smiled at that quirk of our culture. "I'll ask Monaji to invite Mina to our house during her free afternoons. They can go shopping together and pick Anila up from school."

"I think that would help."

"Have you spoken to a doctor?"

"No. You're the first person…"

"Ramesh, in this country you can talk about these things." He smiled. "There are medications that can help relieve depression."

In the following days, Mina spent time with Monaji and Anila, and I located a family physician in town named Dr. Conard who had traveled to India several times and understood the culture. I made an appointment to see him.

Dr. Conard asked Mina questions about how she spent her days, and when and how the feelings of depression overwhelmed her. Gradually, she relaxed and felt comfortable talking with him about her feelings.

The doctor listened carefully to her answers. "Before we try medication, maybe some more focused activity would help. Have you thought about getting a job?"

Mina liked the idea and asked me if her visa allowed that. I told her it did.

"Maybe that would help," she said.

The doctor gave her an encouraging smile. "You would meet people and it would bring some added purpose to your life."

"What about having a baby?" I asked.

The doctor thought for a moment and agreed that could be part of the remedy.

In the following days, things gradually improved to the point that we could function normally *most* of the time. Mina found a job as a bank teller, and we talked seriously about starting a family. In her good moments, Mina liked the idea and we decided to pursue it.

The good days began to grow in number, and a level of happiness filled our lives. With Mina cooking our meals, I returned to a vegetarian diet and this pleased me, although I sometimes made exceptions at business meals.

***

Two or three months later, Mina became pregnant. We enjoyed visiting a baby store to buy a crib and rearranging the apartment to create space for the baby. Mina's parents were thrilled with the news and expected her to follow Indian tradition and come home for the birth.

I had a different opinion. "Mina, the baby must be born in America."

She looked dumbfounded. "But it's tradition to go home for your first child."

"I want our child to have American citizenship from birth."

"Then you tell my father. He may not like it."

Again, tensions rose. I didn't want to be at odds with Mina's father, but my dream was for America to be the child's home for life. I also had a concern that if Mina visited her parents for two or three months while I stayed working in America that she would not want to return.

"The baby must be born here," I said. "This is our home."

27

My Father's Dream

Mina's depression continued on and off throughout her pregnancy. During her second trimester, Hasubhai visited us on a tourist visa to see life in America. Bhabhi stayed in India with their two young children, Hina and Ketan, and my four younger siblings.

I welcomed Hasubhai at the airport and we hugged. His eyes darted everywhere, taking in all the new scenes. "Bhabhi is well and sends her greetings," he said.

"And the rest of the family?" I asked as we walked to the baggage claim area.

"Bhupat, Pravina and their children Hita and Parag are also well. Kirit is very mischievous and does not study and the principal constantly complains."

"You must discipline him. What about Pratibha, Rashmi, and Sadhana?"

"No problem with them. They are pretty mature."

"And the family in Jamnagar?"

"Aunt Jasi is not doing well. The rest are fine."

"Hasubhai, I will continue to send you money: help whoever needs it. I also want to support the charitable trusts that helped with my education. I want to donate money to them for new text books."

He nodded, "I like that idea."

During his visit, I took time off work and we traveled around Florida. We spent many hours discussing what life would be like when he immigrated. He enjoyed all the sightseeing, especially a trip to Disney World in Orlando. "Ramesh, life is very good here. There is clean water, fresh air, and excellent hygiene. I can't wait to immigrate with the rest of the family."

One evening, not long before his departure, we drove to the beach. Mina relaxed in a chair while my brother and I walked a mile or so in the soft, white sand. A warm breeze blew from the Gulf of Mexico.

"Ramesh, how is Mina?"

"You have seen her. Some days are better than others."

"And you felt the same way?"

"At first, yes."

"You never said anything."

"Bhabhi would have insisted that I come home."

He smiled, "That's true."

"They call it culture shock. The subconscious mind reacts to the bombardment of new things, even if those things are better. You will probably feel the same, although this visit may help."

We walked in silence for a while. The sun setting over the Gulf of Mexico silhouetted a group of small fishing boats and created a beautiful scene. We turned and headed back to where we had left Mina.

"What if I can't find a job here?" Hasubhai said. "The accounting rules are different from those in India."

"If you're willing to work hard, you'll be able to find a job in America. Maybe not as an accountant."

He glanced at me. "You mean doing menial work?"

"Perhaps a shopkeeper. Or a job like our father had."

A seagull squawked above our heads. I watched Hasubhai rub his chin. This would be a tough decision for him. "Hasubhai," I said, "Think about your children. They will be educated here and go to college here. Their lives will be so much better. They can be accountants or doctors or whatever they choose to be. That is your gift to them, your legacy. Only you can create that opportunity."

We walked in silence for several paces. I could sense his mind working.

"Hasubhai, our father had a dream. I believe that coming to America is part of that dream. You and Bhabhi and Bhupat all made sacrifices so I could come here. Now you can do the same thing for your family."

He nodded his head slowly. "Where will we live?"

"With us. In two or three years, I will have saved enough to buy a house. I need ten percent for a down payment, and then I can get a low-interest loan. They call it a mortgage.

Everyone who immigrates can live with us until they have a job and enough money to find their own apartment."

We strolled back to where Mina was sitting.

Later that evening, Hasubhai called Bhabhi and talked excitedly about the things he had seen during his visit. A day or two later, he returned to India.

***

On March 11, 1973, Mina gave birth to a baby girl and we named her Sonal. In Guajarati, the word 'Sona' means gold. Caring for the baby gave Mina new purpose and gradually she grew comfortable with life in America. We continued to live frugally so we could send money home and save for a down payment.

Three years later, we obtained a mortgage and purchased a 1,700-square-foot home with three bedrooms, two bathrooms, a family room, a dining room, and a sunroom. It also had central air conditioning and a beautiful landscaped yard where Sonal could play.

Mina persuaded her parents to come and visit us in our new home, and we met them at the Sarasota airport. It was a joy to see three-year-old Sonal meet her grandparents for the first time. After many hugs, tears, and laughter, we headed home.

"The roads are very wide and smooth," Mr. Kanaklal said.

I laughed, "That's the same first impression I had." I proceeded to tell him about billboards and all the other things that had amazed me when I first arrived.

At our home, Mina's mother, Jasiben, trailed her finger across the marble counter top in our kitchen. "Mina, this is a very nice house."

Mr. Kanaklal agreed, "Very nice, much bigger than your 64-D apartment." They both had big smiles on their faces.

"Five times the size," I said. "We are very happy here."

Mina nodded her agreement.

In the evenings, we went for a stroll in the neighborhood. Near the end of our road, we passed Sonal's elementary school, an air-conditioned brick building with a playground and running track inside a fenced area. Mr. Kanaklal cleared his throat, "Rameshbhai, I see your life is much better in America. At a young age, you have a very nice home and Sonal has a nice yard to play in and a wonderful school to go to. I'm glad that Mina feels good about settling down in America."

I could hardly believe my ears and wanted to make sure I'd heard him correctly. "You agree that we should settle in America?"

Mr. Kanaklal glanced down at the young girl holding his hand. "Yes. Your family is better off here."

I peeked at Mina. She had a big smile on her face.

That night, I slept well.

***

Three years after we obtained our green cards, we became eligible for U.S. citizenship. "Let's send off the applications," Mina said. "I have spoken to my three brothers, and they are all interested in coming here with their families."

"I'm busy at work," I replied. "I don't have time to do all the paperwork right now."

"I don't want to wait any more. I want to send off my application now."

"Why the rush?"

She looked at me with a coy grin, "It's the best thing for our children…both of them."

"What's that?"

A big smile lit up her face, "I'm going to have another baby."

We hugged and celebrated.

While I delayed a few more weeks, Mina sent off her application and then focused on her second pregnancy. Things went well and, on October 5, 1977, she gave birth to our second daughter, Rita.

Eight months later, I waited outside a courthouse in Tampa while Mina was sworn in as an American citizen. She walked out with a big smile on her face, clutching her precious American Citizenship Naturalization Certificate: the document that granted her all the privileges of an American citizen, including the right to vote.

"Let me see," I said.

She handed me the certificate and I immediately wished we had done it together.

***

At the age of 36, I entered the same courthouse with hundreds of immigrants from all over the world. I noticed how different groups of people looked so dissimilar. There were people of all shapes, sizes, and ethnicities, and I heard excited conversations in a dozen languages I recognized and others I couldn't place. *What are the unique stories of all these people?*

A court official called for quiet, and the boisterous crowd hushed to pin-drop silence.

The judge entered and started proceedings.

When we all recited the Pledge of Allegiance together, I felt very proud to be an American. It was one of the most gratifying moments of my life. With the blessing of Mahavir, my hard work had paid off.

The following day, I showed Larry, John, and Al my Naturalization Certificate and thanked them for their sponsorship and their trust in me. A few days later, they presented me with a beautiful boxed pen and pencil set with my name engraved on it as a token of appreciation. Soon after that, I was promoted to manager level and started working with Al Gryczka on two patent applications related to the work we were doing together.

***

It took time to sponsor other family members and wait for approval from the country-based immigrant quota system. The influx started in 1983. Hasubhai and Bhabhi arrived first with their two teenage children. They took over the spare bedroom in our home, while our own children—ages ten and six—shared the third bedroom. I found myself with a second, very satisfying job as chauffeur, ferrying Mina to work, children to school, and Hasubhai to job interviews.

At Microlife Technics, Al Gryczka and I celebrated the issuance by the United States Patent Office of the two patents we had worked on as co-inventors.

***

Hasubhai tried to find an accounting job in the Sarasota area. I picked him up from an interview one day, and his slumped shoulders and unsmiling face told me everything I needed to know. He buried his head in his hands. "Ramesh, there is nothing for me here."

"Give it time. Remember our father. 'Tomorrow will be a better day.'"

He grunted, "Not working is driving me crazy. I feel worthless."

"How about some other type of job?"

"Ramesh, I'm forty-nine years old. I can't do a manual job."

"I know a man who owns a 7-Eleven store. He told me that his shop assistant had quit. You could do that."

Hasubhai sat silently for a few moments. "Okay, I'll try it. Any job is better than nothing."

The next day, I spoke with my friend, Gary, and he agreed to a one-week trial. For the first few days, things went well. Hasubhai stocked shelves while Gary served customers and gave him some training. Then Gary had to be elsewhere for a morning and he left Hasubhai in charge of the store.

At around midday, I got a phone call at work.

"Ramesh, come and pick up your brother. I have to let him go."

"Why, what's happened?"

"He's so slow, customers are leaving the store."

"Can he finish the day?"

"No, come now."

I drove to the store and Hasubhai climbed into the car. "It's impossible, Ramesh. They asked me things I knew nothing about."

I calmed him down. "Hasubhai, tell me exactly what happened."

"I did okay with the first customer. He brought items to the counter that had price tags. I took his money and gave him change, no problem. The next customer said something and I wondered if I had misheard him. I thought he asked for twenty camels, but that didn't make sense. I asked him to repeat his request. 'Twenty camels,' he said. I didn't know what to do."

I tried not to laugh. "Hasubhai, they're a brand of cigarettes. He wanted a twenty pack."

He threw his hands in the air, "I know that now. The man pointed to what he wanted and I saw the camel picture on the pack. By then three people were waiting. A woman wanted lottery tickets and I gave her the wrong ones. She reacted like I had tried to cheat her. Ramesh, it was not easy. I did my best, but the line got longer and people started to leave the store without buying anything."

I dropped him at home and returned to work, pondering what to do next.

That evening, we had a serious talk and agreed that Sarasota was not a good place for new immigrants unless they had a technical degree.

"New York would be a better," Hasubhai said. "There's a big immigrant population there."

"Where would you live?" I said.

His eyes flashed with hope, "I know someone there, a childhood friend from Jamnagar."

"Could he help you?"

"We are good friends. I'll contact him."

About a month later, Hasubhai moved to New York to share his friend's apartment and look for work. Bhabhi and the children stayed in Florida. A few weeks later, the phone rang and he sounded excited, "Ramesh, tell Raman to start packing. I have an accounting job."

"That's wonderful. I'm so glad. How did you find it?"

"Narendra has many friends in the Indian community here. One of them does a lot of trade with companies in India and wanted someone who understands their accounting rules. He is very happy with me."

Within a few months, Hasubhai had settled in a small apartment in Elizabeth, New Jersey, and his family joined him there.

Unfortunately, even with a job that suited his talents, Hasubhai struggled with depression in the same way Mina and I had done. Soon, he was calling me daily from New Jersey, sometimes two, three, or four times a day.

One afternoon, Larry Glendenning approached me with a notepad that had a New York telephone number written on it. "Ramesh, do you recognize this number?"

My mouth went dry. "It's the company where my brother works."

Larry took a deep breath. "Did you give him our toll-free number?"

I grimaced, "I gave him my business card when he left for New York."

"He's called that number every day and used up all our toll-free minutes."

I felt sick. "I'm so sorry, that won't happen again. I'll pay the bill."

"It's not the money, Ramesh. We need these minutes for our customers. He cannot call this number."

"Yes, sir. I'll tell him."

I called Hasubhai that evening, wondering how to broach the subject while still showing him respect. I waited until the end of our conversation, "By the way, my boss found out that you are using the 800 number when you call me at work. He was mad with me and asked that we use the regular number. That number is for business only. I offered to pay the phone bill. It would be best if you call me in the evening at home."

"Okay, I understand."

Gradually, Hasubhai overcame his depression, became accustomed to his new environment, and became the foundation of the family in New Jersey. He and Bhabhi had sacrificed many things in India to pay for my education and get me to America, and they continued that unselfish lifestyle in New Jersey as they helped the rest of our siblings settle in America.

***

My younger brothers, Rashmi and Kirit, came in 1987, and Bhupat came with his son, Parag, and his eldest daughter, Hita, early in 1988. They all lived with Hasubhai and Bhabhi in the small apartment in Elizabeth, New Jersey. Bhupat returned to India after three months, leaving Parag and Hita in their care. He planned to sell his business and return with the rest of his family at a later date.

My younger sister, Pratibha, her husband Pradip Kumar, and son Amit arrived later in 1988, and also joined the family hub in New Jersey. My other sisters—Nimuben, Damuben, and Sadhana—decided to stay in India with their families.

Mina's two brothers, Ajay and Nitin, also arrived with their spouses and very young children in 1988. They stayed with us in Florida and went through the same cycle of depression and dejection that we had experienced.

When they acclimated, Ajay and his family settled in Bradenton, close to us, while Nitin, his wife Pragna and their two young children left for New Jersey to look for work in the diamond business.

Mina and I became experienced in managing new immigrants, and we spent our days cooking vegetarian meals and dropping off and picking up family members from jobs, daycare, and schools. We provided moral support, financial assistance and all other necessities until all our family members got established in their new environment.

In some cases, it took more than a year for new arrivals to build up some savings and feel confident about moving to their own apartment. It thrilled our hearts to see our family in America getting larger and our children receiving a good education in the American school system.

***

During this time, we also started planning the next step in our own American dream, buying a plot of land in a gated community in Sarasota and working with a builder to construct a 3000 square feet custom home. This location brought me closer to my work and provided a truly safe environment for Mina and my teenage girls.

When construction finished, we moved into our dream home with great excitement. It had an enclosed, in-ground swimming pool and a lush green lawn, all surrounded by mature palm trees and flower beds. We had the stucco exterior painted a light mauve color. This made our house very visible from the gatehouse across the lake.

One weekend, when I returned from a trip to a nearby Home Depot, I stopped at the gatehouse to gain access because I had left my key card for the automated gate at home. My clothes were very casual and I was wearing a baseball cap. As I eased to a stop, I lowered my window. Before I had a chance to speak, the security guard reached for his daily logbook and fired a question at me.

"Whose home are you painting today?" he asked.

His question puzzled me and I didn't answer immediately.

"Tell me which home you are painting today?" he yelled.

I took a deep breath, convinced my skin color and baseball cap had triggered a stereotype in the guard's thinking. "My dear friend," I said, pointing across the lake, "Do you see that mauve house?"

Immediately, the guard realized his mistake and began to apologize. He opened the gate and saluted with a smile. I chuckled as I drove away.

***

Within months of moving into our new home, Larry and John Glendenning called a meeting and announced they had sold Microlife Technics to a multinational company called Quest International, Inc. A new CEO arrived shortly after and rumors abounded that major changes would follow. Al Gryczka stayed on as V.P. of Operations, and my job did not change.

28

Parenting

In the summer of 1989, Mina and I climbed in our Pontiac Grand Prix with our two teenage daughters to visit our newly immigrated family members in New Jersey. The journey would take fifteen hours or more, so we made sure the girls had books to read and things to do along the way.

Sonal, age sixteen, had completed her junior year at Sarasota high school and was already talking about going to college and becoming a doctor. Rita, in middle school, was also progressing well.

I liked both schools the girls attended. It thrilled me to think that my daughters could be educated to the highest level, a first in our family. I particularly liked the way the high school principal encouraged his pupils to think big and aim high.

"Dad, how many relatives do we have in New Jersey?" Sonal asked about an hour into the journey.

I ran through the list of names, twelve in total.

"They must have a big house," Rita said.

I smiled, "Their apartment is small, but they have big hearts. That's how we lived in India. We will manage. It's more fun."

We arrived very late at night and went straight to bed in the space they had made for us in the crowded apartment. The sleeping arrangements reminded me of 64-D in Bombay. It was not until the next day that we greeted everyone. Parag, Bhupat's oldest son, had already left for school. When he came home, I was surprised by how much he had grown. I had to look up as he approached me to shake my hand.

"Hello, Rameshkaka. How are you?"

"I'm fine. Parag, you look good. What have you been up to lately?"

He smiled, "Not much. We finish school this week."

"What grade are you in?"

"Ninth grade. Freshman."

I liked his good manners and lively personality.

Later that evening, we all sat down for an Indian meal, just like at home in Bombay. We talked about the old days, the daily issues newcomers face, and the persistence each one of them would need to settle down in their new life in America. I looked at Parag and asked about his studies.

"I like the school here, Kaka. I'm doing well."

I noticed he didn't look me in the eye when he said it. "May I see your school grade paper, please?"

"Kaka, I'm doing well."

The room fell silent at this show of disrespect. Hasubhai and Bhabhi stared at their nephew, but said nothing.

I raised my voice, "Parag, did you hear what I said?"

He glanced at everyone watching him. "Yes, Kaka. I will get it from my drawer."

After a few minutes, he returned with his school transcript and handed it to me without a smile. "Kaka, here is my report card. I plan to do better next semester."

I studied the transcript and realized we had a problem. My nephew was not taking advantage of his education. "Parag, I don't see any science subjects here. You have taken carpentry, woodwork, pottery and drawing." I looked at Hasubhai, "Have you spoken to anyone at the school about career choice?"

Hasubhai shook his head.

It was clear to me that my nephew was in serious trouble if he stayed at this school. "Hasubhai, I will take Parag with me to Sarasota. He will go to school there. It's an excellent school."

Hasubhai nodded his agreement.

"Kaka, I'll be okay here. I promise I'll do better."

"Parag, you are ruining your life here. Pack your bags. We will be driving to Sarasota in a couple of days. You have no choice. You are coming home with us."

"But all my friends are here."

Mina reached out to him, "Parag, come with us and go to school in Sarasota. Your kaka is right. Sonal and Rita will be good company for you."

"I want to talk to my dad about it."

"Parag, your dad will agree with Rameshkaka," Hasubhai said. "Go with them."

Tension filled the apartment.

A couple of days later we left for Sarasota. Many miles passed before Parag spoke.

After a while, I looked in the rearview mirror and surveyed the back seat. Sonal and Rita were playing mischievously, but quietly, while Parag stared out the window at passing cars.

"Hi, Parag beta, are you feeling okay?" I said, adding the affectionate "beta" (meaning son) to his name.

He glanced at the rearview mirror, and for an instant we made eye contact. "I'm fine, Kaka."

"Parag beta, this is a good move for you. Sarasota High School is excellent, and Sonal and Rita will be good company at home."

The girls giggled and Sonal leaned toward him, "Parag, we have a big back yard and a swimming pool."

Mina joined in, "Parag, we will take good care of you. You can ride with Sonal to school. She has many friends."

I noticed a hint of a smile on his face.

"Parag beta, everything will be fine," I said. "We will have a good time. If you study and bring home good grades, you will have a better life. Your dad helped me so much with my education. Please, let me do the same for you."

The smile on his face inched wider, "Yes, Kaka."

***

Parag settled in well and soon became accustomed to his new home and his continuing education at Sarasota High. The studies were not easy for him as he moved from pottery, drawing, and physical education to real science and math classes. We were very pleased with his efforts, and told him that his responsibility was to study and maintain acceptable school grades and everything else was our responsibility.

Sonal and Rita were also pleased to have a cousin of their age in the house as a playmate and someone to share daily chores and activities.

Mina and I were thrilled to have him under our guardianship and treated him like our own son. We were determined to support him in every way. He had a bright intellect and had been let down by his previous school.

The high value we placed on achieving top grades at school and moving on to higher education to achieve as much as possible in life was typical of Indian families. My own experiences and success added to that resolve. From the time our daughters first received homework, Mina and I worked with them on a daily basis to maximize their learning. We started the same routine with Parag.

I regularly reminded them of my childhood experiences of poverty and substandard schooling, and of their good fortune to be born in America and go to well-resourced schools.

We also spent a lot of time engaging in out-of-school activities with our daughters such as karate, tennis, and music lessons. We did not want to isolate our girls from American culture, but we did strictly enforce rules about no slumber parties, no going on outings with friends without parental supervision, and absolutely no drinking or smoking. We did relax our vegetarian eating habits, allowing our girls to eat meat at school and occasionally enjoyed peperoni pizza or hamburgers together.

Our parenting efforts and our focus on education bore fruit when, in May, 1990, Sonal graduated with distinction from high school and won the Top Girl Student of the Year award. In three months, she would start her studies for a degree in chemistry at the University of South Florida at Tampa, my alma mater, with hopes of continuing on to medical school.

That evening, we celebrated with a festive meal that Mina had spent hours preparing. After the meal, I noticed Sonal and Rita deep in whispered conversation. It seemed like Sonal wanted to say something but was reluctant to start a dialog.

I beckoned Mina over and asked if she knew what the girls were whispering about. She gave our older daughter a wave to come and join us. "I'll let Sonal tells you."

Sonal approached like Dickens' Oliver advancing to request more food. Mina reached for her arm. "Come on Sonal, tell your dad about your Prom date."

Parag and Rita watched intently from across the room.

Sonal hesitated before she spoke. "Dad, I've been invited to go to Prom next weekend. His name's David. He's a friend of mine."

The request took me by surprise. She had never dated a boy before because that was not part of our upbringing.

"Who is this boy? Do I know him?"

"No, Dad. He's my classmate."

I glanced at Mina. "What are your thoughts?"

"I'm okay with this if you are." She gave Sonal a smile of encouragement.

I paused for a few moments.

"Dad, please?" Sonal said. "I know David. He's a very nice boy."

Before I answered, I wanted to speak with Mina in private. "Let me think about this," I said and gestured for Mina to follow me into another room.

"Our daughter is American," Mina said. "Going to Senior Prom is a big thing. Sonal is a good girl. We can trust her."

"I trust Sonal, but can we trust this boy?"

"Sonal thinks so or she wouldn't ask."

"You don't mind that he's American?"

Mina shrugged. "Ramesh, there are no Indian boys in Sonal's class. And Sonal is American too. You made sure of that."

"You're right. But I don't want her out late at night. And I want to meet the boy."

"I agree," Mina said. "You can tell Sonal when she has to be home, and you can tell her friend the same thing when he comes to pick her up."

Back in the family room, I called Sonal over and told her she could go to Prom with certain conditions. A big smile lit up her face.

"Tell your friend I will speak to him when he comes to pick you up."

"That will be fine," she said.

Over the next few days, many thoughts came to my mind about what could go wrong, but I trusted my daughter. I felt safe.

On Prom day, Sonal had her hair done professionally and dressed in a black evening-dress. She looked gorgeous as she waited patiently for David to arrive.

The doorbell rang on schedule. I opened the door and welcomed David inside. He was smartly dressed in a black tuxedo and shiny black shoes. Sonal formally introduced all of us.

"David, I hear you have asked my daughter to go to Prom Night."

"Yes, Sir," David replied.

"I'm glad you have asked Sonal and I hope you have a wonderful evening. I need to know where you are going and I'd like Sonal to be back home by eleven o'clock."

David gave us the name of the restaurant where he had a reservation and promised to have Sonal home on time.

I handed him a writing pad and a pen. "David, in case something happens and we need to call, please write down your parents address and their phone number."

"No problem, Sir." He wrote the info I requested and handed me the pad.

"Dad, can we go now?" Sonal said.

"Of course, drive safely and remember no alcohol. Back on time please."

Sonal opened the door and the two of them exited and drove away for their Prom night. I kept the address and phone number safe in my pocket all evening while we waited for Sonal's return. I was relieved when I heard the front door open a few minutes before 11PM.

* * *

Summer came and the weather turned hot and humid to the point of exhaustion. It reminded me of monsoon season in Bombay. After a week of frequent thunderstorms and high temperatures we had a very overgrown lawn. Fortunately, a cooler, dry day was forecast for Saturday.

"Parag, let's get the grass mowed this afternoon," I said as we ate lunch.

"Good idea," Sonal said, glancing at her sister. "Rita and I will help pull some weeds."

"Kaka, I'll edge the walkway and trim the shrubs while you cut the grass," Parag said in a cheerful tone.

While the landscaping team went to work, Mina stayed inside to prepare our evening meal.

For the next hour, I battled the overgrown lawn while Parag carefully edged the sidewalks. The noise of our equipment was loud enough to drown conversation so we worked in silence.

After about an hour, I glanced up and noticed a beautiful Cadillac, driven by an older gentleman, stopping in front of the house where Parag was edging.

An elderly lady in the passenger seat lowered her window and said something. I idled the mower so I could hear the conversation.

Parag, looked puzzled for a moment, then pointed to me. "You should ask my boss," he said.

The lady turned in my direction and beckoned me over. I stopped my lawn mower and wiped sweat from my face as I approached. "Yes, ma'am, how can I help you?"

"How much do you charge to mow the lawn?"

From the corner of my eye, I noticed Parag and the girls grinning and waiting for my response to this new instance of racial stereotyping. I turned to survey my beautiful front yard, taking time to enjoy the scenery. The lady watched me, waiting patiently for a response.

"Each weekly cut will cost you around $100," I said.

Her eyebrows shot up.

"Well, someone has to pay for the mortgage on this house."

Her husband realized that I was not the lawnmower boy and shouted an apology as he pulled away from the curb. Parag and the girls began to giggle. I joined in.

* * *

As the summer slipped by, Sonal prepared for college. I spoke to her about her safety as a young girl living away from home and outside of my protection. She laughed. "This is not India, Dad. I'll be fine. There'll be hundreds of girls at USF."

"And hundreds of boys," I said. "Not all of them can be trusted."

"Dad, I'll be very careful. But I can't live my life in a shelter."

I hesitated. We could talk about marriage," I said.

Sonal stiffened. "What do you mean?"

"Marriage brings protection. Your mother and I could find an Indian boy of very high standing who wants to come to America."

"No. I don't want an arranged marriage," she said. Her big dark eyes pleaded for acceptance.

I had expected this day to come. Part of me screamed that it was my role, as her father, to find her a partner for life. Yet my American daughter wanted to go the American way.

I didn't expect her to return to India and marry someone from the Jamnagar Jain Society, but I wanted to have some involvement.

"We would involve you in every step," I said.

"Dad, if you bring a boy from India, I'll kill him. I want to find my own husband."

We knew two other Indian families in the Sarasota area that had been split apart by this issue and I had vowed not to let that happen to us. I had to tread carefully.

"Will you look for an Indian boy?" I asked in a gentle tone.

"Dad, I'll look for the right person. You've taught me that it doesn't matter where someone is born or what color his skin is."

She was right. I'd taught her that—never to discriminate on race, religion or color. And I believed it from the bottom of my heart. But when it came to choosing a husband—was it wrong to be biased toward your own ethnicity? I had some thinking to do.

"Sonal, I want only the best for you," I said. Promise me you'll tell me when you meet someone you're interested in. I'll want to meet him."

29

Love, Loss, & Gain

A year later, in July 1991, my brother Hasubhai went for a simple angiography procedure that was recommended by his physician. Something went wrong, and Hasubhai died during the routine outpatient procedure. He was fifty-six years old. We were all stunned.

I boarded the first available flight to Newark and told Mina to follow as soon as she had made arrangements for the care of our daughters. My brother Rashmi picked me up at the airport.

"How is everybody?" I asked as we drove away.

His eyes welled and his voice choked, "Rameshbhai, we can't control Bhabhi. She's hysterical. We have a disaster on our hands." At that moment, the full impact of my brother's death hit me, and I broke down and wept.

When we arrived at the apartment, I saw an exhausted and very dejected Bhabhi sitting in a corner surrounded by family members and local Indian friends. Her son, Ketan, age twenty-six and studying pharmacy, stood nearby watching over her.

I went straight to Bhabhi and embraced her. Both of us cried as we hugged and comforted each other. Beside us, Pratibha wept in a dazed state, almost like a zombie. I held her and tried to calm her.

The room full of mourners reminded me of the night my father died. I remembered how the elders of the family took over. Here, I was the family elder who had to take the lead. I asked Rashmi and his friends about a local cremation in line with the Hindu/Jain tradition.

"We cannot have an open-air cremation like back home," he replied. "Open pyres are forbidden by law. The nearest crematorium is in Rahway, a few miles away. The body has been taken there, and will be laid in an open casket for viewing prior to cremation."

I nodded. "Has anyone called home to India?"

"I called Bhupatbhai. He is contacting all the family members in Bombay and Jamnagar."

The room fell quiet. I turned to see Bhabhi removing her jewelry in line with Indian tradition when a woman becomes a widow. As she removed each piece, she laid it in her lap. She held all the pieces lovingly for a few seconds before handing them to her son, Ketan, for safekeeping. Finally, she removed the red tika dot from her forehead and left the room to put on a simple white sari. We were filled with sadness and heartbreak, seeing what our beloved Bhabhi was going through.

***

At Rahway Crematorium, Jain religious mantras played at low volume from prerecorded tapes as friends and family members crowded into the open-casket wake room. The body lay in a simple casket, facing south in line with tradition. A single candle burned beside the body. I found the subdued atmosphere painful to bear.

After a few short eulogies from close friends, I gave a final farewell to Hasubhai. Then Ketan, his son, took the honor of closing the casket and pressing the button that rolled the casket through a pair of curtains into the crematory.

Family members and very close friends returned to Bhabhi's apartment. I talked with Bhabhi and Ketan, and we agreed to return to India as soon as possible to scatter Hasubhai's ashes in the Arabian Sea near Bombay.

Late in the evening Bhabhi mentioned that she wanted to go back home with her son and daughter for good.

"Bhabhi, that is not a good idea," I said, but let the matter drop for the rest of the night.

***

The next day, as we drove to collect the ashes, Bhabhi repeated her wishes, "Rameshbhai, I will stay in Bombay. I don't want to live in America anymore."

"Bhabhi, what about Ketan's education? He's in pharmacy school."

She shook her head, "Ketan and Hina will come with me."

Others joined in the discussion and tried to convince Bhabhi not to take this course of action. We all failed.

Bhabhi, Ketan, and I flew to Bombay three days after the cremation. Close relatives and friends had gathered at the family home in Borivali West to receive Bhabhi and comfort her. Our arrival was very sad and subdued. All the attention caused Bhabhi to relive her loss, and once more, her anguish was uncontrollable. It was truly a sad situation and a painful experience. I could do nothing to help.

Later, when others had departed, I had the chance to talk to Bhabhi alone about her decision to stay in India. "Bhabhi, are you sure this is what you want?"

"My roots are here, I want to stay here."

"And what do you want for your son? He is two years from finishing his pharmacy degree. Do you want him to throw that away?"

Her body shook with emotion.

"Bhabhi, you and Hasubhai sacrificed more than anyone to give me my opportunity. You are an inspiration to our family. Give your son the same opportunity."

Eventually she relented and agreed to let Ketan return to America to finish his degree. She also agreed that she and Hina would visit America once every twelve months so their immigration papers did not expire for good.

***

Back in Florida, life returned to normal and we watched our children grow into young adults. Bhabhi and Hina changed their minds about living in India and returned to New Jersey to live with Ketan. Parag thrived at Sarasota High School and went on to study engineering at the

University of South Florida. On more than one occasion, he thanked us for rescuing him from his situation in New Jersey.

At work, Al Gryczka moved to another job within Quest International and, in 1993, the new CEO announced that the Sarasota plant would close in two years' time. All activities would be relocated elsewhere. Later in the day, he spoke with me one-on-one and informed me that my job would transfer to a new head office in the Chicago area. I would be given additional responsibilities, a pay raise, and a new title. The company would also assist with my relocation.

That evening, I shared the news with Mina.

"Ramesh, why do we have to move?" she said. "We are settled here. Rita has three more years of high school."

"Mina, this is a big opportunity. Rumors have been circulating that we'd all lose our jobs. Instead the company has promoted me."

"Can't you find another job here?"

"Not a job like this."

We sat down as a family to discuss the consequences of moving to Illinois. For Sonal, it would mean less frequent trips home from college to visit us. Rita could finish her junior year at Sarasota High School, and then transfer to our new location for her senior year. We took a few days to decide before agreeing to move.

***

In the following months, very little changed in our home life, but at work I learned about the company's restructuring plan and my new role. My title would be Director of Quality

Assurance, North America, and I would be responsible for product quality across six manufacturing plants, five of them in America and one in Canada.

In December, 1994, I took a business trip to Chicago to give my input into laboratory design for the new company headquarters that were under construction and also spent time with a realtor in St. Charles, Illinois, locating a plot of land in a new development and meeting with a builder to begin a discussion about house design. I returned home with lots of information for Mina to sift through. We planned to relocate the following summer.

When I arrived home, Mina informed me that we had been invited to a formal birthday party for Dr. Reddy, a friend of ours, and that I had to dress up.

When I had showered and dressed, Mina handed me a gift bag to carry for Dr. Reddy. I was pleased she had taken care of the gift. After my long trip, I had no energy to run around.

We drove to the party hall and I was pleased to see Kailash and some other mutual friends of Dr. Reddy outside the hall. We chatted for a while and then Kailash suggested we move inside for an evening drink.

He pushed opened the door and to my big surprise everyone screamed happy birthday to me! Mina, Parag and my two daughters had surprised me with a 50th birthday party celebration.

More than 100 friends plus all our family members living in America had gathered. I was completely flabbergasted to see Hasubhai and Bhabhi and other family members from New Jersey; and my brothers-in-law and their families. I looked at Mina and saw the excitement on her face. Everyone cheered and applauded when I hugged her.

For the rest of the evening I mingled with all my friends, thanking them for their good wishes. Sonal introduced me to a well-groomed young man who accompanied her, an American boy. "Dad, I'd like you to meet my friend from USF, Jonathon Rhodes."

The young man stood about six-foot tall and had a muscular build. We shook hands and I continued visiting with other friends, too busy to dwell on Sonal and her companion. Throughout the evening, a DJ played music and the dance floor stayed busy. After a while, I met Sonal again and asked if there was anything I needed to know about Jonathon.

"Dad, we're just friends," she said. "It's not serious."

I moved on and had a blast all evening, chatting, eating, and socializing.

***

The months raced by and I made several business trips to the six sites I now had responsibility for and to Chicago to monitor progress on my new home. During this period, I met Richard Graves, an Englishman who would work alongside me for many years. We enjoyed sharing our immigration stories.

Shortly before we relocated, Sonal visited us from USF and said she wanted us to meet with her friend, Jonathon, before we departed. "He came with me to your birthday party."

"Tell me about him." I said, probably sounding sterner than I intended.

Sonal reached for my arm. "Daddy, he's really nice. You'll like him. He's a chemical engineer."

I noticed Mina looking at me. I had questions for my daughter, but Mina's body language told me this was not the time. I gave Sonal a hug, and we set a date to meet her friend at her apartment in Tampa.

"I shall ask some candid questions," I said.

She nodded, "Ask everything you need to know."

As we parted, I could see in Sonal's eyes the deep respect she had for me.

***

On the way to Tampa, Mina and I discussed the situation. "Do you think they want to get married?" I asked.

Mina shook her head, "Not yet. I think Sonal wants our approval before it gets too serious."

At the apartment, we greeted one another. Jonathon displayed good manners and a strong personality. Sonal seemed more subdued than usual.

We sat down on the sectional sofa and I broke the silence. "Jonathon, how long have you two been dating?"

"A little more than two years."

"And how serious is this relationship?"

He leaned forward, "Mr. Shah, we have a very serious relationship."

I glanced at Sonal. "You didn't mention this earlier."

"We weren't serious then."

My senses told me they had debated a long time about when to tell me this. A hint of a smile crept onto Sonal's lips and her body language screamed encouragement to the young man sitting in the spotlight next to her. Beside me, Mina had a chuckle on her face.

I tried to maintain a stone face. "Jonathon, tell me about your studies."

"I've finished my chemical engineering degree and have enrolled for a master's degree in chemical engineering."

I liked his confidence. "That's very nice. Engineering is a good career."

So far, I couldn't fault him. But there were other important things to probe. "Jonathon, I hope you know what you are doing."

He looked at me, "Mr. Shah, I don't understand what you are trying to say."

I put my hand on the coffee table between us. "Jonathon, put your hand beside mine." He did as I asked. "Look at our skin color. We are different. We have a different religion, a different culture, we are different people. These are important issues. I want to know that you understand them, so there are no shocks or surprises later." From the corner of my eye, I saw Mina nodding her agreement.

Jonathon answered in a clear, calm voice. "I don't see those differences as major difficulties at all." He glanced at Sonal, "We both love each other. We will overcome all the hurdles that are part of our life."

Sonal joined in, more animated now, "Dad, Jonathon and I have discussed all these things. We don't see them as issues. You don't need to worry about it."

Their answers pleased me. Love had not blinded them to the reality of their situation. My frustration at not being involved earlier began to dissipate. "Have you met his parents?" I asked Sonal.

"Yes, I've met his entire family. They approve of our relationship." Her voice sounded firm.

"Mr. Shah, my mom and dad love Sonal. They think she's wonderful and are thrilled to have her in their home."

Another good answer. One of my big concerns was how his parents would react to Sonal. The young man had answered my questions in a respectful and confident way. I couldn't fault my daughter's choice.

At that moment, it dawned on me that this meeting was an important step in our family's acceptance and integration into American society. This was not a time to lament the loss of an Indian tradition, but a time to celebrate.

"Jonathon, as an Indian father, I feel responsible for the future well-being of my daughter. Before I give my blessing to this relationship, I need an assurance from you that you will never bully or abuse Sonal, either physically or mentally."

"I promise you that will never happen to Sonal."

I felt truth and honesty in his reply. "Then you have my blessing."

***

Two years later, in December 1997, Jonathon and Sonal held their engagement party at an Indian restaurant in Chicago. They planned to marry in May 1999 in Tampa, when Sonal graduated from medical school. Every member of our family living in America came to Chicago to welcome Jonathon into our extended family. Mina and I got to know Jonathon's parents and siblings and other family members who attended the party. We felt a very good chemistry between the two families.

***

The day of the wedding approached, and Sonal had only one week between her graduation ceremony and the start of her residency at Baylor School of Medicine in Houston, Texas. By the end of the week, we were exhausted. We had attended the graduation, held two wedding ceremonies—one Hindu, the other Christian, closed up her apartment in Tampa, and helped her settle in Houston.

Mina's parents flew from India to celebrate their first granddaughter's wedding and to welcome the first non-Jain member into their family. Around 250 guests from both sides attended both ceremonies.

Mina and I had a wonderful time chatting with all our guests and were thrilled to see how well our immigrant families had progressed. Only Hasubhai's absence brought tears to our eyes.

Celebrations continued late into the evening with dancing and cocktails. I shared a glass of wine with John Rhodes, Jonathon's father, and we talked at length about our different cultures. Sonal had shared snippets of my early days in India, and he wanted to know more. Memories flowed from my lips. I told him about my father and how, even in the worst situations, he would look at us and say, "Don't give in. Tomorrow will be a better day."

One by one, guests tired of dancing and joined us. The circle of listeners grew and questions flew from all directions.

"Why did you choose America?"

"You washed clothes by hand?"

"Did you go to school on an elephant?"

"When did you first see a television?"

The bride and groom joined us for a few minutes before they departed. Jonathon had heard many of the stories before and laughed at some of the questions.

"Dad," he said, "You have a fantastic story. You should write a book."

Parag Shah, my nephew at Sarasota, Florida

My daughters: Rita and Sonal, Bradenton, FL

Sonal getting married to Jonathon Rhodes, May 22, 1999, Tampa, Florida

Rita married Samit Shah on July 3, 2010 Chicago, Illinois. My family members immigrated to USA.

Epilogue

After completing her residency in Houston, Sonal moved to Naperville, Illinois, to be close to mom and dad and to work as a Board Certified Internist at DuPage Medical Group. Jonathon worked for a number of large corporations and continued to badger me to write this book.

Rita graduated from the University of Indiana Dental School and later settled with her husband Samit in Chicago. Parag graduated from the University of South Florida with a degree in engineering, and later started his own business in northern Virginia. His parents, Bhupat and Pravina, and the families of his three sisters, joined him there.

In May, 2003, my pulse dropped to thirty-five beats per minute and I received a pacemaker implant. This problem was unrelated to my heart murmur. In 2011, the implanted pacemaker battery pack had to be replaced.

In February, 2013, I went for a regular cardiovascular checkup and learned that my heart murmur was becoming more predominant. It was time to investigate my surgical options. Later that year, in November, Dr. McCarthy, a surgeon at Northwestern Memorial Hospital in Chicago, informed me that both my aortic and mitral valves needed replacement to maintain the quality of my life. This entailed open-heart surgery.

I was scared. A few months earlier, we had lost Bhabhi at age seventy-four with a similar heart valve issue. Mina and other close family members encouraged me to go ahead with the surgery. In the end, my desire to be able to play with my grandchildren outweighed my fear.

Before anesthesia on February 3, 2014, I prayed to Bhagwan Mahavir and thanked him for giving me such a beautiful life with so many wonderful opportunities. If the outcome was not perfect, I had no regrets. I prayed silently to my dad, and told him it may soon be time for me to come and see him. I was at peace, knowing how well my extended family in America and my three sisters back home in India were progressing.

When I woke from the anesthesia, I rejoiced. My father's mantra rang in my ears, *"Tomorrow will be a better day."*

Author's Bio

RAMESH SHAH immigrated to the United States from India in 1967. He is currently the Chief Quality Officer of FONA International, a large flavor manufacturing company in suburban Chicago. Ramesh enjoys travelling, reading and photography. He and his wife, Mina, were married in 1971, and they have two daughters and two grandchildren.

Made in the USA
Monee, IL
22 January 2021

57690230R00223